The Instigator

The Instigator

How Gary Bettman Remade the League and Changed the Game Forever

Jonathon Gatehouse

VIKING

VIKING
an imprint of Penguin Canada

Published by the Penguin Group
Penguin Group (Canada), 90 Eglinton Avenue East, Suite 700, Toronto, Ontario, Canada M4P 2Y3

Penguin Group (USA) Inc., 375 Hudson Street, New York, New York 10014, U.S.A.
Penguin Books Ltd, 80 Strand, London WC2R 0RL, England
Penguin Ireland, 25 St Stephen's Green, Dublin 2, Ireland (a division of Penguin Books Ltd)
Penguin Group (Australia), 707 Collins Street, Melbourne, Victoria 3008, Australia
   (a division of Pearson Australia Group Pty Ltd)
Penguin Books India Pvt Ltd, 11 Community Centre, Panchsheel Park, New Delhi – 110 017, India
Penguin Group (NZ), 67 Apollo Drive, Rosedale, Auckland 0632, New Zealand
   (a division of Pearson New Zealand Ltd)
Penguin Books (South Africa) (Pty) Ltd, 24 Sturdee Avenue, Rosebank, Johannesburg 2196,
   South Africa

Penguin Books Ltd, Registered Offices: 80 Strand, London WC2R 0RL, England

First published 2012

1 2 3 4 5 6 7 8 9 10 (RRD)

Copyright © Jonathon Gatehouse, 2012

The NHL creed and the theme song for Canadian NHL expansion are used with permission.

Manufactured in the U.S.A.

LIBRARY AND ARCHIVES CANADA CATALOGUING IN PUBLICATION

Gatehouse, Jonathon
   The instigator : how Gary Bettman remade the league and
changed the game forever / Jonathon Gatehouse.

Includes bibliographical references and index.

ISBN 978-0-670-06592-9

1. Bettman, Gary. 2. National Hockey League—Biography. 3. National Hockey League—History.
4. Sports executives—Biography. I. Title.

GV848.5.B49G38 2012   796.962092   C2012-904428-8

Visit the Penguin Canada website at **www.penguin.ca**

Special and corporate bulk purchase rates available; please see
www.penguin.ca/corporatesales or call 1-800-810-3104, ext. 2477.

ALWAYS LEARNING   PEARSON

To Andrea,
for pulling me up this mountain
and so many more

Contents

1 Sticks and Stones

The full beer cup arcs from the not-so-cheap seats of Vancouver's Rogers Arena toward the home end of the ice, golden contrail spreading out behind. It lands and splatters, short and a little to the left of the intended target, but close enough that he has to notice. Still, Gary Bettman doesn't flinch. Wireless microphone raised to his lips, tight smile firmly in place, free hand tucked casually in his suit pants pocket, the commissioner of the National Hockey League carries on with the speech that no one in the rink can hear over the cacophony of booing and catcalls. Boston's Tim Thomas skates forward to accept the Conn Smythe Trophy as the 2011 Stanley Cup playoffs' most valuable player as the beers—and now plastic water bottles—continue to fly. There's a polite burst of applause, as the burly goalie grins and poses for photographers. Then, just to make sure things haven't been misconstrued, the crowd of 18,860 takes up the chant, "Bettman sucks! Bettman sucks!"

The sequence is much the same when a pair of white-gloved custodians from the Hockey Hall of Fame carry the Cup onto the ice: clapping for the chalice, some high-decibel abuse for the man giving it away. And the odd missile from the stands. Zdeno Chara, the Bruins' towering and glowering captain, doesn't even realize the presentation is underway until Bettman beckons him up to the red carpet. There's a lopsided exchange, in which the 5-foot-6 commissioner looks like the mayor of Munchkinland next to the 6-foot-9-plus-skates Slovak defenceman. Seconds later, the Bruins are celebrating in a pulsating mob at centre ice, while the whipping boy ducks back down the tunnel, surrounded by NHL security.

Afterwards, the commissioner will pretend it was no big deal, chalking up the hostile reception to the Game 7 disappointment of Canucks fans, which was compounded by having to watch a despised opponent celebrate on their own turf. But home or away, the reaction has long been the same. In a sport that prides itself on its rituals, the jeering of the Bettman has become an annual rite of spring, as predictable as undisclosed injuries and bushy playoff beards.

In June 1993, just a few months into the job, he got a pass from fans in Montreal when the Habs beat Wayne Gretzky and the Los Angeles Kings in five with the help of the ghosts at the storied Forum. (How else does one explain the team's ten consecutive overtime wins over four rounds?) And the relief felt in New York the next year when the Rangers finally secured the Cup, ending a fifty-four-year drought with a see-saw Game 7 victory over the Canucks, made the habitually harsh Madison Square Garden atmosphere positively giddy—Mark Messier hoisting Stanley to the strains of Tina Turner's "Simply the Best" and "Iron Mike" Keenan doling out hugs.

But in the wake of a lockout that held the sport hostage for 103 days, there was little respect left for authority at the Meadowlands when the New Jersey Devils trapped their way to a sweep of the Detroit Red Wings in June 1995. The league was in transition. The Quebec Nordiques were already on their way to Denver. The future of the Winnipeg Jets hung in the balance. The LA Kings, laid low by the fiscal implosion and arrest of Bruce McNall, had declared bankruptcy. And even the team Bettman was about to crown Stanley Cup champions was threatening to bolt to greener pastures in Nashville. The problem was a familiar one—building envy. John McMullen, the Devils' owner, had moved the Rockies from Colorado to his native New Jersey in 1982 to take advantage of a shiny new 20,000-seat rink that was begging for tenants. But fourteen years later, Brendan Byrne Arena—better known as the Meadowlands—was no longer so attractive. With only twenty-nine luxury boxes, it paled in comparison to the just-opened United Center in Chicago with its 219 suites, or the 104 corporate lodges planned for Boston's rapidly rising new rink. Claiming his team had lost $20 million and was on track to bleed $2 million more, even as they played to packed houses while on the march to the finals, McMullen was demanding that the New Jersey Sports & Exposition Authority sweeten his lease and pay for extensive renovations—or else.

Bettman disagreed with those who called such tactics blackmail. And he delivered the same message he had been peddling to governments in Quebec, Manitoba, and Hartford, Connecticut: Those who wanted to keep their NHL teams into the next century had better find a way to house them "appropriately." Then, during the finals, the commissioner went further, giving an interview in which he underlined the Devils' tenuous position as the third representative of the fourth most popular pro sport in the crowded New York market. But it was his pointed refusal to rule out a quick off-season relocation that really had people up in arms. The *New Jersey Record* gave its editorial page over to a snarky open letter, suggesting the NHL recruit Atlas Van Lines as a corporate sponsor and painting its boss as yet another out-of-touch New York suit.

"For the sake of the league's stability, you should keep hockey clubs from picking up stakes whenever they smell a fresh greenback," lectured the paper. And at the rink the placards the fans were waving were even more cutting: "Nashville already has enough people without teeth."

So when Bettman stepped out onto the ice following the Devils' championship-clinching 5–2 victory, the leather-lunged New Jersey crowd let him have it, booing and gesturing—thumbs down or middle fingers up—as he presented Claude Lemieux with the Conn Smythe Trophy, and again when he handed off the Cup to Devils captain Scott Stevens. And that night, a tradition was born.

There's no doubt that being a lightning rod for fan discontent is part of the job description for commissioner of a major-league sport. The throng in Philadelphia jeered Bud Selig when he presented the Phillies with the World Series trophy in 2008—rather mildly given that football fans in the City of Brotherly Love once infamously booed Santa Claus during an Eagles half-time show. With an NFL lockout on the horizon in 2011, Roger Goodell got the business at the draft in New York's Radio City Music Hall, forced to stand uncomfortably at the podium until the invective and chants of "We want football! We want football!" petered out. David Stern—Bettman's mentor and head of the NBA for twenty-eight years and counting—figures he has been heckled in every city in the league, although Dallas fans seem to bear him particular animosity. Taking the extremely long view, the seventy year old recalls how everyone used to boo Harry Truman when the president was shown in newsreels at the movies. "I don't know why, but that's what you did," he says. "And I guess I came to believe that if you see the commissioner you boo, too—as the symbol of authority and real or imagined slights and policies you don't like."

Even Bettman's half-brother, Jeffrey Pollack, the commissioner of the World Series of Poker for a time, knows what it's like to feel the fans' wrath: "It's an inherently political job, and public opinion will cover a range of positions."

And, of course, the NHL's head honcho has always been paid handsomely to endure the slings and arrows on behalf of his bosses, the thirty team owners. From his original contract at $1 million a season, to the extension that more than doubled his salary in 1995, to his post 2004–5 lockout pay of $3.7 million, Bettman's salary has grown along with the game. His latest deal, signed in the fall of 2010 and carrying him through to 2015, puts more than $7.5 million a year in his pocket, matching the season take of players like Rick Nash, Marian Gaborik, and Scott Gomez. It places Bettman firmly among the NHL's top twenty earners, but well behind Brad Richards's league-leading $12-million-a-year deal with the Rangers. Certainly, value for money compared with the studiously bland and operationally invisible Bud Selig and his $18.35-million yearly pay packet. (Goodell and Stern both make a little over $10 million a season.)

In one sense then, the stick the NHL commissioner takes is just part of the game: an amusement for the rabble who buy the tickets that ultimately pay his salary. And as with Ron Hextall, the tightly wound Flyers goalie who opposition fans used to be able to drive to distraction simply by sing-songing his family name, there is the added bonus that the abuse so clearly gets under Bettman's skin. Put him in front of a hostile hockey crowd and his shoulders tense, the smile starts to look more like he's baring his teeth, and his eyes flash annoyance. For, despite all his years of experience, he has never quite mastered the trick of nonchalance or sloughing it off as a joke. The closest he's come may have been at the 2008 entry draft in Ottawa, when he responded to the boo-birds by thanking the fans "for making us feel so welcome" and then choked off the audience's laughter with a grin and wink that would have terrified Hannibal Lecter. These days, his underlings tend to treat the problem proactively—limiting the commissioner's time at centre stage, or packaging him with beloved former players, brave military personnel, or victims of recent tragedies during the ceremonial faceoffs.

Still, it goes beyond the office or the fun to be had mocking the rich, famous, and powerful. With Bettman there's something more visceral at play. For many Canadians, who invest the game with all the mythic traits of strong and free nationalism, there's the distrust they feel is due to all Americans: a notion that no one born south of the border can truly understand or appreciate our shared passion. For the hardcore hockey types—including the media, who get paid to be in a perpetual frenzy about the sport's health—there's the conceit that only "insiders," steeped in lore and custom, know what it takes to make it work on and off the ice. And in the darker corners of barrooms and the internet, there's the contingent that simply doesn't like a Jewish lawyer … period.

Those born and bred haters need no excuse. But in his almost twenty years as NHL commissioner, Bettman has provided his other critics with plenty of ammunition: the tilt toward larger US markets and the Sunbelt, which hastened the demise of the Nordiques, Jets, and Whalers. Two lengthy player lockouts—one of which scrubbed an entire season—in the name of altering how the spoils of pro hockey are divided, with yet more labour strife looming for fall 2012. A litany of failed attempts to interest a wider American audience in the game, from glowing pucks to Mighty Ducks to commercials likening players to ancient gladiators. And the stubborn, fifteen-year-long fight to keep the Phoenix Coyotes—whose cumulative losses in the last decade alone top

US$300 million—playing in the Arizona desert, despite the marked indifference of local fans and businesses.

It's the other side of the ledger that tends to get overlooked, though. How Bettman has built a league that routinely draws more fans to its games than the "powerhouse" National Basketball Association—on both sides of the border. Or how the NHL's annual revenues have grown from US$400 million to $3.3 billion on his watch. There's also the new ten-year, $2-billion television deal with NBC and its cable channels that finally has hockey getting paid and treated like a mainstream sport in the United States. His agreement with the International Olympic Committee has seen NHL dream teams participate in the last four Winter Games (although that streak may well come to an end in 2014). The addition of the outdoor Winter Classic was an instant success with audiences and now a major event on the sporting calendar. And what about the run of big-time sponsorship deals with the likes of Molson Coors, GEICO insurance, Reebok, and Cisco Systems? After years of economic uncertainty at the heart of the game, there are now seven financially thriving Canadian franchises (at least, as long as the dollar remains at par). And despite the doom prophets of the media, just one team relocated since 1997—the same number as in the NFL and Major League Baseball. Pro basketball, on the other hand, has moved three clubs over the same period. Hockey's not in as bad a shape as the fans sometimes wish.

As a rule, the NHL commissioner doesn't like to hang around once his duties are done. At the end of the 2011 finals in Vancouver, he awarded the Cup to the Bruins, passed on some congratulations and commiserations, and was in a chauffeured SUV on his way to the airport within minutes. The crowd inside Rogers Arena was unruly after the Canucks' loss, but those who had gathered in the downtown streets anticipating a celebration were far uglier. The rioting started at the intersection of Georgia and Hamilton, only a few blocks from the rink, with people flipping over porta-potties and lighting a vehicle on fire. An initial police charge was beaten back with rocks and bottles, and the youthful and heavily intoxicated mob responded with a celebratory verse of "O Canada." As groups moved throughout the downtown, smashing windows, looting stores, and setting more cars ablaze, those who had stuck around the rink for a post-game reception—including many VIPs and most of the NHL staff—were locked in for their own protection.

At the Flying Beaver in suburban Richmond, a bar and grill just beyond the airport fence that overlooks the mighty Fraser (slogan: Give'r on the River!), the mood was sombre. During the game, it had been standing room only, with fans in Canuck sweaters screaming and clapping thundersticks, and a siren occasionally wailing from behind the bar. Now, only a couple dozen patrons remained, nursing their beers and watching the riot unfold on the big-screen TVs.

The five guys who walked in wearing nice suits would have stood out at the best of times. But it was the little one who drew most of the attention. Less than an hour after people in the pub had been booing him every bit as lustily as the fans at the game, Gary Bettman was suddenly standing among them. "It was like one of those scenes in the movie where the bar goes all quiet and every head turned," he says. The private jet wasn't quite ready to head back to the airfield in New Jersey, so the commissioner, his deputy Bill Daly, spokesperson Frank Brown, NHL vice-president of marketing Brian Jennings, and a hulking ex-cop from league security, had gone in search of dinner.

There was a bit of grumbling at the bar, and a couple of regulars threw epithets over their shoulders as they weaved their way to the washroom. But mostly, people were excited. They approached politely to shake hands and seek autographs. Several had their pictures taken with Bettman. When the floor manager called the owner—who was stuck downtown among the mob—to pass on the celebrity sighting, he had her send over a couple rounds of the house specialty: espresso, vodka, Kahlua, and milk in a rocks glass—a.k.a. The Shaft.

Munching his meal while watching cop cars burn was a bit surreal, but otherwise it was a typical Canadian outing for the NHL commissioner. All that free-flowing abuse from the stands never seems to amount to much when people encounter him face to face. They're respectful, even friendly. It's the kind of thing that allows him to think that maybe, deep down inside, fans really do understand and appreciate him. And the salmon burger at the Flying Beaver was terrific.

When you're Gary Bettman, you take comfort wherever you can find it.

THE SHIELD MAKES A STATEMENT. Four feet wide and almost eight feet high, made of polished stainless steel and black glass with the white letters N-H-L illuminated from within, it's the first thing you see when you enter the league offices in New York City. Placed on a pedestal, it dominates the sparse fifteenth-floor reception area. A shock-and-awe branding exercise designed to be worshipped. Or perhaps in the case of wayward players awaiting their disciplinary hearings—feared.

It takes a visitor a while to notice the game footage flickering silently on the brushed metal walls. When the NHL moved its headquarters just after the 2005 lockout—seeking more space and a fresh start—the designers, TPG Architecture, opted for subtlety, creating a "montage of materials and wintry colors that reflect the

game of hockey," according to a write-up in *The New York Times.*
"Patterned glass evokes the bumpy pond ice that many players
learn on; smooth transparent partitions suggest sleek professional
rinks." Down the hall, there is even a thin line of frost, pulled from
the moisture in the air, running across the top of a brushed-steel
beverage bar. A sweaty sport distilled into the antiseptic comfort of
a first-class departure lounge.

There are whimsical touches scattered over the 133,000 square
feet of office space, like the penalty box, complete with countdown
clock, near the thirteenth-floor elevators. And the mock dressing
room on the twelfth, decorated with the famous words of the late
Flyers coach Fred Shero: "Win today and we walk together forever."
In the cafeteria, there's even a patchwork wall made of numbers and
logos cut from team sweaters. But the floor with the shield is all
about making an impression and doing business: from the alcove
decorated with every name that graces the Stanley Cup (complete
with spelling errors and the *x*'s struck through Basil Pocklington,
after Peter, then owner of the Oilers, was found to have sneaked
his pop in among the 1984 winners), to the high-tech conference
rooms, to the lair of the commissioner.

The corner suite overlooks the Avenue of the Americas and
47th Street. Bettman can see NBC's headquarters—30 Rock—
across the road, and Central Park a few blocks farther on. The
NBA, his former employer, is one avenue over. Fox News and
Sirius Satellite Radio are in the building next door. Power lunches
are held at the Evergreen Diner, a nearby greasy spoon. Midtown
doesn't offer many fine dining choices.

It's the hottest summer day in fifty years in Manhattan, a
choking soup of humidity and ozone, so Bettman is in casual
mode—dress pants, well-polished shoes, and a long-sleeved shirt
with his initials, *G.B.B.*, monogrammed on the breast pocket

(his middle name is Bruce). After a couple of weeks away from the grind—the period after the July 1 free agent frenzy ends and before preparations for training camp begin in earnest in early August, is now the league's only real downtime—he's rested and relaxed. It's a side of the commissioner that the media and public rarely see. At sixty, heading into his twentieth season in charge of the league, Bettman's hair is somehow still dark. He's trim, working out or jogging almost every morning. And he keeps a schedule that would kill most forty year olds. A typical day sees him rise at 6 A.M. at his house in Saddle River, a northern New Jersey enclave that was once home to Richard Nixon and now hosts a hodgepodge of celebrities, including comedian Andrew Dice Clay and thriller writer Mary Higgins Clark. By eight, he's in the back of the car, working the phone or reading during the hour-long chauffeured drive into the city. He's at his desk shortly after 9 A.M., and the day is usually taken up with meetings—operational, long-term planning, or the emergency variety, take your pick—and responding to calls and emails in between. He rarely leaves the office before 7:00 or 7:30 at night, unless he has a dinner meeting. During the season, there are two or three of those a week, usually followed by a hockey game.

Bettman long ago lost track of how many days a year he's on the road—only Debbie Jordan, his executive assistant since his NBA days, knows for certain—but guesses it's near the century mark. He makes a point of visiting each club every season, attending one of their home games and meeting with local media, sponsors, staff, and season ticket holders. Then there are the special events like the NHL Awards, Hall of Fame inductions, the Winter Classic, and the All-Star Game. During the 2011 playoffs he attended close to two dozen games, and with a Vancouver–Boston final, ended up travelling cross-continent eight times. He flies by corporate jet, but travelling with Bettman is hardly luxurious. He prefers to red-eye back, no matter where the game is or how late it finishes: "I hate wasting a day and being out of touch."

The lengths to which he will go to keep his schedule can be extreme. When he found himself grounded in Omaha, Nebraska, in the wake of the 9/11 attacks, where he had flown in for a Warren Buffett–sponsored charity event, his first thought was to rent a car and drive back east. He called Hertz but they kiboshed the plan, saying they were only permitting their vehicles to head west, away from trouble. So Bettman hung up the phone and dialed again, telling another agent that he'd be in Omaha for the next three days and needed a car. He picked it up and immediately set out for the interstate, stopping only for gas, food, and to call the company to tell them that he'd be returning the car in New Jersey instead. He arrived home after nineteen-and-a-half hours of straight driving, had a shower and breakfast, and went into his office in a still-smoking Manhattan to start reworking the NHL's preseason schedule in light of the tragedy.

On board his late-night flights, he likes to listen to music— he's a passionate fan of baby-boomer classic rock like The Doors, Buffalo Springfield, and The Grateful Dead. Or he reads, usually historical biographies. *In the Garden of Beasts*, Erik Larson's best-seller about America's ambassador to Nazi Germany, William O. Dodd, and his family, was a recent fave. Hockey books don't make the cut.

What the commissioner rarely does is sleep. Since university, Bettman has survived on only four or five hours a night. "Sleep is something you do when you have to," he says. And NHL staffers are accustomed to the emails or phone calls that come at all hours. "Gary himself is more accessible, 24/7, 365 days a year, than anybody I know," says his number two, Bill Daly. "And I think he has an expectation that all his senior executives be available any time they're needed. We're never off, from that perspective."

But for all the workaholic tendencies, Bettman prides himself on being a family guy. He and his wife of thirty-eight years, Michelle (Shelli to her friends), have been together since they met as undergrads at Cornell University. The credenza behind his desk is chock-a-block with photos of her, their kids—daughters Lauren, thirty-three, and Brittany, twenty-three, and son Jordan, twenty-seven—and now two young grandchildren. Even during the season there are getaway weekends at the house in Florida or the ski chalet in Vermont. And it's not uncommon to encounter the extended Bettman clan (his eldest daughter and son are both married) at NHL events. Matthew, Lauren's six-year-old son, is a huge New Jersey Devils fan, who starts his day with the NHL Network's highlight show. Sometimes he and his grandpa, unshaven and undercover in jeans, an old sweater, ball cap, and sunglasses, take in matinee games at the Prudential Center, the downtown Newark rink that supplanted the Meadowlands arena in 2007.

It's a contrast to Bettman's own childhood. His parents, Howard and Joy, both native New Yorkers, married young and had Gary—their only child—in June 1952. Four years later, they divorced.

For the most part, Joy raised Gary alone. She received child support, and when he was little worked on and off, sometimes as a shoe model. It seems like an odd calling, but Bettman never thought to ask how or why. "She was petite and had small feet," he guesses. Joy's own parents were dead by the time the marriage dissolved, but there were aunts and uncles who helped out. Howard, who operated the business he had taken over from his own dad—The Bettman Nut Company ("Betty Nuts Are Better!"), located off Canal Street, now the heart of New York's Chinatown—remained a presence in Gary's life, teaching him to sail on weekends when he got a bit older, although it would be a stretch to say that they were close. Growing up in Queens in the 1950s, the circumstances were unusual but not unheard of: "I was fine. It wasn't painful or anything like that."

But Bettman does trace his own, slightly distant relationship with sports to that period. His first trips to Rangers and Knicks games were solo affairs, taking the subway down to the old Madison Square Garden and scoring 50-cent student tickets up by the rafters. Then he'd watch the action while doing his homework and eating the meal he'd packed from home. The excursions were more time killers than pilgrimages—he has no recollection of who the opponents were and can't name a favourite player. And later on, as he did become more of a fan, he gravitated to expansion clubs like the New York Jets, Mets, and then the Islanders. "As I think back on it, that was the coping mechanism. Getting my sport more directly, and not having to worry about having the history passed down. I could be on top of it from the very beginning." He doesn't have any of those memories of father–son bonding at the arena or ballpark. When his father died of leukemia in December 1965 at the age of forty, Bettman was just thirteen.

A year of so before his father's passing, Joy had begun to build a new life for her and her son, marrying another Howard—an accountant by the last name of Pollack. When Bettman was a high school junior, the family, which now included Jeffrey, his baby stepbrother, moved out to Dix Hills on Long Island. The alliterative Half Hollows Hills High (which also boasts Ralph Macchio, the Karate Kid, as a graduate) was different than the school he'd left behind in Queens, a place so overcrowded that the grades had staggered start and finish times. Half Hollows had a planetarium, an auditorium with a Broadway-sized stage, and a lot of green playing fields. Bettman joined the debate club and played halfback for the soccer team. Math was his best subject, although history and politics held more of an attraction.

Bettman had determined that he wanted to be a lawyer at a very early age. Maybe it was because that's what Joy's father had been. Or because becoming a doctor—the other occupation favoured by Jewish mothers—and the fallback option of joining the family nut business were of little interest. Even back then he was meticulous and goal driven. The never-once-deviated-from plan was to go to an Ivy League college and then on to law school. Cornell, in upstate Ithaca, New York, offered a degree in industrial and labour relations (ILR) that had none of the hard science or foreign language requirements of other pre-law programs. The tuition was low because the program was state funded. And it was the best Ivy League school he got into.

It was 1970, the Vietnam War still raged on, and the counterculture ruled, but Bettman's university days were decidedly buttoned-down. He joined Alpha Epsilon Pi, a fraternity whose other notable alumni include Jerry Lewis, Simon and Garfunkel, Facebook founder Mark Zuckerberg, and Jerry Reinsdorf, the wealthy owner of the Chicago Bulls and White Sox who was, for a time, kicking the tires of the Phoenix Coyotes. It was a frat brother who introduced Bettman to Shelli when he was in second year and she in her first. He remembers taking her to see a Bruce Springsteen concert at nearby Hobart College's homecoming celebrations—two tickets, $10 each, tenth row. During his summers off, he taught sailing. Even today during summer getaways, he'll occasionally rent a Laser and head out on his own. He tried to teach his kids, but they never had much interest.

Life in a college town agreed with him. Most of his closest friends date back to those days, including, in a more roundabout way, his best buddy, Lee, a New Jersey veterinarian who is married to a Cornell chum of Shelli's. And ILR, with its mixed focus on sociology, history, and psychology, proved to be right up his alley. (It may be something genetic: All three of his children are now graduates of the same program.) In his senior year, he took a course on the management of complex organizations and produced a thesis examining how Mafia dons structure their criminal enterprises and keep order among their foot soldiers. It was a little unorthodox, but received high marks. Bettman swears that none of his findings have proven applicable to his current position.

What Cornell also provided was his true introduction to hockey. In the spring of 1967, with Ken Dryden in goal, "Big Red" had won their first NCAA championship over Boston University. In 1969–70 the team had won it all again—going 29–0–0 for the only unbeaten, untied national championship hockey season in US college history. (Ned Harkness, the coach, parlayed that success into a job behind the bench for the Detroit Red Wings. But Toronto's Brian Cropper, who sparkled in net with a season GAA of 1.87, never managed to make the jump to the NHL.) And Big Red was still a powerhouse when Bettman showed up in Ithaca that next fall, running up a streak of consecutive home victories that eventually hit sixty-three games. Hockey was the hottest draw on campus, and he joined the crowds camping in tents outside James Lynah Rink to stake his claim for tickets. Bettman had season ducats all four years he was at the university, and it was there, he says, that he learned to love the game. One winter, Shelli taught him how to skate. And he even took a stab at playing pickup once or twice. With his Bambi legs and small stature, though, he soon figured out that he was safer cheering from the sidelines.

After his graduation in 1974, Bettman went on to study law at New York University, and that next summer he married Shelli, who had just finished her psychology degree. She joined him in New York and enrolled at the Hunter College School of Social Work, working toward her certification as a psychotherapist. They were young and temporarily poor.

Bettman likes to say that his ascent to big-league sports commissioner was mostly due to serendipity. "There are only four of these jobs. If that's what you wanted to be, you probably needed to be heavily medicated." But the path between certain US law offices and the inner sanctums of the NFL, NBA, Major League Baseball, and the National Hockey League is surprisingly well worn. Bettman joined Proskauer Rose Goetz & Mendelsohn, a New York firm specializing in labour and litigation, as a wet-behind-the-ears associate in the spring of 1977. It wasn't large, but there were some interesting clients. And it had a few lawyers who would go on to be very influential indeed. David Stern was a partner. So was Bob Batterman, now one of the lead negotiators for both the NHL and pro football. Ditto for Michael Cardozo, who had helped pilot the merger of the rival ABA and NBA in 1976 after a lengthy antitrust tussle with players. Bettman's first real court experience as a young associate—a case about a condo deal that had gone bad—was as an understudy to a senior partner named George Gallantz, who had been the outside general counsel for the National Basketball Association since the 1950s.

Stern doesn't recall much about his protege from those days— just that he was bright and awfully eager. Bettman did some depositions and prep work for him, and he would occasionally give the kid a lift back to New Jersey where they both were living at the time. And when Stern left Proskauer to become the NBA's chief in-house lawyer in 1978, the young associate was among those who came to the goodbye party. One of Bettman's friends remembers his excited reaction that night: "Wow, he has the greatest job in the world. I'd love to work with him."

The problem was that the future NHL commissioner didn't particularly enjoy life near the bottom of the New York legal food chain. He was dissatisfied with the assembly-line aspect of working as a junior and hungered for something more "dynamic," where the cases would be his, start to finish. In 1980, he met another young lawyer at a wedding who ran his own twenty-person firm in New Jersey. They hit it off, and Bettman quit Proskauer to join his practice. His friends and colleagues thought he was nuts.

Bettman regretted the decision almost immediately. He, Shelli, and baby Lauren were living in Connecticut. But a tumbling real estate market was making it impossible to sell their home, and he found himself commuting farther to his new job—fifty miles each way—than his old one. And despite the promises, the work was even less inspiring than the files he had left behind in Manhattan.

If there was a silver lining, it was that the daily drive took him right past his mother and stepfather's new home in Fort Lee, New Jersey. Joy had recently been diagnosed with brain cancer and was declining fast. So Bettman was able to stop in two or three times a week, give Howard a break, and connect with his then-teenage stepbrother. The visits were a comfort to Joy, if not to her first-born son. "When somebody dies of an illness, no matter how old they are, it sucks. I understand that," he says. Joy slipped away a few months later at the age of fifty-three.

His grief made the Jersey job seem all the worse. He was worried about looking flighty, but he had already started to put out feelers, placing a call to George Gallantz to confide how unhappy he was and find out if he had any clients who were looking for in-house help. He had decided that he was ambitious, after all. One gloomy Friday afternoon in December, the phone rang. The

NBA had promoted Stern to executive vice-president. Russ Granik was taking over as general counsel, and they were looking for a young lawyer to do the grunt work. Gallantz wanted to know if he might be interested. Bettman tried to play it cool, feigning a vague interest, but was practically dancing a jig behind his desk.

Stern called the next day and gave him a totally unnecessary sales job. A week later he made the trek into Manhattan for a more formal interview at the league's Fifth Avenue offices. Russ Granik remembers being impressed by the twenty-nine year old, who brimmed with energy and ambition—although also being somewhat taken aback by Bettman's full disco-era beard. The final blessing came in the form of a nighttime meeting with then NBA commissioner Larry O'Brien, in his corner office overlooking the spires of St. Patrick's Cathedral and the twinkling Christmas lights out on Fifth. An old political hand, O'Brien had directed John F. Kennedy's senate and presidential campaigns and was postmaster general under Lyndon Johnson. Later, he served two terms as the chair of the Democratic National Committee (it was his office that was the primary target of the Watergate burglars). Bettman was in awe: "This was the biggest deal person I had ever met in my life." O'Brien, a chain-smoker, spent an hour and a half regaling him with hacking tales of Camelot, then sent him on his way. The next day he was offered the job of assistant general counsel to the National Basketball Association.

The NBA in 1981 bore little resemblance to the multibillion-dollar marketing juggernaut that it is today. Bettman was just its twenty-fifth employee—including support staff. And the league, which had expanded to twenty-three teams after the merger with the ABA and the addition of the Dallas Mavericks, was struggling to find an audience. Games were often played before half-filled arenas, and television viewers were indifferent at best. CBS, the

NBA's broadcast partner since 1975, had taken to showing many of its playoff matchups on tape-delay, after the late local news. The year Bettman joined the league, only three of nine conference final games were carried live, and just two of the six games in a final that saw Larry Bird's Boston Celtics beat out Moses Malone's Houston Rockets. (During the regular season, things were even more dismal, with ABC's *Wide World of Sports* and NCAA basketball regularly clobbering NBA weekend afternoon games.)

To many sports fans, the NBA was more of a violent sideshow than a legitimate major league. On-court brawls were a common occurrence, but it was one particular punch that lingered in the public imagination. In December 1977, the Lakers' Kermit Washington had cold-cocked Houston's Rudy Tomjanovich as he ran to help break up a scuffle. The devastating sucker shot—Kareem Abdul-Jabbar, the great Lakers' star, later said it sounded like a watermelon hitting concrete—broke Tomjanovich's jaw, nose, face, and then his skull when he collapsed to the floor in a pool of blood. Spinal fluid leaked into his mouth and the Houston forward spent two weeks in intensive care. His doctors didn't hide the fact that he came perilously close to dying. Washington received a $10,000 fine and a sixty-day suspension, which cost him a further $43,000 in forfeited salary. But the league became a national joke. On *Saturday Night Live,* the lone black cast member, Garrett Morris, staged a mock defence, suggesting Washington was being treated harshly because he'd beaten up a white guy. "Look at that, look at that! The brother barely touched him," he shouted over the replay. Then came a comic pause. "Maybe we need a different angle."

Three years later, little progress had been made in rehabilitating the league's image. Players still seemed to make the headlines only for the wrong reasons like drug use, infidelities, and violence. And the list of franchises that were bleeding red ink—Cleveland,

Denver, Indiana, and Utah among them—was lengthening. Teams in Kansas City and San Diego almost provoked a strike when they fell behind on deferred payments to former players in 1982— although it was a league-wide problem, with some estimates pegging the amount of compensation due to retired players at US$90 million. At the NBA offices, there were serious discussions about contraction.

It was Stern who turned the ship around, by opening the books and convincing Larry Fleisher and the players association that a new, more cooperative labour model was needed if all their members wanted to keep their jobs. In March 1983, after months of fraught negotiations, the two sides settled on the first salary cap in pro sports, pegging the salary ceiling at $3.6 million per team (plus a bunch of exceptions). In return, the players were guaranteed 53 percent of gross revenue—including ticket sales and local and national TV contracts—going forward. Fuelled by new broadcast deals, an arena building boom, and the arrival of Michael Jordan in the 1984 draft, the league took off. And within four seasons, the cap had doubled. By 1992–93, it stood at $14 million, and the average player salary had gone from $340,000 to $1.35 million.

Bettman sometimes gets credit as the architect of the NBA's system. But he was still on a steep learning curve when Stern, ten years his senior, and Granik, who is six years older, were hammering out the details. As it turns out, Bettman's contribution as the new guy was mostly getting it all down on paper. The kind of legal drudge work that he used to despise, but now embraced with gusto. "He's indomitable of spirit when it comes to working," says the NBA commissioner. It was the next year, when Stern officially took over the reins from O'Brien and Granik moved up to the number-two job, that Bettman really started to prove his worth. Named the league's general counsel, he became the keeper of the cap, charged with frustrating attempts by owners and player agents to circumvent the spirit of the agreement. The so-called Larry Bird exception, which allowed teams to exceed the salary ceiling to re-sign one of their own players, was turning into a massive loophole. "Teams were holding off signing their own guys until after they went out and got free agents, effectively making it a much bigger deal," recalls Granik. And it was just one of the dodges. "We had big accounting and timing issues in the early years."

But that wasn't all that Bettman did for the league. As the organization's number-three man during its decade of explosive growth, he participated in collective bargaining with the players and referees, oversaw licensing and international alliances, and developed the production side of the business, NBA Entertainment. He also shepherded four new expansion franchises—Charlotte, Miami, Minnesota, and Orlando—into being. And he helped negotiate new TV deals—most notably a four-year, $600-million agreement with NBC in 1989—forging relationships that would end up paying off for his next employer years down the road.

The kid from Queens who had dreamed of becoming a lawyer had found a much better job—one that stretched him in all directions at once, demanding the kind of mastery of diverse details that few people are capable of. And his fearsome ability to focus was starting to earn him a wider reputation. Michael Cardozo, then still doing NBA work at Proskauer (and now the City of New York's corporation counsel), remembers being in the league offices one night, working to diffuse a crisis. Bettman, who was one of the first people he knew to have a cell in his car, was driving home to New Jersey, but relaying instructions back to a group clustered around the speaker phone. At one point, he calmly slipped in an aside: "I think you're going to hear a crash in a moment." The car had hit some black ice. Soon there was the sound of crunching metal, but no pause in the lecture. Bettman just kept on talking, even as he slid into the ditch.

THERE ARE MANY THINGS that Bruce McNall could be accused of—and convicted of, as it turns out—but thinking small is not among them. And so it was with his private breakfast meeting with David Stern at New York's Plaza Hotel in the fall of 1992.

McNall, the man who had ransomed Wayne Gretzky to the Los Angeles Kings for US$15 million four years earlier and fundamentally altered the business of hockey, was the new chair of the NHL's board of governors. In late June, the league's owners had abruptly altered course, dumping longtime president John Ziegler and overthrowing Bill Wirtz, the hard-drinking, hard-knocks proprietor of the Chicago Blackhawks who had led their cabal since the 1970s. Part of it was fallout from the first-ever strike by players on the eve of the Stanley Cup playoffs. Ziegler's response had been weak-kneed—even erratic at times—like when he teared up at a press conference, wondering aloud if "our fans will ever forgive us." And despite all his yelling, Wirtz—the old school scion of sports and real estate baron who had grown up sparring with pro boxers, learned to shoot from Hopalong Cassidy, and once took a punch from Rocky Marciano in a barroom brawl—had been unable to do much about it. The one-year deal, clinched just eleven days into the dispute, was a lopsided win for the union and its rookie leader Bob Goodenow. The NHL Players' Association (NHLPA) got its members a bigger share of the playoff money, retained control of hockey card revenues, got the draft shortened by one round, and won concessions on waivers and free agency. All the owners received in return were four extra games each season— and two of those were neutral site affairs from which the profits had to be split with players.

Though more than that, the palace coup was a recognition that the sport itself was changing. The twenty-four-team NHL was drawing 13 million fans a year, filling 90 percent of its seats. But the owners were no longer making the same sort of profits they used to. Player costs were spiralling. The average salary had gone from US$149,000 in 1984–85, when the top earner was the Kings' Dave Taylor at $725,000, to $369,000 in 1991–92, with Mark Messier of the Rangers taking home $2.786 million. And revenues from tickets, concessions, parking, and TV weren't nearly keeping pace.

What McNall offered was hope through hype. He was a self-made—or more accurately, invented—type who had risen from the California middle class to become one of the west coast's highest rollers. The creation myth started with a couple of Roman coins he bought from a strip mall numismatist in suburban Los Angeles for a dollar each when he was thirteen. By fifteen, the chubby kid was trading by mail with fellow enthusiasts all across the country and selling his wares from behind the counter of a liquor store where he had an after-school job. At sixteen, he branched out to the European market and made enough money to buy a car to drive to school—a Jaguar XK-E. There was a stint at UCLA studying ancient Roman history, but by that time he says he was making US$500,000 a year and was a little too busy to give university his full attention. In 1974, at age twenty-four, he set the world record by paying $425,000 for a single coin at auction, outbidding Aristotle Onassis and Valéry Giscard d'Estaing, soon to become France's president, at a Zurich auction.

In the late 1970s, McNall teamed up with Herbert and Nelson Bunker Hunt, Texas oil billionaires who were trying to corner not only the world market for silver, but also the one for ancient coins. They opened the door to the sports world—McNall became a minority owner of the Dallas Mavericks—and Hollywood, too. With the brothers' backing, he started an LA production company that financed one of Sting's early forays into film, the 1982 stinker *Brimstone and Treacle*. (At least the soundtrack made money.) Subsequent efforts proved more successful. By the end of the decade, McNall's name was attached to films like *Mr. Mom, Blame It on Rio*, and *Weekend at Bernie's*.

But coins remained his core business. Jerry Buss, the owner of both the LA Lakers and the LA Kings, was a customer and a friend in the can-you-lend-me-some-money sort of way. "From time to time, he needed dough," McNall chuckles. "Small amounts—$25,000 here, $150,000 there. And it finally got to the point where he owed me a fair amount of money, a million or so." The debt was settled in 1986 when McNall took a quarter interest in the NHL club for what he was owed, plus $3 million down. A few months later he exercised an option to buy a further 24 percent, becoming the Kings' largest shareholder. In March 1988, he bought Buss out completely. And that August, after months of clandestine discussion, he shocked Canada to its core by shipping Jimmy Carson, Martin Gelinas, three first-round draft picks, and a boatload of cash to the Oilers' Peter Pocklington in exchange for Mike Krushelnyski, Marty McSorley, and the greatest hockey player in the history of the game.

Bringing the Gretzky circus to one of America's biggest media markets gave the sleepy little league a jolt like it had never experienced before. In the Great One's first LA season, the Kings took in an additional $5 million at the gate, peddled another $1 million in advertising, got $1 million more for their TV rights, and sold more black-and-silver sweaters than anyone thought possible. And more important, hockey was suddenly cool with the Hollywood crowd. Not just among Canadian ex-pats like Michael J. Fox and

Alan Thicke, but with real, honest-to-God American celebrities like Tom Hanks, Jack Nicholson, and Goldie Hawn, who became regulars at games. Now three seasons later, the jolly, fat ringmaster was being asked to mount the same sort of show on the road. "I think there was a sense that maybe I could leverage what I had done with the Gretzky deal for the whole league," says McNall, "that there was a bit of magic."

His first task was to find a new leader for the NHL. Gil Stein, who had been general counsel under Ziegler, was busying himself as interim president, trying to make a case to hold on to the top job. But the owners were looking for a clean break. They formed a hiring committee, comprising the Habs' Ronald Corey, Mike Ilitch of the Red Wings, Ed Snider of the Flyers, the Oilers' Peter Pocklington, and McNall, and engaged an executive search firm. Several candidates emerged, including the CEO of a large US health-care conglomerate, the president of a major insurance company, and a recently departed and much-hated Canadian prime minister. Interviews were held and a short list was drawn up. McNall was underwhelmed. "I was sitting there, saying to myself, 'This is dumb.' As talented as these people are, what do they know about pro sports or running a franchise or labour unions?"

So, without seeking anyone's permission, he flew to New York, invited Stern to breakfast, and asked the commissioner of the National Basketball Association to switch leagues. The salary offer was generous, the bonus package huge, and it was all rejected out of hand. The Kings' owner then switched to Plan B. What about the NBA's number two, Russ Granik? Stern again said no, although he did propose an alternative—if the NHL really wanted to, it could talk to Gary Bettman. McNall knew the name, but not much else. "David told me he's a lawyer and involved in all our labour negotiations and all that shit." It sounded promising. A meeting was arranged for the next day. Bettman wasn't quite as cocksure as he would become once he got the job, but McNall was impressed by his knowledge and moxie.

Bettman had just turned forty and was again feeling restless. The NBA was riding high, but with two guys in front of him the prospects for advancement anytime in the near future were slim. So he was more enthusiastic about the NHL opportunity than most of the other candidates. As far as McNall was concerned, the search was over. Now it was just a matter of convincing his colleagues to see things his way. "I knew we'd have some problems, because Gary wasn't a hockey guy. He was a little Jewish guy from New York, and that didn't necessarily fit well with folks out of Calgary or other such locations. But I figured I had enough clout to get it done."

Such fears were baseless—at least when it came to the other league governors. Bettman's formal interview a few weeks later went even better than his meeting with McNall. The owners quizzed him on the NBA's salary cap, asked how he would approach the NHL's upcoming labour negotiations, and probed his thoughts on marketing a big-league sport. And for every question, Bettman had a ready answer, highlighting how basketball was succeeding and where hockey was failing. Ed Snider, who was backing another candidate, immediately switched allegiances. "He blew me away. I just felt that he had to be the guy," says the man who has owned the Flyers since their inception. "He was so well-versed in league matters and what was necessary, and the kinds of things he could do with the experience he had at the NBA." And the feeling was pretty much unanimous. Gil Stein was quietly convinced to withdraw his candidacy with the help of a five-year, $500,000-per-annum consulting contract, on top of his

$250,000-a-year pension. And on December 11, 1992, during a meeting at the luxurious Breakers Hotel in Palm Beach, Florida, the board of governors made it official, introducing the NHL's first commissioner to the hockey world.

The production values were somewhat lacking. The scene was a windowless banquet room with a dais and a few rows of white folding chairs. Bettman sat up front at a table, flanked by McNall and Stein. There was a black curtain behind him, to which someone had pinned a large NHL pennant featuring the old black-and-orange shield. The youthful new commissioner, with a thick head of slick, dark hair, looked the part in a sober blue suit—although in hindsight, his garish yellow-and-orange tie might have been somewhat over the top (like "Jerry Garcia tried to draw a map of Portugal," one blogger quipped, when video of the press conference resurfaced on the internet last year). Bettman, wearing a big smile, got off on the right foot with the media, insisting that they call him Gary—a nice departure from their stiff and formal interactions with Mr. Ziegler. And he promised big changes for a league that had been lagging behind its competitors for far too long. "We're going to dispel the myth that this is a regional sport," he said. "The prospects for growth are phenomenal." His first priority would be to get a new national television contract with one of the big American networks.

A reporter asked whether he'd been hired to bring in a salary cap and got a noncommittal response about creating a system that would work well for all sides. Bettman also deftly sidestepped a query about the future of fighting, saying he wasn't yet sure of his personal opinion, but wanted to do the best thing for the business. And when the focus turned to his own connection with the game, he frankly admitted it was tenuous: "I have been a hockey fan at various points in my life. I'm about to become a big-time fan. I'm going to cram. I plan to be around for a while." When the questions were done, the commissioner pulled on an oversized black-and-orange NHL All-Star sweater with number 1 on the back and broke into an ear-to-ear grin for the cameras. He looked like a little kid on Christmas morning.

Bettman's new employers were similarly giddy. "He's a super-star," proclaimed Chicago's Wirtz. "From what we've been told, this guy knows the problem of our own business better than we do," another governor told the *Toronto Star*. "He's going to hit the ground with both feet moving." A former NBA colleague went further. "They're getting the most valuable person in hockey since Wayne Gretzky," predicted John Steinmiller, an executive with the Milwaukee Bucks. Even future foes were willing to believe that this might be the start of something big, with Bob Goodenow faxing his congratulations and best wishes.

Although not everyone who knew him saw him as such a natural fit. "I gave Gary a hockey puck once, and he spent the rest of the day trying to open it," Pat Williams, the general manager of the Orlando Magic, joked.

Bettman's old firm Proskauer had represented the NHL in the contract negotiations, which centred not only on salary and perks but also on the changes he wanted to make to the league's constitution, giving him not just a new title but much more power than the old presidents. Under the terms of the deal, Bettman would be able to set agendas, resolve disputes among clubs, and when necessary, punish team executives—and owners—who spoke out of turn. Michael Cardozo was on hand to work out the final details, and after things were all signed and sealed, he and the new commissioner hitched a ride back to New York on a private jet belonging to Paramount Communications, then owners of the Rangers. It was late on Friday afternoon, and they were both heading to the NBA's holiday party, which was to take place that night.

The weather had been nice in Florida, but a major snowstorm was buffeting the northeast coast. The flight became bumpier, and then it got downright hairy. All the airports around New York were shutting down, and it wasn't clear where they were going to land. There was some not-quite-so-jokey banter in the cabin about whether or not they were going to make it. It was at this point that it dawned on Cardozo and Bettman that all the copies of his new contract, listing the benefits due to his family in the event of his untimely demise, were onboard the aircraft. "I think the two of us looked at each other and said, 'Holy shit! What dumb asses we are,'" recounts Cardozo. When the plane finally did touch down safely, they were still laughing. Gary Bettman was home safe, although he hadn't yet come down to earth.

THE HONEYMOON DIDN'T LAST LONG. The morning he officially took over the job, February 1, 1993, the *Toronto Star* ran a long piece on the new commissioner headlined "Bettman's NHL era begins: 'Everything is under review.'" In the interview with Bob McKenzie, the incoming boss mused about the various changes he might want to make: reducing the number of Canadian offices and consolidating league operations in New York, beefing up staff—especially in regard to marketing, licensing, and broadcasting—and tinkering with the game itself. He singled out fighting, the two-line pass, and icing rules as areas of concern. Bettman also talked about the need to rethink TV broadcasts and find a way to make the action easier for non-fans to follow, perhaps even using computer technology. And then he said "orange puck." No matter that the phrase was actually preceded by the words "I'm not looking at doing anything stupid, like using an ..." Or followed by a declaration that such a move would be "completely inconsistent with everything I've ever learned about running a sports league." "Orange puck" is what stuck in the public imagination.

It was one thing to be a hockey outsider, but it was quite another to be seen as an arriviste trying to remake the sport to suit the needs of an audience that didn't yet exist. The tone of the media coverage started to shift, subtly at first. A sit-down with Réjean Tremblay of *La Presse* during a trip to Montreal the next week resulted in the immortal headline *"Gary Bettman arrive au hockey comme E.T. arrivait sur la terre ..."* (Gary Bettman comes to hockey like E.T. came to earth), which was actually an advantage, according to the writer. Then people stopped even pretending to be nice. Within a few months, the commissioner was firmly on the defensive. "I am not a control freak," he told the *Star* later that year. "I am a good delegator. I hire bright young people who will go through walls to get the job done."

Sometimes it felt like the whole league was ganging up on the new kid. On March 23, 1994, Bettman was at the LA Forum for a Wednesday night game between the Kings and the Vancouver Canucks. On the Sunday before, playing on the road against San Jose, Gretzky had scored the 801st goal of his NHL career, tying his childhood idol Gordie Howe for the all-time lead—in just his sixteenth season, versus the twenty-six it took the Red Wings great to do it. Now the commissioner was on hand for the big moment. The plans were set. When Gretzky scored—there were no "ifs" with Wayne—the action would stop for a special, red carpet presentation at centre ice with his wife Janet, mom Phyllis, father Walter, and Bruce McNall standing at his side. Bettman would emcee. There was a gift: a thick book containing the score sheet from every game in which Gretzky had tallied. (Not quite as impressive as the $275,000 Rolls-Royce convertible the Kings owner would present his star a few days later.) And Bettman had even worked out what he was going to say. "You've always been the Great One. But tonight, you become the Greatest."

The magic moment didn't come in the first period. Still, Bettman followed through with plans for a live, between-periods TV interview in a studio down at ice level. By the time it finished, just before play was to resume, he was in desperate need of a washroom. The nearest at hand was in the visitors' dressing room. But while the commissioner was using the facilities the Canucks departed for their bench, padlocking the door behind them. Bettman didn't have his cell phone with him, so for long minutes he screamed and pounded on the door, hoping to attract someone's attention. He got lucky. A Vancouver trainer returned to the room to sharpen a skate and set him free. The commissioner made it back to his seat just in time to see Gretzky snap a Marty McSorley feed past the Canucks' Kirk McLean at 14:47 of the second period. (Vancouver went on to win 6–3, spoiling the party.)

Almost two decades later, the indignities persist. But sitting in his Manhattan office on a summer's morning with his feet up on a coffee table, far removed from the booing crowds, Bettman claims that none of it bugs him, that it matters little if hockey fans ever embrace him. "The fact is, when you are in the public eye this much, people come to their own understanding and beliefs without knowing you. They believe what they want to believe." The real Gary Bettman is more relaxed, and happier, than is portrayed, he says. "I'm not sitting around plotting the things the media would suggest. That view is somebody's fiction, for whatever reason."

Brian Burke, the pugnacious president and general manager of the Toronto Maple Leafs, spent five years working for Bettman as the league's vice-president of hockey operations in the mid-1990s, and remains one of his most ardent defenders. The big, quick-tempered Irish American has always had his own fraught relationship with the media, but argues that his former boss gets treated even more harshly. He ticks off a bunch of reasons for why things are the way they are: the proprietary attitude that Canadians have toward the game, old prejudices, and the commissioner being perhaps a little too smart for a dumb sport. Burke, a Harvard law grad, says he routinely used to have to lean over in meetings and ask him to slow things down so he and everyone else could catch up. And within the Leafs organization, Bettman's intelligence has become a sort of measuring stick: "We'll say, is that guy smart? Yeah, he's Gary-smart." Burke might be the only one who takes his friend at his word when he says he's indifferent to the critics and the boo-birds. He likens him to the man who buys a house near the airport. When people come over for a barbeque they wonder how he can stand the noise. And his response is, "What noise?" What rings truer is his observation that Bettman, like most people, would prefer to be liked, but often doesn't have that luxury in his job. "If the question is be popular or do the right thing, he's always going to do the right thing," says Burke.

One thing's for sure, the displays of antipathy do bother Bettman's family and his friends. They avoid reading what's written about him or watching the intermission shows where the pundits regularly tear him apart. In all these years, Shelli has never really given an interview or let the public have a glimpse of their private life. When he first got the job, *The Hockey News* pitched a profile where they would follow the commissioner through a typical day, starting with his 6:30 A.M. jog. Bettman put the proposal to a vote at the dinner table. His wife and kids were unanimous in their opposition. When her husband took over the NHL, Shelli was still working as a psychotherapist in New Jersey treating substance abuse patients, but she gradually phased out her practice. Her focus switched first to raising the kids and then to protecting Gary. Their home and getaway places are refuges, where he doesn't have to be amped up and engaged all the time. "She's the foundation," he says. "To me, driving around with the roof down in Florida for twenty minutes is a vacation." And that's about as much of an escape he ever allows himself.

The fact that it's lonely at the top suits Bettman just fine. For after twenty years in the commissioner's job, he has become the most powerful figure the game has ever known. He's changed the economics of the sport and carved a path for other major leagues to follow. He's transformed the way hockey is played on the ice, how it's packaged for sale, and how it's consumed at home. He has preserved the game in Canada and dragged it onto the national stage in the United States. The owners, his titular employers, now interact with him—and each other—according to his rules. And even if the fans claim to loathe him, for all those reasons and more, they long ago swallowed his marketing vision, forever finding reasons to celebrate hockey's traditions in places where the game has no history.

He's sometimes prickly, often tone deaf, and infuriatingly evasive about the NHL's problems and intentions, but on his watch the sport continues to prosper. And in the end, the animus that hockey fans bear toward him says as much about them—and the national insecurities of Canadians in particular—as it does his preening and pettiness. Long accustomed to defending an under-appreciated sport, they've come to believe that fandom is more of a calling than a choice—and that when the game succeeds in unlikely spots, that uniqueness is somehow diminished. It's like when music fans lament that their favourite band has finally hit the big time. And for two decades, Gary Bettman has been to puck purists what

Casey Kasem is to indie rockers. Hockey is a cult, and its followers too often find validation in its failures.

On his office wall, just to the right of his desk, there are two needlepoints that Shelli made for him years ago. One features some law books sitting atop a desk and the inscription "Gary Bettman, Esquire." The other is a hockey puck with the old NHL shield above two crossed hockey sticks and the initials G.B.

He takes a visitor on a tour of the mementos he's acquired over the course of his career. In a corner, there's a life-sized replica of the Stanley Cup, made from 6000 pieces of Lego. The Lester Patrick Trophy he won in 2001 for his service to US hockey sits on a shelf next to two Emmys and the *SportsBusiness Journal*'s 2011 plaque for professional league of the year. On the coffee table, there's a copy of Andrew Podnieks's book *Canada's Olympic Hockey History: 1920–2010*, inscribed, "To Gary Bettman, a great friend of Canada—Stephen Harper," a keepsake he never fails to point out to Canadian journalists. In an anteroom near his desk, the wall is adorned with photos of him posing with former US president Bill Clinton and former prime minister Jean Chrétien. And there's a large poster of the commissioner as a costumed superhero, rendered by Marvel Comics legend Stan Lee.

But it's the adjoining bathroom that wins the prize. Inside, there's a large framed picture of Bettman, McNall, and Gretzky standing on the ice that night at the LA Forum, autographed by the Great One himself.

Maybe the commissioner even has a sense of humour.

2 From Failing Hands

Maurice Richard stepped off the red carpet and pitched forward, dropping the Stanley Cup with a clang onto the freshly cleaned ice. As the chalice rolled to his left, the crowd at the Montreal Forum let out the sort of anguished "*ohhh*" usually reserved for a cannonading drive that had just missed the net. But it was soon clear that the seventy-two-year-old Rocket was more sheepish than injured. Guy Lafleur gently took him by the elbow and lifted him back up on his skates as Jean Béliveau bent to collect the dented hardware. Then the three aging stars began a slow victory lap around the rink, arthritically handing off the NHL's Holy Grail to the strains of Metallica's "Enter Sandman." It was not an auspicious beginning.

The idea was to commemorate the soon-to-be hundredth anniversary of Lord Stanley's mug. In the 1892–93 season, the much smaller (and lighter) Cup had been awarded to a team affiliated with Montreal's Amateur Athletic Association. They won it again the following year, then lost it to another local club. In the trophy's first two decades, it rarely left the city, awarded to Montreal squads on sixteen different occasions. And after the National Hockey League was formed in 1917 the trend continued. The Montreal

Maroons, long since defunct, won the title in 1926 and another time in the mid-1930s. The Canadiens captured it at least once in every decade, and virtually owned the Cup through the 1950s, '60s, and '70s. The three former captains on the ice had a hand in eighteen of the franchise's then twenty-three championships.

Maybe the stumble wouldn't have garnered so much attention if what followed had borne even a passing resemblance to the playoff memories they were summoning. The 1993 All-Star Game was anything but glorious, however. Mike Gartner, a last-minute replacement for his injured New York Rangers teammate Mark Messier, scored the Wales Conference's first goal on a tip three minutes in. Seventeen seconds later, he had his second, when Chicago's Ed Belfour charged out almost to the blue line to clear a puck and whiffed, letting it right through his legs. "Oh, baby!" John Davidson exclaimed on the NBC telecast. "That's why goaltenders wear masks." By period's end, Gartner had a hat trick and was well on his way to the new car awarded to the game's MVP, and the Wales Conference was leading 6–0.

Calgary's goaltender Mike Vernon fared no better in the second, letting in six more goals on just fifteen shots. Although his Campbell Conference teammates did at least manage to hit the back of the net twice and keep the gap to ten. There were eight more goals in the third, including a tally by Brad Marsh—the lone representative of the truly awful expansion Ottawa Senators. Closing in on his thirty-fifth birthday, he had played more than 1000 games in the NHL and was among the final few veterans still not wearing a helmet. But with just twenty-three goals in fifteen seasons, the big defenceman was not known for his touch around the crease. The final score was 16–6 in favour of the Wales Conference. "You know you're in big trouble when Marsh scores," was the headline in the next day's *Montreal Gazette*.

Gary Bettman, only a couple of days into his new job as commissioner, tried to remain upbeat. "I think the players wanted to make me feel comfortable. I came from a place where there was a lot of scoring," the former NBA executive told an interviewer. But he was a stranger in a strange land. The educational component of the weekend had already gone far beyond the copy of Ken Dryden's memoir *The Game* that he was lugging around. Some helpful soul had advised him that with all the transportation the league was providing between the hotel, the parties, and the rink, he wouldn't even need an overcoat—in February, in Montreal. And sitting in the stands, he and his party had quickly been brought up to speed about how the players viewed the All-Star contest. "The goalie looked like he was having trouble bending over," recalls Bob Batterman, a colleague from Bettman's old law firm who was helping the NHL prepare for the upcoming labour negotiations. So he asked Gil Stein, the outgoing league president, what the problem was: "He told us that the goaltender had come in at about three o'clock in the morning, drunk as a skunk, and that he was terribly hung over."

Afterwards in the dressing room, a dispirited Wayne Gretzky— no points, just a couple of shots, and captain of the losing side—offered a blunt assessment of the afternoon's festivities: "I know you guys are looking at this and thinking it's a piece of crap. Well, you're probably right." The game's biggest star wasn't himself. A herniated disc in his back had kept him off the ice until early December and away from practice until after Christmas. He had fourteen points in fourteen games since returning to play on January 6, but he hadn't scored in a dozen matches. At the All-Star Skills Competition, Gretzky had fallen trying to make a tight turn around a pylon. And during the game he was almost invisible— except for the time he failed to bury a perfect Brett Hull feed into a wide-open net. At thirty-two he suddenly looked old. In the press box, the reporters had taken to calling him "the Good One."

Eric Lindros, the nineteen-year-old Philadelphia Flyers rookie dubbed "the Next One," wasn't even at the game, but rather back at his parents' home in Toronto, awaiting a verdict in his assault trial. He'd been the league's dominant headline maker since June, when the Quebec Nordiques finally traded him following his year-long holdout—to two different teams. The swap with the Flyers came first: Mike Ricci, Peter Forsberg, Steve Duchesne, Ron Hextall, Kerry Huffman, Chris Simon, two draft picks, and US$15 million for a kid who had yet to play a game in the NHL. Then, ten minutes after Marcel Aubut, the principal owner of the Nords, had verbally shaken hands, he called Philadelphia back to say that Lindros was instead on his way to the New York Rangers. That agreement would have seen Doug Weight, Tony Amonte, John Vanbiesbrouck, prospect Alexei Kovalev, three first-round draft picks, and a similar amount of cash head to Quebec City. The embarrassment was punted to an arbitrator, who quickly ruled that a deal was a deal, even if Aubut did get a better offer. By month's end, Lindros had a six-year contract with Philly and was among the league's best-paid players.

His first season hadn't gone according to plan, however. Yes, Lindros did have twenty-one goals and sixteen assists by the All-Star break, but he had also missed twenty-three games due to injury. His 6-foot-4, 235-pound frame and physical style belied his fragility. Four months into his NHL career, he was already contending with two wonky knees and a chronic inflammation of the right elbow. And despite being paid like a superstar, the fans around the league were treating him more like a villain. In October, during his first visit to Quebec's Colisée in a Flyers uniform, Nordiques fans held up mock tombstones and littered the ice with baby pacifiers, coins, batteries, and golf balls while rattling the rafters with a heavily accented "Fuck Lindros" chant. In many rinks, he was booed every time he touched the puck. Then there was the incident that made Koo Koo Bananas famous.

In late November, when Lindros was recovering from his first big-league knee injury, he travelled back to Ontario to seek treatment and blow off steam with some friends. On a Saturday night, they headed off to an oddly named bar in a suburban Toronto strip mall to watch the Flyers play the Islanders and have a few drinks. Long after midnight, Lindros was taken by the urge to dance. Some bumping on the nightclub floor led to a confrontation. A beer was poured down the hockey star's back and, in turn, he spit a mouthful of suds in the face of twenty-four-year-old Marie Lynn Nunney. More alcohol was senselessly wasted and the cops were called. Out in the parking lot, an officer tried to broker a mutual apology, but an enraged Lindros just kept talking about how much money he made and the type of legal counsel he could afford. A couple of weeks later Durham Regional Police issued a warrant for his arrest. When he flew back home, he allegedly threatened a *Toronto Sun* reporter he found waiting for him at the airport if he didn't put down his camera. There were no consequences for that, but the pictures in the next day's papers captured an even lower moment— an unshaven Lindros, hair thickly gelled and dressed all in denim like an outcast from Menudo, being perp-walked into an Oshawa police station with his wrists cuffed. "I got a little ink on my hands, but I smiled for the mug shot," he later told reporters.

The trial in early February took three days and drew press from across North America. Despite the testimony of nine witnesses, Ontario Court Justice J. Rhys Morgan was unable to determine who had been the first to go ape that evening. He dismissed the charge of common assault the day after the All-Star Game, delivering a ruling from the bench that suggested he might have been questioning his own life choices: "Should a court be asked to view, through the prism of criminal law, behaviour that would best be described as rude and insulting?"

Waiting to learn his fate that weekend, however, Lindros must have surely wondered at the welcome Montreal fans gave Mario Lemieux. The Pittsburgh Penguins star, winner of back-to-back Stanley Cups and Conn Smythe awards, had started the 1992–93 season on a tear, racking up twenty-seven points in his first eight games. He was on pace to top his 1988–89 total of eighty-five goals and 114 assists—199 points—and perhaps even challenge Gretzky's single-season record of 215 points set almost a decade earlier during the run-and-gun glory days of the Edmonton Oilers. In October, on his twenty-seventh birthday, Lemieux signed the richest contract in league history—$42 million over seven years for his marketing rights as well as his on-ice skills. He was becoming the face of the game.

Then things started to fall apart. In early November, on an off-night in Minnesota before a tilt against the North Stars, Lemieux and his teammates Bob Errey and Rick Tocchet went for dinner at a Hooters restaurant in the Mall of America in suburban Bloomington, near the rink. Dan Quinn, a former Penguin then playing for the Stars, joined them. Beers were consumed, and the group flirted with a waitress and two of her young friends, who were there waiting for her to get off shift. Errey eventually called it a night, but everyone else went back to Mario's room at the Marriott to continue the party. Later, one of the women—a nineteen year old—went to police alleging that Quinn had sexually assaulted her. The North Stars player claimed that what happened was consensual, but he was arrested and then released on $30,000 bail. The incident made the papers, and soon it emerged via a police affidavit that Lemieux had been present in the room during the alleged attack. The district attorney declined to move ahead with formal charges against Quinn, but the damage to Lemieux's squeaky-clean image—his fiancée in Pittsburgh was then pregnant with their first child—was considerable. Especially back in his home province of Quebec.

On January 5, during a game against Boston, Lemieux left the ice in the middle of the second period with back spasms. Disc problems had hampered him since the 1989–90 season, and even after surgery his spine was wonky enough that a Penguins trainer was tasked with doing up and loosening his skates. The team doctor came down to the dressing room to check him out—nothing was out of the ordinary, except for a small lump on his neck. A specialist performed a biopsy later that week, and Lemieux was diagnosed with Hodgkin's lymphoma. The disease was in its earliest stage—confined to just one lymph node—and 95 percent of such patients made a full recovery. But cancer was cancer. At a press conference on January 15, Lemieux talked about his own shock. "I could hardly drive home because of the tears," he said. "I was crying all day." There would be surgery to remove the affected node, then twenty-two radiation treatments over the next month. The Penguins star hoped to be back on the ice in time for the playoffs.

His absence cast a pall over the All-Star celebrations—until its dramatic dissipation right before the puck was dropped. "During the opening ceremonies, the towering man in the dark suit stood hidden in a back corridor while familiar names were announced amid polite applause and uneven cheering," Roy MacGregor wrote in *Road Games*, his chronicle of the 1992–93 season. "He heard the crowd roar when the hometown hero, Patrick Roy, was introduced, and he heard the more familiar cheer—the sudden snap of sound only the real heroes bring forth—when Gretzky's name was called. When he heard the lead-in to his own name he moved through the doorway and into sight of those nearest the entrance, and the sudden snap was replaced with a roar of surprise, the sound building as the fans spotted him and reacted to the presence of a god they feared might be dying."

The standing ovation lasted for minutes on end, and thundered again when Scotty Bowman, the coach who had guided the Penguins to their second Cup, gave him a hug and the white All-Star sweater with the number 66 on the back and the captain's C on the front. Lemieux shrugged off his suit coat and tugged the sweater over his head. The crowd went wild again.

It was Bettman who had made the phone call and talked him into coming to Montreal, engineering the catharsis for a wounded star and his fans. But he got little credit for his deft manipulations. Instead, the media were focused on the question of whether he had any instincts for the game itself. One of his first moves as commissioner was to order up some new commercials to promote hockey on both sides of the border. The slickly produced spots focused on players' grace, speed, and skill in an effort to overcome what Skip Prince, then the NHL broadcast director, termed the "toothless goon theory." Predictably, however, purists were not impressed by the images of glimmering skate blades carving pristine ice sheets in slow motion, or the "Share the glory" tag line. If that is what hockey is all about, "they might as well show Kurt Browning or Elvis Stojko," Ron MacLean, the host of *Hockey Night in Canada*, sniffed to the *Toronto Star*. Although what was really under the microscope was Bettman's view on fisticuffs. Would he mess with hockey's most violent tradition to make the sport more palatable to a mass American audience? While attending games in Toronto and Montreal just prior to the All-Star break, he had pointedly remained seated when the crowds rose to their feet and cheered on the heavyweights. Pressed by reporters, he claimed to be somewhat baffled by the on-ice scraps. "I don't get particularly excited by fighting," said Bettman. "Fighting doesn't turn me on, and it doesn't turn me off. I'd like to understand it better."

The death of John Kordic the previous summer had reignited the debate. The twenty-seven-year-old enforcer won a Stanley Cup with the Canadiens in 1986 and became a fan favourite in Toronto after the Leafs traded away Russ Courtnall's speed for his ham-sized fists in the fall of 1988. But his problems with alcohol and drugs soon sent his life and career into a nosedive. A stint with the Washington Capitals ended after two suspensions and a failed trip to rehab. Then he signed with the Nordiques for the 1991–92 season and played just nineteen games, collecting two points and 115 minutes in penalties, before he was cut loose over discipline issues. He finished the year in the AHL, playing for Edmonton's affiliate in Cape Breton.

On the evening of August 8, 1992, Kordic walked into a low-rent hotel in the Quebec City suburb of L'Ancienne-Lorette, dropped a $100 bill on the counter, and demanded a room. His face was bruised, his knuckles bloody, and he'd been drinking, although he convinced the clerk he just wanted to sleep. A couple of hours later he began to make abusive and threatening calls to the front desk, and the frightened manager called the police.

When officers arrived, they found him pacing like a jungle cat inside his trashed suite. He was sweating heavily, hitting himself and swearing, and there was blood all over the bed and the walls. Recognizing whom they were dealing with, they called for backup. In the end, it took nine cops to wrestle him to the ground and cuff his hands behind his back. They carried him outside and placed him in a waiting ambulance. On the way to the hospital Kordic stopped breathing. The official cause of death was heart failure and a collapsed lung, but a coroner would later testify that the man—238 pounds of pure muscle—had more cocaine in his blood-stream than he had ever encountered in twenty years of practice. Inside the room, police found forty unused syringes and more than a dozen vials of anabolic steroids. The fluid found inside his lungs, it was theorized, may have been a side effect of his chronic abuse of the muscle-building drug.

"People would say isn't it great to get $150,000 a year to sit on the bench just to beat somebody up and the answer is 'yes,' but after four or five years of that I want to play," Kordic had told TSN a couple of years before. "You walk away from the rink and people are calling you a goon and a freak and say you can't play the game ... it starts to bother me."

Even prior to his death—and all the attendant bad publicity—the NHL was having a crisis of conscience about fighting. Harry Sinden, general manager of the big, bad Bruins, had introduced a resolution at the spring 1992 meetings to have it banned from the game, which was surprisingly seconded by Jay Snider, son of Ed and president of the Philadelphia Flyers, a team that won two Cups in the 1970s by beating the crap out of all comers. A nine-man committee was established to study the pros and cons of fighting, and the proposal was scheduled to go before the full board in late August. Gil Stein, hoping to remove the "interim" from his job title, seized the opportunity to burnish his media profile and launched a noisy crusade against on-ice thuggery. But when it came time for the vote, the traditionalists won handily. The only change made to the rulebook in the wake of the Kordic tragedy was a slight tough-ening of the instigator rule. If a player was determined to have single-handedly started a fight, there would now be an automatic game misconduct rather than a ten-minute penalty. Referees, who already applied the rule sparingly—naming an instigator in just a quarter of all fights in 1991–92—reacted by making the call in just 15 percent of the bouts in the season following the change.

And fights still had a way of overshadowing the rest of the game. In February 1992, the Rangers' young tough guy Tie Domi had taken on Detroit's Bob Probert, the league's undisputed champion, in a game at Madison Square Garden. Their tilt at centre ice had lasted for more than a minute, and surprisingly it was Domi—who was giving up five inches and twenty-five pounds—who got the better of the veteran, cutting Probert over his left eye. Then on his way to the box, the twenty-three year old added insult to injury by wrapping an imaginary title belt around his waist.

An anticipated rematch in March failed to materialize because Domi was out with a knee injury. But early in the 1992–93 season, the New York goon made it clear he was willing to give Probert a chance at redemption, telling a *Toronto Sun* columnist that he had Boxing Day circled on his calendar, except in his case the celebration would be on December 2 when the Wings again visited Manhattan.

Their second bout, which came just thirty seconds into that game, was a lopsided affair with Probert landing twice as many punches as Domi—forty-seven to be exact—and pummelling his foe into the ice. Red Wings captain Steve Yzerman handed the imaginary belt back to his teammate. "I didn't like the way he was building himself up. And when people start going to the press and mouthing off, well, that's not cool," Probert recalled in *Tough Guy*, a memoir that was published shortly after he died of a heart attack in July 2010 at the age of forty-five. Although all those years later, he was somewhat chivalrous in victory: "To his credit, he was a tough little bastard. He could really take a punch." Neither player was assessed an instigator penalty.

Stein, who was proudly trumpeting a 56-percent drop in

fighting majors through the early part of the season, was apoplectic. He had sent warning letters to both teams prior to the game, but to no effect, so he launched an investigation. In early January 1993, he released a rambling eleven-page report that laid the blame for the "premeditated" fracas at the feet of Domi and Rangers coach Roger Neilson. Both men were fined $500, and Domi was handed a two-game suspension—to be served the next season. There was no punishment for Probert.

Domi's stock had never been higher. Just prior to New Year's, he and fellow Rangers bruiser Kris King were traded to Winnipeg for centre Ed Olczyk, a thirty-two-goal scorer the season before. The move came one day after a member of the North Stars broke his stick over the back of the Jets rookie sensation Teemu Selanne. The Finnish Flash had scored twenty-four goals in his first twenty-nine NHL games, but opposing teams were taking a lot of liberties and his production was tailing off. When Domi arrived in the Winnipeg dressing room, Selanne ran up and gave him a welcoming hug. Suddenly, there was a lot more room on the ice for the budding star.

In mid-January, Selanne hit the thirty-five-goal mark, and speculation turned to whether he'd be able to break Mike Bossy's rookie record of fifty-three. On February 28, the twenty-two year old notched four against Minnesota to bring his season total to fifty-one. Two nights later, he added a hat trick against the Quebec Nordiques and set the new benchmark for freshman goals and celebrations, throwing his glove high in the air, then dropping to one knee to sharpshoot it with his stick. In the month of March, Selanne added twenty more goals and surpassed Peter Stastny's rookie record of 109 points in a season. He finished the year with 132 points, including seventy-six goals, putting him in a tie with another European import, Alexander Mogilny of the

Buffalo Sabres, for the top sniper honours. Selanne was the unanimous choice for the NHL's best rookie award, the Calder Trophy. Domi finished the season with 344 penalty minutes—249 of them acquired in service of the Jets—and fifteen points.

Bettman's opportunity to prove there was a new sheriff in town came soon enough. In 1992–93, New York Islanders centre Pierre Turgeon enjoyed a career year, counting fifty-eight goals and seventy-four assists to finish tied with Selanne for fifth in overall scoring. And with just twenty-six minutes in penalties over eighty-three regular season games, the twenty-three year old went on to win the Lady Byng Memorial Trophy as the league's most gentlemanly player. Riding his strong numbers, the Islanders finished third in the Patrick Division, setting up a first-round playoff matchup against the Washington Capitals. The series was closely fought, with Washington taking the first game, then New York winning the next three in extra periods, two of them in double overtime. Then the Capitals won Game 5 at home, setting up another do-or-die match on Long Island.

Game 6 on April 28 wasn't nearly so tight. Halfway through the third, with the Islanders up 4–1 and the crowd already singing, "Hey, hey, hee-ey, goodbye …" Washington defenceman Al Iafrate corralled a loose puck in his end and fired it around the boards up the left side of the rink. His teammate Dale Hunter, a veteran centre with a mean streak a mile wide, cut it off on its way out of the zone and then flipped it toward one of his wingers coming through the middle of the ice. He didn't see Turgeon until it was too late. The puck hit the Islander in his midsection and tumbled down onto to the blade of his stick. Gliding to the net, Turgeon froze goaltender Don Beaupre with a head fake and then fired it into the lower left corner to make it 5–1, sealing the series victory. He was several seconds into his ecstatic celebration—stick raised high, right arm pumping—when Hunter finally arrived on the scene and blindsided him into the boards. Throughout the many minutes of scuffling that followed, the Islanders star lay dazed on the ice, clutching his separated shoulder.

Bettman, who was at the Nassau Coliseum that night, sitting only a few rows away, was horrified by the cheap shot. Still in the midst of hiring an experienced deputy to oversee hockey operations, the new commissioner took it upon himself to mete out the punishment. He reviewed videotapes and deposed witnesses with his characteristic thoroughness, and quickly determined that Hunter, who topped 200 penalty minutes in a season eleven times in his career, was a habitual offender. Bettman threw the book at the Capitals centre, levying the longest violence-related suspension in league history—twenty-one games—and fining him $150,000, a full quarter of his next season's salary. "Under my watch, this is how I plan to deal with such incidents. If this isn't a suitable deterrent, I don't know what is. I feel this is a very severe penalty," said the commissioner.

For once, there was applause. "The Bettman era was launched when the Hunter verdict came down," columnist Jim Proudfoot wrote in the *Toronto Star*. "Make no mistake about what's ahead. Gary B. Bettman has a mandate to change the look of hockey in dramatic ways. And he's going to. Goonery is extinct. Fighting? Well, he hasn't decided yet. But maybe. Certainly the premeditated, strategic kind." After fifteen years of Ziegler's waffling, there was an appetite for decisive leadership. But what Bettman would soon come to understand was that it was awfully small. And that all the issues that had bedevilled the league before he took over were now well and truly his problems.

In the end, it was the tired and true superstars who saved Gary Bettman's first season. After missing twenty-three games, Mario

Lemieux returned to action on March 2, the day of his final cancer treatment, with a goal and an assist in a 5–4 loss to the Flyers. He was held off the scoresheet in the next game, a loss to the Rangers, and was feeling so fatigued that he wondered if he'd made the right choice. The answer came soon enough. Starting with a 3–2 victory over Boston on March 9, the Penguins won a league record seventeen games in a row. Over the streak, Lemieux—who wasn't even practising in order to conserve his energy—scored twenty-seven goals and set up twenty-four others. In the final game of the regular season, a 6–6 tie with New Jersey, the Penguins captain added two more goals and an assist to finish the year with 160 points and capture his fourth league-scoring title—despite having played just sixty games. *Sports Illustrated* put Lemieux on its cover with the headline "Miracle on Ice," anointing him "the world's dominant pro athlete." And his feel-good story was carried far and wide in the US media, placing the NHL front and centre on everything from the morning talk shows to the evening news. It was the first positive publicity the league had received in a good long while. The fairy tale never got the ending the NHL desired, however—the Penguins' quest for a third consecutive Cup stopped in the second round of the playoffs with a Game 7 loss to the surprising New York Islanders. Turgeon, who suited up for the first time since his injury wasn't a factor, but his teammate David Volek—a healthy scratch for much of the season—had a pair of goals, including the overtime winner. Lemieux, for once unable to bend the game to his will, finished the night with one assist, for a total of eighteen points in eleven post-season games.

For Gretzky, 1992–93 was the worst season of his career— at least since he was six and scored just one goal in his first year of organized hockey. As a nine year old, he piled up 196 goals in seventy-six games, then notched 378 in eighty-two games the following season. Turning pro at age seventeen, he had forty-six goals and 110 points playing through the death throes of the World Hockey Association. And when the Oilers joined the NHL the next year, Gretzky made the jump effortlessly, winning the 1979–80 Hart Trophy as league MVP. He had scored more than 200 points four times in his pro career, and more than 150 on five other occasions. Now, hampered by injury and falling out of love with both Los Angeles and Bruce McNall—whose money troubles had seen the team mothball its private jet and trade Paul Coffey, one of Wayne's best pals, to Detroit—he finished the campaign with sixteen goals and forty-nine assists. Still almost a point-and-a-half for each of the forty-five games he played, but with gritted teeth rather than an easy smile.

As the playoffs approached, however, Gretzky suddenly seemed to rediscover his mojo. The surging Kings knocked off Calgary in six high-scoring games in the first round. Then they took down the division-winning Vancouver Canucks in the second. The conference final against the Toronto Maple Leafs may have been Gretzky's greatest—and most infamous—post-season performance. Through the first five games, the Kings captain again looked like a spent force and was drawing heat from the media in both cities. But with his team facing elimination, he found a way when it mattered most. The Leafs, who had clawed their way past both Detroit and St. Louis during their deepest playoff run in a generation, had set the stage for greatness in Game 6. After staking the Kings to a 4–1 lead, they roared back in the final twenty minutes, with Wendel Clark's third goal of the night tying the score with just 1:21 remaining. The game went to overtime.

Early in the extra frame, with LA on the power play, Gretzky unleashed a shot that was blocked by Toronto defenceman Jamie Macoun, and in the midst of trying to retrieve the ricochet, caught

Doug Gilmour flush in the face with his stick. The Leafs centre crumpled to the ice and came up bleeding. Under NHL rules, intentional or otherwise, it was supposed to be an automatic five-minute major and a game misconduct. But referee Kerry Fraser either didn't see it—or didn't dare to. After worriedly conferring with his linesmen, he motioned the teams back to the faceoff circle. The power play resumed, and less than a minute later, Gretzky tapped in the winning goal. The Kings lived.

Game 7 was back in Toronto, but the Great One appeared completely at home. On the penalty kill in the first, he was set free on a short-handed break with Marty McSorley and finished a pretty give-and-go. A few minutes later, leading a 3-on-2 up ice, he feathered a pass that Tomas Sandstrom ripped past Felix Potvin to make it 2–0. And when the Leafs battled back early in the second with goals from Clark and Glenn Anderson, it was Gretzky who restored the lead, somehow shaking off a check, walking into the slot, and unleashing a point-blank slap shot. With three minutes remaining in the third, and the Kings up 4–3, Gretzky finished the hat trick by bouncing the puck off the skate of Leaf defenceman Dave Ellett and into the net. Los Angeles was on its way to the Stanley Cup Final.

The matchup against Montreal wasn't a New York market-er's dream, but it offered everything a fan could want. Hockey's greatest player, supported by the best cast that money could buy—including self-help infomercial king Anthony Robbins as their dressing-room guru—against a group of upstarts playing well above their station. The 1992–93 Habs had finished the regular season third in the Adams Division and boasted only one star, goaltender Patrick Roy. In the first round against Quebec—a team that had their number all year long—they dropped the first two games and escaped Game 3 with an overtime win, thanks only to a lucky bounce. Then they won the next three straight to take the series, and swept Buffalo in the second round (albeit with three overtime wins). In the conference finals, Montreal pushed past the Islanders in five. But they were hardly an offensive juggernaut—over the first three rounds they scored forty-eight fewer goals than Los Angeles (although the Kings did play four more games).

When the final began at the Montreal Forum on June 1, it was LA who drew first blood—winning 4–1, with Gretzky setting up the first three goals and adding a late empty-netter himself. In Game 2, the Kings were up 2–1 with just 1:45 remaining when Montreal coach Jacques Demers made perhaps the greatest gamble in Stanley Cup history, calling for a measurement of McSorley's stick. After being fired by the Red Wings following the 1989–90 season, Demers had spent two years waiting for his phone to ring. More than thirty NHL coaching vacancies were filled and he never got a sniff. It got to the point where he asked his agent to make some inquiries about whether he had been blackballed. But in the summer of 1992, Montreal GM Serge Savard gave him another chance. Now it all rested on the size of the curve on a right-handed wood Christian-brand stick. Kerry Fraser got out the ruler, deemed the cue illegal, and sent McSorley to the box. Demers then doubled down by pulling Roy for a sixth attacker—praying that Montreal's 0–31 streak on the power play would finally come to an end. Just over thirty seconds later, Eric Desjardins blasted a sixty-foot shot from the point past the Kings' Kelly Hrudey to tie the score. In overtime, the Montreal defenceman scored his third goal of the game to hand the Habs a 3–2 victory.

The next two games also went to overtime, and Montreal won them both, courtesy of goals by John LeClair. Patrick Roy had transcended to a higher hockey dimension, playing ninety-six minutes and thirty-nine seconds of extra time over ten games without surrendering a goal—so comfortable in the net that he winked at the Kings after robbing Sandstrom on the doorstep in Game 4.

The outcome of Game 5 back in Montreal seemed predestined. Paul DiPietro, an AHL call-up who only ever played one full season in the NHL, scored his seventh and eighth goals of the post-season. (In 2006, DiPietro would prove that he still had a flair for the dramatic, scoring both goals for Switzerland in an epic upset of Canada's Olympic hockey team at the Turin Games.) Kirk Muller and Stephan Lebeau tallied, too. McSorley had Los Angeles' lone goal. And Gretzky, who finished the post-season with fifteen goals and twenty-five assists, didn't register a shot.

Gary Bettman stood on the ice and handed Montreal captain Guy Carbonneau the franchise's twenty-fourth Stanley Cup. It was the only time a Canadian-based team would win an NHL championship during his first twenty years as commissioner. When it was Roy's turn to hoist the chalice, he turned and looked dead into the lens of the camera. "I'm going to Disneyland!" he shouted. And just to be sure he got his money—US$100,000 courtesy of Mickey Mouse—the Conn Smythe winner repeated his declaration twice more. In English and French.

It's safe to say that most of the people in attendance that night thought that hockey's golden age was at least twenty, if not forty years in the past, when Mayor Jean Drapeau had quipped about the victory parade following its "usual route." But nostalgia also moves with the times, and two decades later it's now the early 1990s that seem like the best of hockey times. High-octane offences, original six buildings, two towering superstars, and a Cup that spent as much time north of the border as down south.

If those were the good old days, however, the new commissioner hardly got to enjoy them. A few minutes after the trophy presentations, as the crowd from the Forum merged with fans out on Rue Sainte-Catherine, the celebrations started mutating. What began as people taking street signs as souvenirs quickly escalated to vandalism, then an all-out riot. Storefronts were smashed and looted along the length of the city's main shopping strip. Police cars were overturned and set ablaze. By the time the cops, carrying shields and wielding batons, finally gained the upper hand, there had been more than $2.5 million in damage and 168 people injured, including forty-nine officers. It was hard to imagine what would have happened if the Habs had lost.

IN SEPTEMBER 1993, *Sports Illustrated* published a list estimating the price that every franchise in the NFL, NBA, Major League Baseball, and National Hockey League would fetch on the open market. At the top of the column were the New York Yankees, valued at US$225 million, followed by the Dodgers, Mets, and Toronto Blue Jays (soon to win their second consecutive World Series), all at $200 million. The most valuable NFL team was judged to be the Dallas Cowboys at $175 million, sixth overall. And the Chicago Bulls, coming off their third straight NBA title, occupied the twentieth slot with a worth of $140 million. The Detroit Red Wings were the first hockey team to show up on the list—in sixty-first place—with a notional sale price of $80 million. Five more NHL clubs, including Boston and Montreal, were valued at $75 million. The Leafs, Flames, Flyers, and Oilers could fetch $65 million each, while Quebec, Vancouver, Anaheim, and Florida—two teams that had yet to play a regular season game—were worth $50 million apiece, the same price as the Utah Jazz. The last nine places on the table were occupied by NHL franchises, from Buffalo at $40 million to Ottawa, Tampa, and Winnipeg, all at $35 million. According to America's sports bible, the NFL's then twenty-eight teams were collectively worth $3.64 billion, baseball's twenty-eight clubs $3.6 billion, and all twenty-seven NBA franchises $2.16 billion. The NHL's twenty-six teams were valued at $1.42 billion.

It was no secret that hockey was the poor cousin of North American pro sports. A 1992 study in *Financial World* magazine pegged the combined annual gate and broadcast revenue of football at $1.31 billion, $1.23 billion for baseball, and $807 million for basketball. The NHL's yearly take was $440 million. And when it came to merchandising, the league hardly deserved to be called "big," flogging just $800 million worth of sweaters and other products—a full $2 billion less than the NBA.

The new commissioner's job was to somehow fundamentally alter that business fact, plus a lot more. "Bettman's mission is simple," Joe Lapointe wrote in *The New York Times*, tongue planted firmly in cheek: "Put a stop to labour unrest; sell the product in television's mainstream marketplace; change the violent image of the game; curb salary inflation; force enlightened self-interest on reluctant, old-fashioned owners; expand contacts with European developmental leagues and markets; settle the divisive issue of possible Olympic involvement; and help launch several new expansion teams."

The NHL had grown from the original six teams to twenty-six, but its culture had hardly changed at all—the owners were still basically in it for themselves. Ed Snider, who after he was awarded the Philadelphia franchise in 1966, named the team, designed the logo, and built a rink for them to start playing in that next season, remembers the first expansion as less than a golden era. He and his partners paid $2 million to buy in, but soon discovered that their colleagues in Detroit, Toronto, Boston, Chicago, Montreal, and New York still ran the show. "When we got into the league, we had very small revenues, as did all the other expansion teams. We couldn't afford anything," says Snider, now seventy-eight and the longest-serving member of the board of governors: "So we wanted to pay a percentage of our revenues to the league office as dues, and (Leafs president) Stafford Smythe refused. 'No, we're all equal, we all pay the same amount.' That was my first of many frustrations."

And Bettman's predecessors were hardly the types to start a revolution. Clarence Campbell, who guided the league for thirty-one years beginning in 1946, was a tough customer—sitting calmly in the stands at the Montreal Forum as a riot brewed following his season-ending suspension of Rocket Richard in March 1955—and he knew the game. Born in Fleming, Saskatchewan, he played growing up and continued through his university days in Alberta, then at Oxford where he was a Rhodes Scholar. When he returned to Canada in the early 1930s to practise law in Edmonton, Campbell moonlighted as a referee, and by 1936 he was overseeing NHL contests. He was officiating the night Howie Morenz, the Stratford Streak, broke his leg in four places in a game at the Forum against Chicago. (The Canadiens star was confined to a hospital bed and died a few weeks later of an apparent heart attack at age thirty-four.) He once swore at Boston's Dit Clapper during an argument about a call, got a punch in the face in return, and publicly admitted he deserved it. But his on-ice career ended after a 1939 game, when Toronto defenceman Red Horner was clipped and cut by a high stick, and Campbell assessed only a two-minute minor. Conn Smythe, the Leafs' blustering owner, was incensed and success-fully lobbied to have him fired. They later became friends as fellow Canadian officers in World War II, but Campbell took the lesson to heart. When he was welcomed back into hockey's fold after the war, he never again crossed the people who paid his salary.

Even as the league continued to expand through the 1970s, eventually growing to twenty-one teams, it remained a sleepy oper-ation. The NHL offices in Montreal shut down entirely in July. "It was governmental in nature," says Howard Baldwin, the former owner of the Hartford Whalers, Minnesota North Stars, and Pittsburgh Penguins. As one of the principal negotiators for the World Hockey Association when the two leagues tried, and tried again, to merge through the latter part of that decade, he quickly discovered the negotiators on the other side of the table were more than a little reactionary. When the Quebec Nordiques filed their expansion application in French, Baldwin recalls getting a phone call at home on a Saturday morning from "Mr. Campbell," telling him that even if the NHL was headquartered in the same province, its language of business was English. And after the melding finally did occur in 1979, Baldwin and the other former-WHA types, all young businessmen who liked to party, found the NHL culture stultifying. The highlights of the annual board of governors meeting at the ultra-luxe Breakers Hotel in Palm Beach, Florida, included a croquet tournament on the lawn—mandatory whites— and a fancy-dress party where the owners and their wives danced the night away to the sounds of a fifteen-piece orchestra.

Campbell was eased out of the job in 1977, shortly after he was charged for bribing a member of the Canadian Senate in connection with a non-hockey business deal. The NHL presidency wasn't really a full-time gig, and he had several outside interests, including a company that held the duty-free concession at Montreal's Dorval Airport. Back in 1972, when a rival pried away the lucrative contract, Campbell had asked Louis Giguère, a longtime Liberal bagman whom Pierre Trudeau had elevated to the Upper Chamber, to intervene, and the decision was quickly reversed. Just before the news was announced, however, Campbell sold Giguère 5000 shares for $1 apiece, which he sold a month later for $20 each, earning a quick $95,000 profit. When their arrangement became public a few years later, it blossomed into a major political scandal—the so-called Sky Shops Affair. Giguère, who was charged with influence peddling, was acquitted at trial for lack of evidence. But Campbell wasn't so lucky, receiving one day of jail time and a $25,000 fine—a postscript that has been pointedly omitted from his Hockey Hall of Fame biography.

John Ziegler, the Detroit lawyer who took over hockey's reins, becoming just the fourth president in the NHL's sixty-year history, quickly discovered that it wasn't much of a business. "Three weeks into the job, I asked to see the monthly financial statements and was told that we didn't have any," he recalls. Then Ziegler asked what kind of shape the NHL's budget was in and was cheerfully informed that the league was in fact insolvent. "My priorities changed very quickly," he says dryly. Competition with the WHA, which began play in 1972, had pushed costs steadily upward. In the first head-to-head season, the average NHL salary jumped from US$28,000 to $44,000. By the year Ziegler took charge, it stood at $96,000, significantly more than baseball's $76,000 or the $55,000 an average NFL player made. The accumulated operating loss for the NHL's eighteen teams was approaching $100 million—or so the owners claimed. Although, their relationship with the players' union in those days was a lot more amicable. In early 1977, the Cleveland Barons—née the California Golden Seals, who relocated after the 1975–76 season—missed a couple of payrolls and were about to fold. When the other owners turned down a cash call, Ziegler went to Alan Eagleson, then head of the NHLPA, who arranged a $750,000 loan from union funds to keep the franchise afloat. The money didn't address the fundamental problem, however—attendance in Cleveland was worse than it had been in Oakland. And in June 1978, the franchise was put out of its misery and merged with another sad-sack operation, the Minnesota North Stars.

Ziegler, like Campbell before him, found it next to impossible to tame the owners. Some were irascible just for the fun of it. In 1977, when the new president mandated that players' names be put on the back of sweaters, Toronto's Harold Ballard, who feared the move would cut into his program sales, had them attached in the same colours—white on white, blue on blue—so they were impossible to read from the stands. Ziegler was a "know-nothing shrimp," Ballard declared. And even the more enlightened proprietors often bristled at changes designed to benefit the league rather than their own pocketbooks. "I used to say to my staff that our goal was to get the owners to move forward and believe that it was their own idea," Ziegler says.

Then there was the press, especially north of the border. For years when his name appeared in the papers, it was almost invariably followed by the words, "the American-born president of the NHL." The message was implicit: Hockey was a Canadian sport. Ziegler, who had been a pretty decent player in high school, chafed at that notion, but it wasn't anything new. When he showed up for his first year at the University of Michigan in 1951, the varsity squad was entirely made up of skaters from Canada. Only the coach, Vic Heyliger, was American, and he was less than encouraging when Ziegler asked for a tryout with the reigning NCAA champs. On the second day of camp, he called the future NHL leader over to the boards and unceremoniously cut him. "You skate like an American," Heyliger said, suggesting he join an intramural team instead. The Wolverines went on to win the NCAA title again that season, and repeated the feat three more times over the next four years.

Despite the obstacles, Ziegler enjoyed a fair amount of success during his fifteen years helming the NHL, taking head office revenues from a $600,000-a-year loss to a $10-million annual profit and, most notably, delivering some fat expansion fees to the owners. The former WHA franchises—Hartford, Quebec, Winnipeg, and Edmonton—paid $6 million each to join the league. And when the NHL threw open the doors to further growth a decade later in 1989, he managed to convince groups in Ottawa and Tampa Bay to pay $50 million apiece for their teams—significantly more than the $32 million the NBA got that same year for birthing the Minnesota Timberwolves and Orlando Magic. (The Hamilton, Ontario, contingent led by Tim Hortons honcho Ron Joyce was among those who balked at the price, quite possibly dooming that city's pro hockey hopes forever.)

But Ziegler's aloof style—he rarely gave interviews, or attended games—rubbed both the press and his bosses the wrong way. When hot-tempered New Jersey Devils coach Jim Schoenfeld got in a scuffle with referee Don Koharski during the 1988 playoffs, calling him a "fat pig" and suggesting he "have another doughnut," Ziegler was nowhere to be found. And he remained MIA even when officials went on a wildcat strike in support of their spherical colleague, leaving it to his deputies to defuse the crisis. The brief April 1992 strike by the players was the final straw for the owners. Ziegler, then just fifty-eight, was ushered out the door with a $2-million payout and a $250,000-a-year pension. But he didn't entirely disappear from the game. The mercurial Bill Wirtz named him an alternate governor for the Blackhawks, an association that has continued under Wirtz's son Rocky. And twenty years later, Ziegler still regularly attends league meetings.

Hockey wasn't exactly a model of professionalism at the team level either. Trevor Linden, who broke into the league in 1988 with Vancouver, remembers the Canucks front office as a "mom-and-pop" type of operation—a dozen people at most taking care of the day-to-day administration of the franchise as well as selling tickets and advertising. And the romance of the original six buildings was elusive when you were the one sitting in the dressing room at the old Boston Garden, shaking the cockroaches out of your gear. "Now the dressing rooms are fully equipped with fitness facilities, player lounges, and movie rooms where you study game footage," he says. "We didn't even have video back then." The team employed a head coach, one assistant, a medical trainer, and an equipment manager—no nutritionists, masseuses, sleep experts, or sports psychologists. The sticks were made of wood, the gear was much heavier and hotter, and you generally finished the season wearing the same pair of skates you started it with: "Now guys use four or five pairs a season, and these composite sticks, they go through them like toothpicks." Travel was another thing that improved drastically over Linden's twenty-season career. Through the mid-1990s, most teams flew commercial, and players had to wait in line to check their bags, just like everybody else. That made the west coast disadvantage—more time zones and distance to cross—even more pronounced. "From Vancouver, the only places we could fly direct to in the US were Chicago and LA. We spent so much time waiting for connections at O'Hare, I used to joke about buying a condo there," says Linden. The trips home from the east coast were the worst: "We'd play in Hartford and then wake up the next morning at 5 A.M. for a seven o'clock flight to Chicago." The final leg back to British Columbia was usually on a 737 with three-seat rows: "You're crushed in with other people, you played the night before. It was awful. And then we'd get back to Vancouver and practise. You could hardly move."

The LA Kings were the first team in the league to get the pampered treatment when Bruce McNall purchased a Boeing 727-100 in 1990 so that Gretzky and company could fly in style. Whether the 1960s vintage aircraft did formerly belong to the president of Mexico or cost $5 million, as McNall claimed at the time, remains uncertain. But it was luxurious, with twenty-four large leather seats up front and thirty-six regular ones in the back, as well as a dozen TVs and VCRs, massage facilities, CD players, and an extra-large galley. The colour scheme, inside and out, was the same as the team's uniforms—silver, black, and white. Bill Clinton rented it for a couple of weeks during his 1992 presidential campaign. And McNall delighted in showing it off, using it to ferry twenty-five celebrity friends, including Jim Belushi, Mariel Hemingway, and Super Dave Osborne, to Toronto for the debut of Raghib "Rocket" Ismail with the CFL's Argonauts—a team he co-owned with Gretzky and comedian John Candy—in the summer of 1991.

By the beginning of the 1992–93 season, however, the party was winding down. McNall grounded the plane—ostensibly because of the Kings' poor play—but the truth was that his financial empire was unravelling. The coins, trading cards, and other assets were all mortgaged to the hilt, and they weren't worth nearly what he had claimed to the banks. He was in desperate need of cash. So he listed the jet in an Upper Deck sports collectibles catalogue for $5 million, promising to have it autographed by his entire hockey team.

He didn't succeed in selling the aircraft (it was eventually seized by creditors and auctioned off for just $500,000), but the move did lead him to a far more lucrative payday. One of the few people who bothered to stop by the airport to check it out was Wayne Huizenga, the owner of Blockbuster Entertainment, a chain of 3000 video rental stores. He had started his empire with three garbage trucks in 1968 and was now worth $600 million. And at age fifty-five he was busy spending his money on one of his passions—sports. In 1990, he had purchased a 15-percent stake in the Miami Dolphins—he'd go on to buy the whole team and their stadium in 1993—and Major League Baseball had just awarded him the Marlins expansion franchise in exchange for a cool $130 million. McNall, who knew a gift horse when he saw one, seized the opportunity and started hard-selling him on the idea that Miami needed an NHL club, too.

The Kings owner had already been talking with Michael Eisner, then CEO of The Walt Disney Company, about putting a team in the $103-million, 19,000-seat rink that the City of Anaheim was building not far from their iconic theme park. Eisner's kids played the game, and he was sort of a fan, although he wasn't convinced that greater LA needed a second pro-hockey franchise. Eisner did, however, have an ego the size of Space Mountain. So McNall played him by saying that Blockbuster was definitely going to catch the hockey wave. And then he spun a similar white lie about Disney to Huizenga. Within a matter of weeks, he had both men hooked. McNall's reward would end up being a finder's fee of $25 million.

The NHL gives its clubs an exclusive "home" territory that stretches 80 kilometres in every direction from their city limits. And in the past, interlopers like the Islanders and New Jersey Devils had paid millions in indemnification fees when they horned in on the New York hockey market. The problem that McNall and interim NHL president Gil Stein faced was that Disney wasn't willing to pay more than $50 million in total to join the league. So a deal was cut that saw the Kings owner get half of the Anaheim expansion fee in compensation. It was a neat trick—getting paid off after basically begging someone to invade your backyard—and there was some grumbling among the other owners. But the prospect of divvying up $75 million ($50 million from Huizenga and the remaining Disney money) as well as having two corporate titans onside made the pill easier to swallow.

So on December 10, 1992, the day before Gary Bettman's hiring was announced, the NHL officially embarked on its strategy to transplant hockey to America's Sunbelt. The board of governors approved the Minnesota North Stars' relocation to Dallas and awarded expansion franchises to Miami and Anaheim. The press conference had a cobbled-together feel—Eisner was wearing a Goofy baseball cap and a godawful green, yellow, and purple Mighty Ducks' sweater, while Huizenga was dressed in a sober blue suit and tie. And the only Blockbuster tie-ins were the video rental cassettes that somebody had placed in the lap of a large Minnie Mouse doll that was sitting on the table. But the two men were there, standing next to Bruce McNall and his Cheshire cat smile. Eisner told reporters that his market research was the children's movie he had borrowed the sweater from and its $50-million box office gross. He mused aloud about what to name the team: "We might as well call it the Mighty Ducks even though I've been told no hockey player will play for a team called the Ducks. Of course, if we don't win we'll be called the Unmighty Ducks—or worse." (When the name was made official at an event in California in March, Eisner obliged McNall, and a distinctly uncomfortable-looking Bettman, to toot duck calls in unison with him in "the quack heard round the world," as the Disney chairman called it.) Huizenga, newly minted as owner of the Florida Panthers, just looked pained by the whole affair. "It wasn't that I wanted a hockey team, but the opportunity was there to get it," he would later tell a biographer, so it became a case of "let's go ahead and do that and we'll figure out what happens."

For all that effort, the money didn't end up being much help to McNall. "Disney being Disney, they gave me a long-term promissory note with a low interest rate that was eventually discounted," he says. "I probably got $12 million or $15 million total." A drop in a very large and leaky bucket. By late 1993, McNall had defaulted on two different $100-million loans and the Kings were up for sale. (The Rolls-Royce he gave Gretzky in March 1994 was paid for by the people who were about to buy the team.) That May, he resigned as chair of the board of governors, just before he was charged with fraud. A few months later, he admitted to bilking $236 million from six financial institutions over the course of a decade and was sentenced to seventy months in jail. He served much of his time in a prison south of Detroit, and a few of the Kings would trek out to visit whenever they were in town to play the Wings. Eisner wrote him letters and received a special present in return—a wallet that the former NHL owner crafted in the penitentiary leather shop.

MCNALL'S DOWNFALL WAS EMBARRASSING, but the timing worked out perfectly for Bettman. He inherited a league that was on the upswing, and his hands were clean of the messy dealings that had launched the growth spurt. Better still, there was now a clear break with the past, right down to his empty office at NHL headquarters. Ziegler had taken all the furnishings— lots of antiques and paintings of horses, nothing whatsoever to do with hockey—leaving only picture hooks on the bare walls. (The massive carved table in the conference room stayed behind. It had once belonged to Ivan Boesky, the broker who was the inspiration for the Gordon Gekko character in the movie *Wall Street*. The league, which took over his offices when he went to jail for insider trading in 1987, got it for $700 because it was too heavy to be moved.) The new commissioner had been hired to bring some of basketball's magic to hockey, and now he set about remaking the NHL in the image of the NBA. "Going in, I had a vision, but it was from 10,000 feet up," says Bettman. "I believed that we needed a more stable economic system, which was something I had discussed with the owners. And I also believed that we needed more exposure."

The makeover was swift and unsentimental. He replaced the vice-president of broadcasting and the head of the business division, NHL Enterprises. Within a matter of months, the size of the staff had doubled and the budget for league operations was soon $30 million a year, three times what it had been under the last president. There was a new marketing campaign hyping hockey as "the coolest game on earth." And there was a new attention to detail around head office. Brian Burke, who left the Hartford Whalers in the fall of 1993 to join the league as a senior vice-president, and Bettman's designated "hockey guy," recalls running into his new boss in the washroom. The commissioner was busy picking up scraps of wet paper from the floor. When Burke suggested he leave it for the cleaning crew that would be in later that evening, Bettman exploded: "Every guest, every sponsor, every vendor, every owner, and any and all club personnel will use this restroom. And it *will* be neat and tidy."

Hockey's fortunes were quickly changing. By 1994, licensing revenues—spurred by the new franchises—had grown to $1 billion a year. The Mighty Ducks' logo, a bill-shaped goalie mask over crossed sticks, was the hottest thing in sportswear, outselling even the LA Raiders and Chicago Bulls (although much of that money was going directly to the Magic Kingdom under an agreement that Eisner had brokered giving the company all the proceeds from Ducks gear sold at its 500-plus Disney stores). And NHL sweaters were suddenly "trendy fashion," noted *The New York Times*, showing up at nightclubs and in "gangsta" rap videos like Snoop Dogg's "Gin and Juice." "There is a wonderful opportunity to make hockey hip," declared Tommy Hilfiger, the fashion designer. "We've had the football jersey, the baseball jersey, basketball trends. Hockey is like the virgin." The sport was triumphing with video gamers, too. Electronic Arts' official NHL series was selling more than 1 million copies a year—almost double the sales of the most popular NBA game—despite its hefty $60 price tag. Jean-Claude Van Damme, Hollywood's up-and-coming action star, was busy filming *Sudden Death*, a movie in which he played Darren McCord, a Canadian-born firefighter with a heavy Belgian accent who foils a tortured plot to assassinate the US vice-president during a Pittsburgh Penguins game. The movie, produced by then Penguins owner Howard Baldwin and featuring cameos by Chris Chelios, Luc Robitaille, and Markus Naslund, went on to gross $64 million worldwide. And on TV's hottest new show *Friends*, Joey, Ross, and Chandler were diehard Rangers fans who regularly attended games.

The apex of the boom was the 1994 Stanley Cup Final, featuring New York and Vancouver. Not only did it pit Mark Messier, a legendary leader who had already captured five championships with Edmonton, against the Russian Rocket, Pavel Bure, the most exciting young player in the game, it had an irresistible storyline. The Rangers hadn't won a Cup since 1940—a fact that rival fans delighted in pointing out in sing-song chants—and for a while it had seemed the drought was destined to continue. The best team in the league during the regular season, they swept the Islanders in the opening round, then took the Capitals in five, but stumbled badly in the semi-final against New Jersey. Down three games to two and facing elimination, Messier went to the press to personally guarantee a win, and then delivered by scoring a natural hat trick in the third period for a come-from-behind 4–2 victory. Game 7 went to double overtime, when Stephane

Matteau scored a dramatic wraparound goal to clinch a date with Vancouver.

The Canucks, who had finished seventh in the Western Conference, were Cinderella, knocking off heavily favoured Calgary in seven games in the opening round, then taking both Dallas and Toronto in five. Winners of Game 1 in overtime at a hostile Madison Square Garden, they seemed to have seized the momentum. But the Rangers rallied and took the next three. Vancouver dominated Games 5 and 6, setting up one last showdown in New York. The Rangers won 3–2, with Messier scoring the Cup-clinching goal. Brian Leetch, who became the first American-born winner of the Conn Smythe Trophy, even got a post-game phone call from President Bill Clinton at the White House: "Congratulations, man," said the bubba-in-chief. The next night, Messier, Leetch, and goalie Mike Richter brought the Cup along for an appearance on the *Late Show with David Letterman*. The NHL had never been so cool.

That week, *Sports Illustrated* devoted its cover to hockey's ascendancy, seeking to explain "Why the NHL's Hot, and the NBA's Not," and the new commissioner got much of the credit. "Gone is the image of the NHL player as a toothless face-buster. Fighting in the playoffs, this year and last, has been practically nonexistent," E.M. Swift wrote admiringly. "Even the fans' image has changed: Pre-Bettman, when the NHL was the boil on the pro sports boom of the 1970s and '80s, hockey's spectators looked like the spillover from Wrestlemania. This year elegant couples like John F. Kennedy Jr. and Daryl Hannah (also Knick attendees) and Farrah Fawcett and Ryan O'Neal were spotted at NHL games." New York mayor Rudy Giuliani was also in on the act, building an outdoor rink à la Walter Gretzky in the backyard of Gracie Mansion for his eight-year-old son. Riding the crest of expansion excitement—Tampa was averaging 21,000 fans a game, and a solid playoff run had made the Sharks a northern California sensation—Bettman was downright cocky about the future: "We're not just a cold-weather sport," he told the magazine, "we're getting a national footprint."

Basketball, on the other hand, was a mess—fights on the court and in the stands, trash-talking run wild, and playoff ratings that were down 30 percent. The real reason behind the slippage was the absence of the game's biggest star, Michael Jordan. In October 1993, just two months after his father was murdered, he had abruptly retired at the age of thirty, declaring his intention to follow another dream and become a pro-baseball player. The timing of the announcement, just days before the league was to release the results of an investigation into Jordan's off-court gambling activities, lent itself to whisperings of a secret suspension. But the end result was the same—with MJ's high-flying show temporarily grounded, the plodding Charles Barkley, "The Round Mound of Rebound," was now the face of the NBA.

Of course, it didn't last. The hype and excitement about hockey did little to alter its fundamental business challenges. The league was still without the kind of big-money, wide-exposure TV deal that enriched all of its competitors. It remained heavily gate-dependent, with 65 percent of all revenues coming directly from ticket sales—more than any other pro sport. The collective bargaining agreement with the NHLPA, which had been extended for one year shortly after Betttman took over, would expire in September 1994, and relations were frosty. Seeing the boom in merchandise sales, the players had sought a cut of the royalties being made—roughly $2.5 million per team—from placing their names on the backs of pricey "authentic" sweaters. The commissioner stonewalled, and when the NHLPA tried to cut its own deal with vendors he took them to court, personally serving the Rangers'

Mike Gartner, the union president, with legal papers just before a home game against Edmonton. Gartner, who became a born-again Christian while playing for the Washington Capitals in the early 1980s, was inclined to turn the other cheek. But Bettman seemed to be developing a taste for the rough stuff. He had already taken a tough stance against the NHL's referees and linesmen when they went on strike in the fall of 1993, demanding that their pay packets start to reflect the rising fortunes of both the players and the league. (The annual salary for a first-year ref was $50,000, and just $33,000 for a rookie linesman.) Scab zebras were hired at the bargain rate of $800 per game for refs and $500 for linesmen. And when the officials returned to work after seventeen days, it was with a far more modest salary and benefit package than they had originally been seeking.

The owners were also playing hardball with their former players, contesting an Ontario court decision that had ruled the NHL had illegally scooped more than $40 million in surpluses from the pension fund. The injustice at the heart of the case was evident to everyone—Gordie Howe, who had played more games than anyone in history, was getting around $14,000 a year, and the sainted Bobby Orr, who had crippled himself for the greater glory of the game, just $8,400. Yet the league appealed the matter all the way to the Supreme Court of Canada before settling in the summer of 1994. Bettman claimed that his hands were tied, but he defended the strategy with his typical zeal, ensuring that he was soon seen as just as much a villain in the matter as his bosses. Tone deafness that seemed all the more egregious when Alan Eagleson, the former head of the players' union, who had facilitated the pension grab and a host of other schemes that enriched him rather than his members, later pled guilty to charges of theft and fraud and served six months in jail.

Bad publicity was something that the commissioner was getting used to, however. In February 1993, he had been unable to broker a deal with the NHLPA and the International Olympic Committee to replicate the NBA's "Dream Team" success and have the world's best pros participate in the hockey tournament during the 1994 Lillehammer Winter Games. The failure annoyed fans, especially those in Canada, where the national team hadn't won hockey gold since 1952. Glenn Anderson, who wore the red and white at the 1980 Lake Placid Games, was desperate to suit up for Canada again, and had even negotiated a clause in his contract with the Toronto Maple Leafs allowing him to go. But the move required the permission of the league, and the longstanding policy was that only players with less than a year of experience were free to join the Olympic squad. Anderson was in his fourteenth season, and Bettman denied the request.

Tiffany Williams was an eleven-year-old girl from Trenton, Ontario, who happened to be one of Anderson's biggest fans. Outraged by the decision, she started a petition to ask the NHL commissioner to reconsider, and in a matter of a couple weeks had collected more than 5000 signatures. In early February, she reached out to John Nunziata, a Toronto-area federal MP who had a well-earned reputation for grandstanding. He arranged a meeting with Bettman in New York and flew down with Tiffany to help present her demands.

Maybe the NHL didn't understand whom they were dealing with, but the Canadian media certainly sensed a looming debacle. And they were camped outside the door waiting when the two-hour session ended. Bettman had stuck to his guns, and Williams was disappointed. "They didn't have a very good argument," she said. "They were very weak." Nunziata, who made his bones as a member of the opposition Liberal "Rat Pack" that savaged the government of Brian Mulroney during daily question period—so effectively that the prime minister once described them as "Nazis" who "deal in lies and calumnies"—did not disappoint either. "Bettman is as phony as they come," he fumed. "It's clear to me he's just a little dictator."

Behind closed doors, the new NHL commissioner sometimes wondered what the hell he'd gotten himself into. Jeff Pash, who was hired as the league's general counsel in 1993 and served four years before moving on to the same job at the NFL, admits there were many moments of frustration. But Bettman had his unique way of marking them. "From time to time, something would happen and he would turn to me or Burkie and say, 'Write that down. That's going in the book,'" says Pash, now executive vice-president of the NFL. "And he even had a title for it: *You Can't Make This Shit Up.*"

3 Kicking the Can

As training camp wound down and the league's deadline loomed, the players began to chafe. And the message they decided to send out to NHL fans across North America was anything but subtle. In Montreal, Habs defenceman Mathieu Schneider skated onto the ice for practice with a piece of white stick tape plastered to the front of his helmet on which he'd scrawled the words *Bettman Sucks*. Joe Sakic, the quiet young captain of the Quebec Nordiques, suggested the new commissioner "knows nothing about hockey and doesn't care." Cam Neely, sitting in the Boston dressing room in his long underwear and an NHLPA ball cap, predicted a dire future for any sports league that would dare to lock out its players: "They're not shooting themselves in the foot, they're shooting themselves in the head as far as I'm concerned." And even Wayne Gretzky, a man so averse to controversy that he invited Alan Thicke to emcee his wedding, weighed in. Wearing a suit, tie, and sour face, he met the media at the LA Kings' practice facility to make it clear that if the 1994–95 season didn't start on time, there would only be one man to blame. "I've played this game for thirty years, and for someone to come along who has only been in our sport for one year and tell us that we're not going to play is very frustrating and extremely disappointing," the Great One said. "I've worked too damn hard to help push our sport … Hopefully it doesn't all come down because one person wants to change the format."

It was Chris Chelios who grabbed the headlines, however, with some inelegant ad libs to the carefully scripted vitriol. Just off the ice and still sweating, the Blackhawks D-man glowered into the cameras and gave Gary Bettman a taste of the menace with which he played. Not only was the former NBA executive out of his depth, he was a little Napoleon who couldn't even recognize the game's biggest stars when they weren't wearing their names on their backs, said Chelios. He should be worried about the safety of his family and his own well-being: "He's going to affect a lot of people, and some crazed fan—or maybe even a player, who knows—is going to take things into their own hands. And figure they're going to get him out of the way and maybe things will get settled. You'd hate to see something like that happen, but he took the job."

The relationship, such as it was, between the players and the owners' front man had been unravelling for months. In early January, Bettman had confirmed suspicions about his hiring—his main task was indeed to bring a basketball-style salary cap to hockey. His initial proposal for the new collective bargaining agreement was a "compensation pyramid" where the league would set the figure for each team's payroll and then let the players on the roster fight over how to divvy it up. The union rejected the idea—a cap in all but name—without even putting it to a vote. Talks had continued through the spring, but Bettman's subsequent demands were no more palatable. The NHL didn't just want to link salaries to revenue, it was also seeking a firm limit on rookie pay, to do away with guaranteed contracts and the arbitration system, as well as to cut roster sizes and reduce the amount of money it handed out for the playoffs from $9 million to $2 million. Then in August, the NHL commissioner delivered the bargaining equivalent of a face wash, announcing his intention to roll back perks and benefits when the existing deal expired in September. The players were still welcome to attend training camp, but they would have to pay for their own flights, medical and disability insurance, and meals— moves that would apparently save the league's cash-strapped franchises between $20 million and $40 million. And to top it off, Bettman let it be known that he wasn't going to start the regular season as scheduled on October 1 unless a new labour deal was in place. "We need a player-employment system that avoids making this a league of haves and have-nots," he wrote in a letter to the union. "Unless we develop that type of system, our recent success will not solve our economic and competitive problems. This situation must be addressed, and addressed now."

The players dug into their own pockets for camp and the exhibition schedule, but there wasn't much optimism about a quick solution. The NHLPA gave each of its twenty-six team reps a credit card with a $50,000 limit—to buy the players one-way tickets home when the inevitable happened.

For all the focus on the new commissioner, this battle had been brewing for years. In 1989–90, there were only four hockey players making a million dollars or more a season—Gretzky, Lemieux, Edmonton's Mark Messier, and the Red Wings' Steve Yzerman—and the average NHL salary was just $232,000. The Great One's Hollywood-worthy contract with Bruce McNall set a new benchmark for the game's superstars. But it was the St. Louis Blues who pried the lid off Pandora's box that summer by breaking an unwritten rule and actually signing a free agent. Hard-rock defenceman Scott Stevens, who had forty points in fifty-six games for the Capitals and earned $345,000, was suddenly making

$1.29 million a season. Retribution came in the form of a league arbitrator, who awarded Washington the Blues' next five first-round picks in compensation, but the deed was done and teams now had to worry about the true market value of their regular stars as well. Ray Bourque's deal with Boston was renegotiated up to seven figures. And the same thing happened for both Chris Chelios in Chicago and Denis Savard in Montreal. During the next off-season, Ron Caron, the Blues' fiery GM, shook the league's foundations again, signing Brendan Shanahan away from New Jersey—a move that backfired when the Devils sought and won Stevens as compensation, yet loosened the purse strings even further. And once the Rangers and Philadelphia finished bidding up the services of Eric Lindros in June 1992, making the rookie holdout the fifth highest-paid player in the game, the spending spree was fully on. By the 1993–94 season, there were seventy-five millionaires in the NHL, and the league's average salary had almost doubled to $560,000.

The owners' cozy compact with the union had also broken down. Alan Eagleson, the founder and longtime head of the NHLPA, had been more than friendly with management—he was their partner in every way, helping to stage international tournaments, keeping salary expectations low as an agent, and even abetting their efforts to skim pension funds. Contract negotiations under his leadership were basically a sham, with all the details ironed out in advance with John Ziegler, one of his best buddies. The NHL president "seemed to know in advance what the players would probably agree to in the negotiations and the price the clubs would have to pay to get it," Gil Stein, the league's former general counsel, wrote in his memoirs. And when the owners and players met for face-to-face bargaining sessions, it was simply theatre: "Eagleson would first make a number of demands on behalf of the players, including, of course, those Ziegler and he had already agreed would likely, at the end of the day, be granted by the NHL. Next came the various owners, speaking on their assigned topics, letting the players know of the precariousness of the NHL's financial picture and why the players' desire for free agency could never be agreed to." Speeches were made, brave stands taken, tête-à-têtes held, but nothing substantive changed. And once the deal was struck, the owners treated the player reps and their wives to a lavish banquet. "Everyone who was there could attest to how difficult the negotiations had been," wrote Stein. "To us, it appeared the players never suspected the scenario might have been carefully scripted in advance."

Part of it was certainly the players' fault. Marty McSorley never frightened easily in his nineteen-season career, amassing 3381 penalty minutes, chiefly as Gretzky's protector in Edmonton and LA, but he still remembers how hard it was to speak out on labour issues. Team guys by nature and trained to be deferential to coaches and managers, hockey players made lousy militants. When McSorley jumped into a dressing-room debate to advocate salary disclosure during his rookie campaign with the Penguins in 1983–84, a veteran teammate told him, "Shut up, kid. You don't know what you're talking about." There were also consequences for those who broke ranks. When the tough guy later became part of the group challenging Eagleson's leadership, he saw his hockey career directly threatened: "Bill Wirtz called up Bruce McNall and told him to get rid of me. 'Don't trade him. Fire him,' is what he said." The Kings owner took the request from the then chairman of the board (and most powerful force in the league) seriously enough to broach the subject with Gretzky, but deferred to his superstar's wishes. For once, it was Wayne saving Marty's bacon.

Things began to change rapidly after the arrival of Bob Goodenow on the scene. Raised in Detroit, he had been a good enough player to captain the varsity hockey squad when he was at Harvard and was drafted by the Washington Capitals, playing two seasons for the IHL's Flint Generals before heading on to law school. Like Bettman, he, too, was attracted to labour relations, and for a time practised on the management side. In 1983, representing a Pittsburgh firefighting equipment manufacturer, he kept a group of Teamsters on the picket lines for eleven months until they surrendered. "He's the most difficult man I've ever dealt with," Frank Caputo, a retired official with the local, told the *Chicago Tribune* a decade later. "It makes me sick to my stomach he's head of a union." He was just as uncompromising when he became an agent in the mid-1980s, representing players like Mark Howe—son of Gordie and a childhood friend and teammate—and later Brett Hull, making him one of the NHL's early millionaires following his seventy-two-goal performance for St. Louis in 1989–90. Intense to a fault, the pale-eyed redhead wasn't much for small talk, but the players recognized him as one of their own—he was missing five of his upper teeth thanks to a cross-check in junior—and chose him to take over as they started to ease Eagleson out the door that summer.

At the time, the NHLPA had just three employees—a secretary, a business manager, and Eagleson—and was still being run out of its founder's Toronto law offices. Goodenow was provided with a space about the size of a broom closet, and the atmosphere, tense from the beginning, worsened when the FBI launched an investigation into Eagleson's past dealings following a series of revelations in the US media. (A grand jury was convened in Boston a year later, and the hockey strongman was indicted on thirty-two counts of racketeering, fraud, and embezzlement in March 1994.) Goodenow, who officially became executive director at the beginning of 1992, quickly found the union new digs and set about beefing up its staff.

And he went on the road to prepare his members for a new, far more confrontational era in management–labour relations. Right from the beginning, Goodenow encouraged players to start putting their change aside in case things got ugly—the NHLPA, funded for decades only on union dues, had no strike fund whatsoever. And the money would soon be needed.

The last Eagleson-negotiated collective agreement had expired at the beginning of the 1991–92 season, but the two sides had agreed to keep talking while the players kept playing. The owners, who had adopted the former union boss's nickname for his successor— Jingle Nuts—figured they still had the upper hand. The NHL was on shaky ground, they contended, with player salaries now eating up 63 percent of all revenues, versus just 49 percent in the mid-1980s. The league was already set to lose $52 million in the current season and more than $100 million the year after that. And if the salary trend continued, the NHL would be paying 173 percent of the take to its employees within five years. It was time for concessions, not raises.

Goodenow and his charges were unmoved. The league had just added three new teams—San Jose, Ottawa, and Tampa— pulling in US$125 million in expansion fees, and was coming off a $51-million, three-year US cable television deal. And massive profits were being made in the post-season—$29 million in 1991, $24 million the next year—of which the players received only a paltry share, as little as $10,000 each for going all the way to the Stanley Cup Final. The NHLPA took a strike vote on April 1, 1992, and the result was 560 to 4 in favour.

The walkout—the first-ever strike by NHL players—came just a week before the playoffs, when the owners made so much of their money. The high-stakes disruption finally vaulted hockey to the front of the sports section in the US papers. And in Canada, it eclipsed all other news. With the season, and the Cup hopes of fans, hanging in the balance, Goodenow certainly came across as a cold fish—especially compared to John Ziegler's tearful good-of-the-game pronouncements: "If it will make the players happy. If it will be the thing that gets them back to what they do best, playing the game, I will call it surrender. I will call it unconditional surrender." But there was no way to score the one-year deal, struck after just eleven days, as anything but a decisive victory for the new union boss. One former NHLPA employee remembers the league president as a defeated man during the final negotiations, more concerned about the prospect that someone might drip mustard from their takeout deli sandwiches on his office carpet than the details. And within months, Ziegler was gone from the job.

When Bettman took over, he arranged a number of dinners and outings to watch games with Goodenow to try and create a rapport. They were both the same age and had followed similar Ivy League and career paths, but they found they had little in common. Some of the standoffishness was tactical—a signal from the union head to players and the media that the chummy Eagleson days were long gone. More than that, however, there was a real antipathy. If Bettman was prickly, Goodenow was even worse. "With Bob, you were either a friend or an enemy," says Ted Saskin, his deputy and later his replacement at the NHLPA. "And probably more people fell into the enemy category."

That dynamic quickly became apparent during the 1994 negotiations. The players beat up Bettman in the press (although after Chelios's comments, the commissioner was concerned enough about metaphor becoming reality that he hired a bodyguard), and his gang responded with their own blunt-force rhetoric. "The most important thing of all when you deal with a union is to have an intelligent union leader," John McMullen, the Devils owner, declared a couple of days after the lockout began on October 1. "And we don't have one today." Philadelphia's Bobby Clarke, a former Goodenow client, suggested that it was the NHLPA head who was really out of his depth. "Those of us who know him felt from the start there would be no chance of a deal being made. He's not a deal maker." And a deliberate link was made to the ongoing labour strife in baseball, where a strike had kept players off the diamond since early August and led to the cancellation of the entire playoffs and World Series—much to the chagrin of fans of the Montreal Expos, holders of a league leading 74–40 record. Goodenow was taking his orders from Donald Fehr, then head of the Major League Baseball Players Association, went the line. "If baseball had a deal today, we'd have a deal today," declared David Poile, the Washington Capitals GM. "I don't think it's a coincidence that their tactics are so similar."

Fans sitting at home with nothing to watch on Saturday night were left to try and sort out who was telling the truth. Did the expansion Florida Panthers really lose $4 million in 1993–94, despite having one of the smallest payrolls in the league at $12.9 million and playing to more than 14,000 fans a night? Could it be possible that the Vancouver Canucks, losers of the Stanley Cup Final in seven games, really did turn a profit that was less than the average player makes? Bettman said that he was heading a league "with a profound financial problem," with collective losses of more than $37 million the previous season and $30 million the year before that. Less than Ziegler had claimed, but still unsustainable.

Yet, as far as Goodenow was concerned, it was all "creative accounting." The NHL's revenues had jumped to $700 million—a $150-million increase from 1992–93—and the league had signed a new $155-million, five-year TV deal with Fox just two weeks before it locked out the players. And the owners were hardly practising restraint. In the run-up to the lockout, there was a flurry of player signings: Jaromir Jagr got $19.2 million for five years from Pittsburgh; Dominic Hasek received $6.9 million for three years in Buffalo; and Eric's brother Brett Lindros took $7.5 million for five years from the Islanders. The off-season splurge of signings totalled more than $200 million.

The only thing that was certain was that as the lockout dragged into its third month, both sides were forgoing a lot of revenue: more than $170 million at the gate for owners and close to $88 million in paycheques for the players. Proposals were still being traded—Bettman's latest gambit was a graduated luxury tax on team payrolls that were above the league average, with the money going to small-market franchises—but there were no real nego-tiations. Wayne Gretzky and some other big-name players were preparing for a barnstorming tour in Europe with the proceeds to go to charity. There was loose talk about starting a rival league, or perhaps mass defections to the IHL and turning the minor circuit into a major one. And the NHL had taken to sending information packets on its position directly to player agents, hoping to provoke a rift.

At the Hockey Hall of Fame induction ceremonies in Toronto in November, all twenty-six GMs sat down for breakfast with the media to again press the case against the union. Boston's Harry Sinden likened Goodenow's latest proposal to "giving a canoe to an Arab," saying that what were billed as concessions were useless. Vancouver's Pat Quinn said that not a single one of the issues the two sides had been discussing for ten months had been addressed. And when the question of the credibility of the league's numbers came up, Edmonton's GM Glen Sather got so angry that he invited a reporter from *The New York Times* to step outside. A few days later, Brian Burke, the league's vice-president of hockey operations, escalated matters even further, accusing the doubting Thomases in the Toronto media of not just anti-Americanism, but anti-Semitism as well. A columnist for the *Toronto Sun*, who made a habit of referring to Bettman as a "New York lawyer," was singled out and accused of using coded language to invoke the commissioner's religion.

The mood inside the bargaining sessions was no brighter. Jeff Pash, the NHL's general counsel, had been warning—publicly and privately—that there were real problems in Winnipeg, Quebec City, and Hartford, but never sensed the message was getting through to the union. Goodenow in particular seemed blasé about the challenges ahead, he says: "He really wasn't very sensitive about the concerns of owners. We put a lot of information in front of him, but he was unwilling to engage on most of those issues." Pash, who later returned to the NFL and led that league through its 2011 lockout, was frustrated by the narrow focus, but understood it all the same: "Bob Goodenow was a player guy first and foremost, and he wasn't particularly concerned with the health of the business. If the cheque cleared, that was probably the most important thing to him."

Tempers were fraying. At a session in Buffalo—an easy flight from Manhattan and quick drive from Toronto—Bettman himself threw a tantrum, screaming about the unreasonableness of his opponents before stomping out of the room. One of the NHLPA representatives still wonders to this day whether it was real or a tactic—an attempt to channel the NBA's David Stern, a famed and feared yeller: "It didn't really work. It was almost like he was trying it on for size. It was kind of comical, actually." Bettman's strength was more the cutting remark, or the menace behind the cold smile. Marty McSorley, who brought some muscle to the players' bargaining committee, still bristles at the memory of how the commissioner refused to call the players anything but "labour" during the talks. Although the man with the fourth-most penalty minutes in NHL history did manage to goad Bettman to anger once. The topic under discussion was league discipline, and McSorley, a frequent recipient, suggested it was a conflict of interest for someone employed by the owners to sit in judgment over a player. "He asked me if I was questioning his integrity, and I made an off-hand remark about the lack thereof," says the former tough guy, now an analyst for Sportsnet. It was a small satisfaction that he grew to regret.

In February 2000, when McSorley was playing for Boston in the twilight of his career, he found himself on the ice in the final seconds of a game that the Bruins were losing 5–2 to Vancouver. As the puck rolled into the Canucks end, he skated up behind Donald Brashear, a fellow enforcer whom he had already fought once that evening, and swung his stick, hitting him in the side of the head with its heel. Brashear, who was out cold even before he fell back and smashed his helmet into the ice, suffered a severe concussion. To this day, McSorley maintains that it was a mistake—he was only trying to hit Brashear on the shoulder and make him fight: "I know in my heart I did some bad things on the ice. But that wasn't one of them." But the explanation didn't wash with the NHL, or the police. Suspended by the league for the remainder of the season, he was also charged, and eventually convicted, of assault with a weapon, sentenced to eighteen months probation. McSorley says he wanted to mount a better defence, but the NHL frustrated his lawyer's attempts to call team personnel and officials as witnesses. They even refused to give him a copy of the videotape of the attack. And when he considered appealing the judge's decision, his agent was quietly informed that McSorley would have to sit out until a new judgment was rendered—a process that could take up to four years. As it was, the veteran of seventeen seasons never played again. When he applied for reinstatement in the fall of 2000, Bettman called him personally to deliver his decision to extend the suspension until late February 2001—a full calendar year after the incident and just before the trading deadline. McSorley knew the jig was up—no team was going to take a chance on a guy who was closing in on his thirty-eighth birthday and hadn't played in twelve months. "Was what I did really the worst thing in NHL history?" he asks. A decade later, and now walking like he's permanently on skates thanks to two artificial hips, not being able to leave the game on his own terms is still a sore spot. "Gary's a vindictive guy," he says, absently twisting the 1987 Cup ring that sits atop one of his gnarled knuckles. Or maybe just one who always finishes his fights.

In late November 1994, the players had made a significant concession, offering to sell out the undrafted and cap the salaries of future rookies if the league dropped its demands for similar fetters on veterans. But the board of governors flatly rejected the proposal, and as the Christmas season approached, it began to look like neither side had the will to make a deal. The All-Star Game, which was to have been the kickoff for the new Fox broadcasts in late January, was cancelled. Then on day seventy-four of the lockout, the owners moved a step closer to the nuclear option, voting unanimously to give their commissioner the power to scrub the entire season and playoffs—just like baseball—if a deal wasn't soon reached. "This is not about a league fighting with a union. It's about a league fighting for its future," pronounced Bettman.

Many of the players were already giving up hope. Kelly Kisio, who had moved from the Sharks to the Flames as a free agent, signing a three-year deal at the age of thirty-five for $1 million a season, enrolled in an apprentice carpenter's course at the Southern Alberta Institute of Technology. His teammate, the veteran defenceman Zarley Zalapski, opened up his own specialty coffee shop in Calgary, while tough guy Sandy McCarthy, still on an entry-level contract for $150,000 a season, made ends meet by starting an office cleaning business. Geoff Courtnall, who had scored nineteen points for the Canucks during their run to the Stanley Cup Final, busied himself waiting tables at Double Overtime, the Vancouver burger joint he owned, and bought a big pickup truck in preparation for a new career as a builder of luxury homes. Montreal winger Vincent Damphousse picked up an easy $40,000 for an eleven-game stint with the Ratingen Lions of the German Elite League, a cellar-dwelling club that managed to win only twice with a bona fide NHL star in its lineup. Down at the Tim Hortons, there wasn't much sympathy for the players, but it could be tough to make ends meet, even with the $3000 monthly cheques from the union strike fund. When an Edmonton radio station called Kelly Buchberger's house to see if the Oilers grinder would appear at a store opening for $1000, his wife accepted on his behalf before he could even get to the phone. There were some cracks in solidarity—Stephane Richer of the Devils told a newspaper that he figured most of his fellow players would settle immediately if they were ever allowed to vote on an offer. And the *Montreal Gazette* detailed a tense NHLPA conference call during which Larry Murphy, the Penguins' player rep, was taken to task for suggesting he liked the sound of the owners' latest proposal. "Hey, Murph, where's your balls?" McSorley reportedly barked. "I don't think with my balls, Marty," was the retort.

As it turned out, it was the fault lines among the owners that were more profound. After the first week of the lockout, Bettman started getting phone calls from team executives who were already desperate to get back on the ice, recalls Brian Burke. Generally it was the clubs—both US and Canadian—that had recently opened new buildings or had the most lucrative local TV contracts and were therefore forgoing the most revenue. But some of the other doves just couldn't understand what the hell the NHL thought it was doing. "I voted against the lockout on every single occasion," says Howard Baldwin, then Pittsburgh's owner. His team, locked into a lease at the old Mellon Arena, was struggling to find the means to pay the contracts of Mario Lemieux, Jaromir Jagr, and Kevin Stevens, losing between $5 million and $9 million a season. But to Baldwin's mind, not playing wasn't going to help. And coming off the excitement surrounding the Rangers' Cup win and the new TV deal, a protracted labour war seemed shortsighted: "Hockey had what was really, really hard to get—momentum." The most hawkish owners, like Chicago's Wirtz and the Red Wings' Mike Ilitch, took him aside and argued that the players would cave as soon as they missed a paycheque, but Baldwin remained doubtful. "I thought we were forgetting why we overpaid them—they're competitive guys. And I was pretty sure that they were going to want to cook our asses."

The league had started backing away from a salary cap, or even the luxury tax model, a couple of weeks before Christmas, agreeing to head down parallel negotiating tracks—one with their preferred system and one without. And when bargaining resumed after the holiday, a breakthrough seemed imminent. Time, however, was running out. Bettman, keen to squeeze in at least a fifty-game regular season and the entire playoffs by the end of June, had circled Tuesday, January 10, 1995, as the drop-dead date for a settlement. Just before New Year's, there was a small group meeting in Chicago between Pash and Burke and their NHLPA counterparts, Bob Riley and John McCambridge, two American labour lawyers, where the outline of a deal started to come together. But Bettman and Goodenow would need to sit down and make the difficult trade-offs. Hired to bust heads only two years before, the commissioner's brief was now to broker a compromise with an opponent who was just as stubborn as he was. And having locked the players out, any failure would be his alone.

It wasn't until January 9, less than twenty-four hours from the league's deadline, that the make-or-break bargaining session was convened. The meeting at the Four Seasons hotel in Manhattan started at 10:30 A.M., with the commissioner tabling what the Bruins' Harry Sinden had called the owners' "final, final, final, final, final offer." Progress was fitful, and it was getting close to midnight when Bettman and Goodenow repaired to Shun Lee Palace, a Chinese restaurant that advertises itself as the ideal location for Upper East Side socialites, to hash the last details out over dinner. But things dragged on long after the egg rolls got cold. It was 6 A.M. when both negotiating teams, red-eyed and rumpled, met up in Goodenow's hotel suite for what was supposed to be one final examination of the terms. The list was read aloud: An escalating cap on rookie salaries, beginning at US$850,000; check. The continuation of the existing arbitration system, but with a new right for owners to walk away from decisions they didn't like up to three times every two years; check. A six-year term, with both sides retaining the right to reopen the deal after the 1997–98 season; check. Then came the provisions about free agency, and that's where things went sideways. "Gary thought they had agreed on one thing, Bob thought they had agreed on another," John McCambridge recounts. "People were getting pretty hot. The whole deal almost blew sky high." What sounded to outsiders like a trifling matter—whether the age of unrestricted free agency would drop from thirty-two to thirty-one after the first year of the new agreement or the third—now threatened to derail the entire enterprise.

Bettman was eventually convinced to take Goodenow's version of the terms to the owners for a vote, but expressed doubts he could push it through. He was prescient, but not enough of a soothsayer to predict just how virulently some of his bosses would react. Bettman had barely begun to spell out the details via conference call when Abe Pollin, the owner of the Washington Capitals, cut him off demanding to know who had given him the authority to depart from the ultra-final proposal they had presented a couple of days before. The real estate developer, who would later change the name of his NBA franchise from the Bullets to the Wizards because of his concerns about gun violence in DC, was anything but peaceable. He moved to reject the settlement and send a message back to the players telling them to accept the league's past best offer ... or else. "That's the dumbest motion I've ever heard," responded the Flyers' Ed Snider. Bill Wirtz jumped into the fray supporting Pollin, as did Ilitch, Marcel Aubut in Quebec City, and Winnipeg's Barry Shenkarow. The screaming lasted for close to two hours, and when a vote was finally taken, the owners rejected the commissioner's deal fourteen to twelve. (Although someone from Bettman's camp made sure to share all the gory details with the reporters waiting outside, ensuring that fans knew just who was standing in the way of a settlement. "I can't believe my partners would do this," the Capitals' owner complained. "I think this is schlock.")

It was Goodenow who saved the season, agreeing to give the NHL two more years of control over the fate of its thirty-two year olds. When the revised deal came back to the board of governors later that evening, it passed nineteen to seven. The dissenters were Chicago, Detroit, Washington, Boston, New Jersey, Quebec, and Winnipeg. After 103 days, the NHL's first lockout was at an end.

The early draft of history the next morning suggested the

league and its new commissioner had triumphed. "Owners by a knockout!" screamed the *New York Post*. The NHLPA "held off the cap and slipped on a straitjacket," declared *The Boston Globe*. While a columnist for *The Vancouver Province* pronounced that "the owners won this thing so cleanly it's obscene." Many of the players also felt that it was a lopsided defeat. "We're getting raped," said the Canucks' Trevor Linden. There was some public grousing from the few owners who had wanted an unconditional surrender rather than a settlement, but Bettman positioned himself as the voice of reason. "If all twenty-six owners had said that they had to have a tax or a cap, we could have pursued them, but in my judgment it would have cost the entire season," he told an interviewer. "Many people, including me, thought that if there was a way to preserve the season, then that should be done." The illustration of what could happen in the absence of compromise was obvious—baseball's strike was entering its sixth month with no end in sight, and now there was talk of starting spring training with replacement players.

The NHLPA was content to take the heat. They had gone out of their way to portray their side as the giving party during negotiations, with the sole goal of skating away from a cap. And while a framework for the collective bargaining agreement (CBA) had been reached—just a ten-page term sheet, really—the guts of the agreement remained to be worked out, with lots of potential for designing a contract that tipped the balance back toward the players. "There was no question that Gary understood the cap system. But if he had an edge, it was in a system that he didn't end up getting," says McCambridge. The former player agent Goodenow and his team knew the NHL's free agency and arbitration system inside and out, far better than the ex-NBA types they were facing off against. And now they could set about leveraging that knowledge. When the new CBA was finally completed five months later, it was not nearly as owner friendly as many had predicted. "We were very confident that we got what we wanted," says McCambridge.

The union also felt like it had discovered the secret to dealing with Bettman: Feed his ego as much as it could take until he fell into blissful self-reverie. "He definitely has the smartest-boy-in-the-room syndrome," says another person who was involved in the negotiations. "It's so obvious when he's trying to trick you. He's not dumb, but it's the people who work for him who call him a genius." During negotiations Goodenow's side had played to the commissioner's vanity by suggesting that he was bright enough to succeed where others had failed and make the NHL work as a free market, without the crutch of a cap. And such attempts at manipulation continued even after the deal was done. In June 1997, with the NHL's first Olympics in Nagano on the horizon, Bettman came to the Players' Association seeking an extension of the CBA to ensure that the anticipated post-Games bump to business wouldn't be overshadowed by labour strife the following summer (not to mention his plans to expand the league by four more teams). The union had an opinion—they wanted to prolong the deal for as long as possible—but they kept it quiet and instead asked the commissioner to walk them through the numbers: "We said we're not really capable of evaluating these business matters. We'd like to be educated by you. So, he gets all puffed up and gives us a big lecture and we ended up with what we wanted." And on June 25, 1997, the day that Atlanta was awarded an NHL franchise, the league and its union also announced an agreement to extend their current deal through the end of the 2003–4 season.

Bettman says he did learn a crucial lesson from the labour disruption and its fallout: "You have to make sure that your constituents, your clients, however you want to characterize them, are telling you everything you need to know." He had presented his negotiating strategy to the board of governors and received unanimous support. But once the lockout began, the solidarity proved to be a mirage. "I kind of knew early on that not all of the owners were in a position to go the distance."

Jeff Pash, who now has three decades of experience negotiating labour agreements for sports leagues, says the emphasis on picking a winning and losing side might mirror what happens on the ice or playing field, but it doesn't reflect the reality of the business: "If your goal is a perfect deal, you won't ever make one." At the time, he and the other NHL negotiators thought they'd done pretty well for the owners. And for a couple of seasons, the numbers seemed to bear them out. By the time Joe Sakic and the transplanted Nordiques hoisted the Stanley Cup as the Colorado Avalanche in June 1996, sweeping the Florida Panthers in four games, league revenues had hit $936 million—$200 million more than in the pre-lockout season. Attendance had bounced back, with thirteen franchises showing gains over 1993–94 for a league average of just under 16,000 a game, 1300 more than before the lockout. (Although in Canada, where fans were so rabid that the CBC drew more than a million viewers for Saturday night reruns of "classic" games during the dispute, there were concerns about continuing low turnouts in Calgary and Edmonton.) The US franchises were generally thriving and would soon welcome another refugee Canadian club when the Jets finished their long goodbye and headed to Phoenix. The Olympics beckoned, with the promise of a tournament that would finally showcase the NHL's product to a global audience. But the good times would prove to be fleeting, just like Bettman's supposed victory over the union. "That's the lesson we learned," says Pash. "You can kick the can down the road a little bit, but not get to where you have to go."

THE PREPARATIONS FOR WAR began in the early part of 2000, more than four-and-a-half years before the deal was set to expire. Broad strategy sessions were held in the commissioner's office at NHL headquarters, where Bettman brought together the in-house and outside lawyers to start refining the league's demands, and to try and predict how the NHLPA would attempt to parry them. The meetings were sporadic at first, but two years out from the September 15, 2004, end of the CBA, they became weekly fixtures in everyone's calendar—10 A.M. on Tuesday in Gary's office. Sometimes they would last just half an hour, other times they could drag on for an hour or two, spinning off the week's events and the latest rumours. They discussed the business model they were shooting for, and the ones they might be willing to settle upon. They crafted the message that would be sold to the press and the fans. They discussed the nuances of labour law in the United States and Canada. But mostly they obsessed about how to get the better of Bob Goodenow this time around. The commissioner liked to map out decision trees, tracing paths for the negotiations if the union did x or y, or even x, y, and z. As the deadline approached, the frequency of the meetings was bumped up to twice a week. And once the NHL's lockout began, they were a daily obligation. "I have never had an experience like I had in that negotiation," says Bob Batterman, one of Bettman's former bosses at Proskauer and the league's outside counsel since the early 1990s. "I've sat in collective bargaining sessions for forty-five years, I've been the chief nego-tiator for hundreds of contracts, and I have never had the degree of preparation and client involvement that I had then. Gary was not going to leave a single stone unturned. He was not going to run any unnecessary risk to the business or the process. He did it right."

Bettman had made his opening gambit in March 1999, sending Goodenow a letter detailing his concerns about the league's changing financial picture, and asking the union to start talks immediately on a new CBA: "If the current trend continues, I cannot predict what shape the league will be in in 2004. I can, however, tell you with certainty that the potential for conflict will be greater because we would, under this scenario, be likely to insist on a significant re-trenching (not just limiting increases) of player costs." The threat between the commas was ignored.

So, too, was common sense. The near-death experience of the first lockout had quickly faded from the memories of NHL owners, who had cashed in on $320 million in expansion fees—$80 million apiece for the Thrashers, Blue Jackets, Wild, and Predators—in just three seasons. In the summer of 1999, the Anaheim Ducks made twenty-four-year-old Paul Kariya, a gifted player, but one who had never won a major award, or even led the league in any statistical category, the NHL's first $10-million-a-season man. And the rising salary tide was lifting all sorts of boats. In 2001, the Boston Bruins signed free agent Martin Lapointe, who had exactly one NHL season where he had scored more than sixteen goals, to a four-year, $20-million contract. In 2002, the Rangers lured Bobby Holik, who had never topped sixty-five points, away from New Jersey with a five-year, $45-million deal. By the end of the 2002–3 season, league revenues were approaching $2 billion, a 171-percent increase since 1994. But the average player salary had ballooned from $560,000 to $1.79 million, a 244-percent increase. And even the median numbers were getting into the high-rent district—half of all NHLers were now making in excess of $1 million a year.

The owners appeared unable to help themselves, yet they remained eager to have someone else impose discipline on their finances. In June 2000, the board of governors voted unanimously to give Bettman the power not only to negotiate their next deal with the players but also to override their baser instincts. If the commissioner was in favour of an agreement he now needed the support of just a simple majority, rather than two-thirds of the owners. And if he was against a settlement, he would be able to scuttle it with the votes of just eight like-minded franchises. In January 2002, the governors gave him a further vote of confidence—a new $3.7-million-a-year contract that would carry him through to the end of the 2008 playoffs.

Bettman had learned from the spanking that Wirtz and the other hard-liners had administered to him in the final hours of the 1995 negotiations. This time, the owners needed to be united and to follow their leader without question. In the months before talks began, he personally visited each and every one of them to outline the strategy, and drive home the fact that it might well cost the NHL a season—or two—to get the deal that they wanted. "Gary really got into it with them about what this would mean if we were going to go down this path," says Shep Goldfein, another NHL legal adviser who accompanied him on many of the trips. There was a formal presentation with lots of numbers and all those various decision-tree scenarios neatly sketched out. Few of the owners expressed any reservations. "In some ways, it was a little bit easier to sell because it cost the league less to shut down than to play," says Goldfein. "The system just wasn't working." And just to make sure that there would be no loss of will when the bills came due, each club was required to obtain a new $10-million line of credit and file the papers with the league. There would also be a steep price to pay for departing from the company line—it was agreed that any owner who divulged details of internal NHL discussions or divisions would be subject to a fine of up to $1 million to be levied at Bettman's sole discretion. (The NHLPA was also wielding a big hammer, threatening to decertify any agent who publicly questioned the union's position.)

Negotiations opened just after New Year's in 2003 with a meeting between Goodenow and Bettman in New York City. But whatever hopes existed for an easy settlement quickly dissipated. The Ottawa Senators, who had been struggling to restructure a $160-million debt tied to their new rink in suburban Kanata, filed for bankruptcy on January 9. And four days later, so did the Buffalo Sabres—left insolvent by the spectacular financial implosion of owner John Rigas, who had looted billions from his public company, Adelphia Communications, and was about to be indicted on charges of bank, wire, and securities fraud. Bettman tried to spin the twin disasters as indications of just how unworkable the finances of hockey had become. And an incensed Goodenow responded with a press release that basically called him a liar.

Having the main antagonists from the last lockout face off across the table was clearly not going to be a recipe for success. So a decision was made to embark on a different course: a series of informal, without-prejudice meetings where the two sides could freely explore all the options for a new collective bargaining agreement. The NHLPA would be represented by their deputy director, Ted Saskin, and outside lawyer John McCambridge. For the NHL, it would Bob Batterman and Bettman's major domo, Bill Daly.

Daly had been involved on the fringes of the 1994–95 negotiations as an associate working for Shep Goldfein at the Manhattan offices of the law firm Skadden, Arps. And when Jeff Pash left the league to return to the NFL in 1996, Daly was tapped to replace him as the NHL's new general counsel. Just thirty-two at the time, he didn't have a lot of experience, but he was a verifiable sports freak and added some much-needed testosterone to the league offices. A New Jersey kid, he'd grown up playing football and had a decent mix of size and speed—running the forty-yard dash in

4.6 seconds. He was recruited by Dartmouth and played four seasons of Ivy League ball as a tailback, although a knee injury early in his university career transformed him from burner to a short-yardage grinder. But Daly's true passion was hockey, and more specifically, the New York Rangers. He came by it naturally; his mom was from Saskatchewan and his father, a businessman, shared her Canadian enthusiams. The family had season tickets, and Daly attended a lot of games while growing up. He can still rattle off the rosters and rhapsodize about the team's run to the Stanley Cup Final in 1979. (His favourite all-time Rangers are Lou Ferrigno look-alike Barry Beck and Don Maloney, now the perpetually put-upon GM of the Phoenix Coyotes.) It was something beyond regular fandom. Each year when the Blueshirts were eliminated from the playoffs, Daly used to fashion a black armband out of electrical tape and wear it to school.

Bettman had come to rely on him for both his hockey knowledge and his people skills. Blunt and bear-like, Daly is a guy's guy, right down to the man-cave basement at home with the bar and five TVs hooked up to two different satellite dishes. And he got on well with pretty much everyone, including the rep from the NHLPA, with the notable exception of Goodenow. "[Bob] had a great run at the Players' Association. He could do anything he wanted to do and the players gave him a lot of rope because he'd been so successful," says Daly. "But I don't think he had a relationship with anybody. I don't even think Bob had a relationship with his own side."

The secret talks, dubbed Project Blue Fin after a seafood and sushi restaurant in the W Hotel in Times Square, the site of the initial meeting, were focused on finding a compromise. The mood was cordial and no subject was verboten. There were close to a dozen sessions over four months and it seemed like progress was being made, but then in early June, Goodenow and Bettman joined the group and things started to fall apart. In the presence of the main combatants, all the bad blood from the first lockout suddenly flowed back into the room. And winning became a lot more important than bargaining. The positions quickly hardened. The league wanted some type of firm ceiling on the amount of money going to the players, and the NHLPA wouldn't budge.

"Goodenow was inflexible. He was a prick. And he didn't think he had to do anything because he didn't think there was a snowball's chance in hell that the owners would hang together," recalls another person who was involved on the NHL side. "He wasn't going anywhere. He wasn't making any concessions."

The union made its first formal proposal at the beginning of October—a 5-percent across-the-board salary rollback, more limits on rookie pay, and a luxury tax tied to a new revenue-sharing system. It was rejected almost immediately, and the NHL countered with a hard-to-swallow figure—$31 million was as much as it wanted any one team paying its players, less than half of the $69 million the Rangers had spent in 2003–4.

The gloves came off and the two sides spent the fall trading blows in the press rather than negotiating. When the league pronounced that its thirty teams had lost an astonishing $300 million in the 2002–3 season alone, the Players' Association revealed that it had been allowed to look at the books of four of them—two US and two Canadian—and uncovered $52 million in hidden revenues. (A piece in *Forbes* that estimated the NHL's collective loss to be more in the order of $96 million a year further inflamed the debate. The Islanders were only counting half of their $17-million cable deal, it reported, while the Blackhawks' revenue figures showed none of the income they earned from the United Center's 212 luxury boxes. Saskin praised the magazine's independence and integrity.

Daly questioned its methodology and accused the editors of "irresponsible journalism.")

Bettman countered by hiring Arthur Levitt, the former chair of the U.S. Securities and Exchange Commission, to conduct what he called a "super audit" of league finances. His findings, released in February 2004, were not as forensic as billed, but did back up the league's doomsday scenario. In the previous season, the NHL had a combined $273-million operating loss on just under $2 billion of revenue. Four teams had lost more than $30 million apiece, and eight others more than $10 million. Only eleven teams showed a profit, and just two of those made more than $10 million. Levitt pegged total player compensation at $1.5 billion, or 75 percent of the take. "The current relationship between League-wide player costs and League-wide revenues is inconsistent with reasonable and sound business practices," he concluded. At a press conference in New York City, the ex-watchdog was even more pointed: "I would not underwrite any of these ventures as a banker, nor would I invest a dollar of my own personal money in a business that, to me, appears to be heading south."

There were sporadic bargaining sessions through the spring and summer, but they were mostly exercises in public posturing. A final stab at a deal—twenty hours of talks over three days during the World Cup of Hockey in Montreal in early September—was followed by one last proposal from the NHLPA, which again featured a token rollback and more revenue sharing. "We're not even speaking the same language," Bettman carped.

When the lockout officially began in mid-September, everyone involved knew it was going to be a drawn-out affair. Within a week, more than 150 NHLers had already signed deals to play in Europe, and by the beginning of 2005, the number had swelled to 350—almost half the league. Not everyone was happy to see them arrive. Goaltender Corey Hirsch, who had moved on to the Langnau Tigers of the Swiss league after his big-league career had sputtered out, wrote an opinion piece for the *Calgary Sun* in which he labelled his former colleagues as scabs: "I think some of these players should have a talk with my pregnant wife and kids who moved their lives to Europe, only to watch me sit in the stands game after game, because I have been bumped by an NHL player." His point was somewhat undercut by the fact that his replacement was the Carolina Hurricanes' Martin Gerber, a Swiss-born netminder who had started his career with the Tigers and was the go-to guy for the country's national team as well.

Trevor Linden, the heart and soul of the Vancouver Canucks and president of the NHLPA, didn't have the option of leaving town. The big centre had met Bettman for the first time during the 1994 Stanley Cup Final and had come away unimpressed. The new commissioner just didn't seem like a hockey guy. It was an unfavourable opinion that hardened during the lockout that began later that year, when Linden served as the team rep, waiting at home by the fax machine for updates on negotiations from the NHLPA office in Toronto. Over the ensuing years, he'd become more involved in union business, serving on the licensing committee. And when Mike Gartner retired from the game and stepped down as the union head at the end of 1998, Linden had put his name forward as his replacement. His first term was uneventful. The league was expanding, there were more jobs for players, and the competition was driving salaries steadily up. But when he decided to stand for re-election in 2002, he knew that a reckoning was coming. "There was going to be a major war. The expansion money had been spent, the difference in the Canadian dollar was enormous, there was inequity in what large-market and small-market teams could afford to spend," he says. "There were huge problems."

This time, the Players' Association had a sizable war chest, and Goodenow had done his best to prepare his charges for the long struggle ahead. Players had been given ample warning to build up their savings or prepare to find other work. And plans had been put in place to help those who never learned to balance a cheque-book. The message had been consistent: It would take at least a year to break the owners this time. "It was no cap, no cap, no cap," Linden recalls. "In those ten years between the lockouts, we had been indoctrinated with all the pitfalls of that system."

And solidarity was zealously enforced. When Montreal winger Pierre Dagenais gave an interview to *La Presse* saying that he wouldn't mind playing under a cap and that there were a growing number of guys who felt the same way, he was told in no uncertain terms to shut up. A few days later, he was paraded before the media at a union briefing session in Toronto wearing an NHLPA ball cap and sweatshirt. Asked about the cap, he declined to express an opinion. "All I want is to play hockey, and these guys are working hard to fix the problem," said Dagenais.

But as the lockout entered its fourth month, there was growing unease among the players. In early December, the union invited the NHL back to the table and made a stunning proposal—a 24-percent rollback on all existing contracts coupled with more concessions on rookie salaries and arbitration plus a luxury tax. Goodenow walked the media through the details with a PowerPoint presentation and suggested an agreement was now close at hand. He was wrong. Bettman rejected the deal and countered with an offer that treated the rollback as a starting point, piling a cap and other draconian conditions on top. Goodenow was apoplectic, decrying the move as "completely useless and phoney." The union had been beaten with its olive branch. "In hindsight, it was something we just gave up and didn't get anything for," says Linden. "But if the year was cancelled, it was a 100-percent rollback."

As 2005 dawned, and the second lockout eclipsed the record set by the first, reality started to sink in. Goodenow taped an audio message for the players and posted it on a password-protected website. There would be no more offers, he said, and he encouraged members to look for work in Europe, since it was more than likely that there would be no NHL season. The next negotiating window would be in the summer as the owners looked toward training camp, and if those talks failed, there would be nothing until close to Christmas, as pressure to save at least part of a season again built to its peak. Beating the owners and avoiding the cap could take at least another year, if not two.

What was meant to reassure had exactly the opposite effect. Linden, feeling pressure from his constituents, took matters into his own hands and invited the NHL to a meeting in Chicago. No Bettman, no Goodenow. Just himself, Saskin, and McCambridge trying to hash things out with Daly, Batterman, and Harley Hotchkiss, the co-owner of the Calgary Flames and chairman of the board of governors. The talks at a hotel attached to O'Hare Airport lasted five hours and were followed by another meeting a couple of days later in Toronto. Both sides were still unwilling to blink, but Hotchkiss's vivid descriptions of the challenges facing small-market owners and evident passion for the game moved Linden, and started him thinking that this time it might be the players who had to give.

The NHL made two more cap proposals in early February, but neither were acceptable to the union. And Bettman finally set a drop-dead date, indicating that if a deal wasn't completed by mid-month he would cancel the season. Linden's phone was burning up. "I fielded call, after call, after call, after call where the guys were like, 'I just want to understand what we're fighting for. Please help me out with this,'" he says. The prospect of losing not just money but a full year or more of a short professional career was daunting to many: "I think they started to lose sight of what the fight was about. Was it ideological? They had just sacrificed a year, and they weren't exactly sure why."

What was clear was that the fans had had enough of the dissembling and pettiness of both sides. Archie Bennitz, an eighty-four-year-old Leafs supporter, arranged to have a posthumous message placed in his death notice after he passed away at an Ottawa hospital in January: Bettman and Goodenow were "skunks for denying him the pleasure of watching the NHL on TV this year." His son David told the press that hockey was the only thing his father had ever watched, and that he became increasingly livid over his final months as the lockout dragged on. Another group of rec hockey players in Edmonton got talking about the fate of the Cup over post-game beers and became tipsy enough to pony up the money for a legal opinion on the question. Informed that the chalice was still technically a challenge trophy, they tried to convince the trustees from the Hockey Hall of Fame to allow them to stage one of their regular "dark versus white" contests as the 2005 final. It wasn't an original idea—the Hockey Hall of Fame ended up receiving 400 such submissions—but the Edmonton boys were the most determined. When their request was denied, they filed suit in Ontario Superior Court seeking a declaration that the league didn't own its ultimate prize. The matter was eventually settled out of court, with the NHL agreeing to give $500,000 over five years to leagues for women and underprivileged children.

On February 13, the US government forced the league and union to sit down with a mediator in Washington. And it was there that the NHLPA finally agreed to discuss at least the possibility of players limiting themselves to a set percentage of the league's gross revenues. The next morning, Valentine's Day, Ted Saskin got in his car and drove from Toronto to the Honeymoon Capital of the World, Niagara Falls, New York, to meet Bill Daly at the Four Points Sheraton. Love wasn't in the air, but a compromise seemed possible. With the commissioner's deadline looming, the NHL proposed a cap of $40 million, and the players countered with an offer that set the ceiling at $52 million. On the fifteenth, there was another meeting in New York, where the league came up to $42.5 million and the union down to $49 million. "We cannot afford your proposal," Bettman snapped. "You'll receive nothing further from us," was Goodenow's icy response.

Despite the tough talk, ideas did continue to fly back and forth throughout the afternoon and evening. But it wasn't just a matter of sawing off the difference. Sharing revenues would demand a whole new system of reporting and accounting, concepts that had never previously been discussed. And soon it was evident that there wasn't enough time. When the death knell sounded, the two sides were still miles apart—Bettman and his crew in a boardroom in Manhattan, and Goodenow, Linden, and their negotiating team, which had grown to include players like Bill Guerin and Brendan Shanahan, gathered around a table in Toronto. "It was a very somber mood," recalls Saskin. "You're getting closer and closer, and then we just felt like we had gone as far as we could go. And they felt the same way." At 11 A.M. the next morning, a haggard Gary Bettman stepped up to a podium in New York and became the first, and so far the only, big-league commissioner to scrub an entire season of play. "We are truly sorry," he told the fans.

There was one more desperate salvage attempt—a meeting in New York a couple of days later that brought Wayne Gretzky and Mario Lemieux into the picture—but no one had anything new to say. "I was very clear that we weren't going to make a deal just for the sake of making a deal," says Bettman. "If you have problems, you have to fix them." The progress that had been made seemed to be ebbing away. A couple of weeks after the cancellation, the commissioner vowed that there would be hockey in the 2005–6 season, and the league started to prepare the ground for the use of replacement players, filing a challenge with the US National Labor Relations Board over a Players' Association policy that would financially penalize anyone who crossed the line. The NHLPA responded by seeking official certification as a union in Ontario and Quebec, two provinces that had anti-scab laws.

If Bettman was worried about his owners breaking ranks, it didn't show. And soon he was to receive an unsolicited gift that helped keep his side focused on the prize. In March, Bain Capital, the investment firm founded by Mitt Romney, made a $3-billion bid to take over all thirty teams and run the NHL as a single entity. The buyout was hatched by Game Plan LLC, a Boston company that brokers the sale of sports franchises. Randy Vataha, one of the principals, was a former wide receiver for the New England Patriots who had once been active in the NFL Players Association, leading his team out on strike in 1974. Later, he became an owner himself, buying into the Boston Breakers of the USFL, a short-lived rival football league. Vataha and his partner, Bob Caporale, looked at the NHL and saw a business that could make a lot of money, but not with thirty different bosses. The idea that they sold to Bain would have left individual club management in place, but seen the league set the payrolls, collect the revenues, and pay all the bills. Bettman allowed them to make their pitch directly to the owners. "You'd be surprised at how many calls we got after that," Caporale says. "There were governors who understood it and thought it had some value." The bid fizzled out before things got serious, but it did serve the commissioner's purpose—demonstrating that a firm that had made pots of money investing in enterprises as diverse as Sealy mattresses and Burger King saw lots of potential in hockey.

In April, the players came back to the table with a new proposal, a floor and a ceiling for team payrolls, tied to revenue. It was something the owners felt they could live with and negotiations gathered steam. In May and June, the two sides met more than thirty times, mostly at the offices of Skadden, Arps, on the thirty-eighth floor of a building that overlooks Times Square and offers commanding views in all directions. By the end of the process, the conference rooms provided to each side were so beaten up, and the rugs so stained with takeout food, that they had to be completely redecorated. Bettman was there constantly, recalls Shep Goldfein, involving himself not just in negotiations but in the drafting of the CBA as well. The carefully crafted provisions about buyouts and contract averaging are covered with his thumbprints. "Gary kept saying that he had been through all this with the NBA and that we needed to have very particular examples in our agreement to explain how it is intended to work," says the lawyer. Same with the sensitive issue of revenue sharing: "There were some real politics, because some teams were going to have to give money to their opponents and these guys are as competitive as can be."

The one person who was rarely present throughout the final months was Goodenow. And even when he did stop in, he made a point of not attending any of the meetings with the NHL side. The union's very public, no-cap-under-any-circumstances stand had been his strategic decision, and when the players began to balk at their limited options it had provoked a rift with their longtime executive director. "Bob was willing to wait for the owners to cave and accept our December proposal with the 24-percent rollback," says Linden. "And I didn't think that was going to happen." He had always told the players that it would be impossible to get the owners to fully disclose their revenues. And now it seemed that that wasn't true. The complex and comprehensive definition of hockey-related revenues being worked out between the two parties was adding $200 million to the pot they would share—54 percent to players and the rest to the owners. Goodenow, who was spending much of his time back in Detroit caring for his dying mother, was still in the loop, but no longer in charge. Linden and Saskin were calling the shots.

The deal was finally concluded on July 13 during an all-night session at the league offices, on the heels of ten straight days of bargaining. Saskin, who had to catch a flight to Italy that evening for a nephew's wedding, had set his own deadline, and Daly met it. After 301 days, the NHL was back in business.

The agreement, which called for a $39-million-per-team salary ceiling for the 2005–6 season and a $22-million floor, coupled with the 24-percent rollback, was greeted with more relief than enthusiasm by the players, who voted 87 percent in favour. The owners gave it their unanimous approval. Bettman made some brief remarks, noting the enormous cost of the "new partnership" and vowing to repay the fans by giving them all the fun they could handle. Goodenow marked the end of the battle, and a deal he did not endorse, with a short press release. Only July 28, he called a news conference in Toronto to announce that he was stepping down and that Saskin was taking over as executive director of the NHLPA. The reality was that Goodenow was pushed out—his severance package, later leaked to the *Toronto Star*, was worth $8 million. Linden hasn't spoken to him since August 2005. Neither has Saskin. And Goodenow himself has maintained a discreet silence, refusing all interview requests since he parted with the union.

Saskin found himself embroiled in controversy within weeks of officially taking over the top job. His appointment was targeted by a group of dissident players, led by Chris Chelios, who objected to his $2.13-million-a-year salary, negotiated one-on-one with Linden without the input of the team reps. There were repeated challenges within the union and even a lawsuit. And in the spring of 2007, facing an independent outside investigation into the circumstances surrounding his hiring, Saskin was accused of having tapped into players' private email accounts to glean details of the campaign against him. That May, he was fired. He later sued for the remaining $6.5 million on his contract, ultimately settling for $400,000.

Saskin, who now does some consulting and works for a family-owned real estate development firm in Toronto, traces his troubles right back to Goodenow's bargaining strategy. "In hindsight, I think it was a mistake to make the cap an all-or-nothing win–lose fight," he says. "If you cast cap as bad and non-cap as good, and then you end up in a cap system, the simplicity of that message remains out there afterwards. And a small, yet vocal group who were unhappy with the way the negotiations ended chose to have a large impact."

Paul Kelly, a Boston lawyer who as a young assistant US attorney had prosecuted Alan Eagleson, was hired as the new NHLPA executive director. He lasted just two years, pushed out in the summer of 2009, amid accusations that he had been too friendly with the NHL hierarchy—a perception that may have had its roots in his decision to invite Bettman to address a union meeting held in Las Vegas at the end of the previous season. His severance package was worth a reported $1.5 million. Ian Penny, his interim replacement, lasted just three months, succumbing to yet more infighting. Bettman's crushing lockout victory had left opponents in complete disarray.

It had taken a dozen years and two extended labour disputes, but the league's first commissioner had finally delivered what he had promised—real restraints on player costs. And the NHL was now the envy of the pro-sporting world, boasting what was effectively a triple cap: the total league-wide salary amount fixed as a percentage of revenue, a team-by-team ceiling, and individual player compensation limited to a maximum of 20 percent of his team's envelope. All accomplished within a system that shared less revenue than football or baseball, guaranteeing that the NHL's most successful franchises would become even richer.

Heading into another round of negotiations in the fall of 2012, Bettman is cagey about his last victory. "The fact is that we did what we had to do at the time," he says. It was the fans—not the owners—who were the driving force, demanding a rebalancing of the league, he contends. "Our research showed that they were supportive of what we were doing because they wanted the problems fixed. They didn't want a Band-Aid. They wanted better competitive balance and better economics in terms of franchise health and stability." The commissioner skates around the question of whether he really would have kept the NHL idle for a second season just to get a salary cap. But bluff or not, it was a potent threat.

When play finally resumed in the fall of 2005, there was no denying the obvious: Hockey was Gary Bettman's game.

4 Lost and Found

The last time Gary Bettman visited Winnipeg, it was with police protection. A half-dozen of the city's finest, standing guard outside the meeting room and subsequent press conference just in case an angry Jets fan decided to try and save the franchise through regicide. He'd been shamed into coming to town. Perhaps even bullied.

The day before—Friday, April 28, 1995—the *Winnipeg Free Press* had broken out the D-Day-landing-sized type for a headline declaring that the city had been "Shafted by the NHL." A deal to sell the team to a consortium of seventy local business leaders and to finally build a new arena was unravelling amid charges that Bettman had altered the rules of the game in the final minutes. Facing a May 1 deadline to conclude the sale, the prospective owners, the Manitoba Entertainment Complex—MEC for short—had launched a blistering attack against the commissioner and his "outrageous" demands.

They had thought things were on the right track until Thursday afternoon. MEC's chairman, John Loewen, had joined Mayor Susan Thompson in her office along with the city's chief commissioner and outside auditor for a conference call with Bettman at the NHL's New York headquarters. It was their *ta-dah* moment: The money was in place to buy out Barry Shenkarow and the Jets' three other private owners at the hometown discount price of $32 million Canadian and move ahead to the next phase, a $120-million replacement for the old Winnipeg Arena, with the costs split between three levels of government and the private sector. (City and provincial taxpayers, who had poured in $18 million and counting since 1991 to cover the team's losses, would retain a third of the club.) But Bettman was less than receptive to their plan. The first problem, he said, was with their payroll projections. In the lockout-shortened season that was just then drawing to a close, the Jets had spent US$13 million, with their highest-paid player, Keith Tkachuk, taking home a prorated $1.16 million of his $2-million salary. MEC had budgeted US$18 million annually for the coming years—slightly above the league average. Now the commissioner was telling them that $30 million would be a middle-of-the-pack expenditure in the near future.

Then Bettman let off a stink bomb. The deal could still go ahead, but only under certain conditions: There needed to be a primary owner, and the group couldn't sell until they had collectively lost at least $25 million. If they wanted to move the team before the end of the 1999–2000 season, they would have to pay the league a $50-million transfer fee. And they couldn't mortgage the Jets for more than $50 million—the notional value of the team for the transaction—to finance the new rink.

For those gathered in Thompson's office, the terms came out of the blue. Meeting just one of them would be difficult enough, but collectively they were an almost certain deal killer. They hung up and started working through their options—and the stages of grief. Calls flew back and forth to the commissioner all afternoon. Loewen, a tall, aw-shucks type who had recently sold the family payroll services company to a major bank, almost tossed the phone through a window after one heated exchange. Thompson, a more natural scrapper who had left behind the family-owned saddlery and western goods store on Main Street to become the city's first female mayor, was even angrier. Through it all, Bettman hardly raised his voice. He sounded like a man who had given up on Winnipeg long before.

Still steaming, the mayor and the MEC head threw open the office's big oak double doors and started venting to the reporters who had been milling around in the hallway outside. She publicly questioned whether Canada's game was destined to become a strictly American one. He called Bettman's new stipulations an "ambush." But even as he spoke, the rage was giving way to despair. Loewen, then in his early forties, had taken on the chairman's role and become the public face of MEC because the sale of his business meant he and his family could leave town if things got ugly. Now he was wondering what things were going to be like for his kids at school the next day, and whether he really was a Toronto sort of guy. The icing on the cake came when he finally made it outside to find his car had been towed away.

Friday morning's headlines and some vigorous drum-beating on local talk radio saw more than 1500 people take to the streets at the noon hour to express their extreme displeasure with the NHL commissioner—albeit in a polite, Prairie way. "Bettman is a jerk!" read one of the homemade signs. Another called him "two-faced." "Wise up, Bettman," warned a third. After blocking traffic at Portage and Main for a while, the crowd—mostly young and dressed in Jets paraphernalia—wandered over to the Manitoba legislature to chant at Gary Filmon, re-elected as premier earlier that week, in no small measure because of his promise to do whatever it took to keep the team in place. Once outside to address the mob from the building's steps, he didn't exactly calm the waters. "NHL hockey was born, raised, and developed in Canada," he shouted. "Gary Bettman and his little group of wealthy owners have no right to take Canada out of the game." Mayor Thompson was busy banging the same gong, writing open letters to Prime Minister Jean Chrétien and the civic leaders of Quebec, Edmonton, Ottawa, and Calgary, begging for a concerted front to stop the league's "implicit strategy" to abandon all the country's smaller markets. The national media were eating it up.

The spat, coming on the eve of the playoffs that were supposed to help fans forget and forgive the 103-day lockout, was quickly becoming a public-relations disaster. The NHL offices in New York put out a release blaming erroneous reporting for the turmoil, maintaining that MEC had been informed of all the changes weeks before the conference call. And Bettman and his chief legal officer, Jeff Pash, the California-born son of a former Winnipegger, agreed to catch an early Saturday flight from New York to listen to people's concerns.

The meeting took place in a sterile conference room at the old Winnipeg airport terminal. The premier and mayor were joined by Liberal heavyweight Lloyd Axworthy, the federal minister of employment, immigration, and goodies—via his Western Economic Diversification portfolio. Loewen brought along MEC's big dogs, including Sandy Riley, CEO of the brokerage house Investors Group, and Hartley Richardson, president of the agriculture, oil and gas, and financial services conglomerate James Richardson & Sons—the core who had hatched the plan to rescue the Jets over the May 24 long weekend the year before at their Lake of the Woods cottages. Under the fluorescent lights, they took turns trying to convince the NHL commissioner and Shenkarow—the man who was desperate to sell the team—that they had the means, know-how, and support to stabilize the franchise. Bettman just kept coming back to the idea that he wanted one owner he could point at and say, "This is your team. Make it work. Pay your bills." Susan Thompson, who had instantly disliked everything about Bettman—from his "arrogant" tone to his body language to his lawyerly speech—the first time she had met him months before in Edmonton, sat silently fuming. Filmon, also not an admirer, figured the game was up: "He didn't give us any sense that the league really wanted us to make the effort. He just kept saying that he had all these wealthy Americans in southern US markets of five million people or more who were willing to put big money into a team."

Afterwards, Bettman and Shenkarow travelled downtown to brief the press. The commissioner (still under police protection) acknowledged that he wasn't the most popular guy in town, but chalked it up to misplaced anger: "It's too easy to pick on me because I'm an American." The situation Winnipeg found itself in wasn't of his making. He was simply the guy in charge of trying to clean it up.

Larger forces certainly seemed to be conspiring against the NHL's smaller markets. Free-spending teams in New York, Los Angeles, Pittsburgh, and St. Louis were driving up player costs at a rapid rate, and the lockout had failed to do much to slow them down beyond curbing rookie salaries. (The average team payroll the year before the work stoppage was US$12.9 million. The season after, it was $19.9 million.) Clubs in the Great White North, required to pay players in American greenbacks, found themselves further disadvantaged by a weak loonie, which sank as low as 65 cents US. And the arena-building boom that was providing flusher franchises with access to even more revenue streams like luxury boxes, club seats, and swanky restaurants only widened the gap. Canadian owners were lobbying fiercely for federal and provincial assistance to acquire their own shiny new barns, but it was an uphill battle. Struggling to tame their deficits and fix priority programs like medicare, Ottawa and the provinces were big on moral support, but less forthcoming with actual dollars. And public sympathy for the bunch that had just deprived them of four months of pro hockey was not running high.

A template for a move to sunnier and larger locales had already been established the day before Bettman took over the league's reins at the December 1992 owners' meeting, when the board of governors cut a deal to let Norm Green relocate the Minnesota North Stars to Dallas at the end of the season. Just two years removed from a lucrative trip to the Stanley Cup Final (Mario Lemieux and the Pittsburgh Penguins defeated them in six games) and located in America's unquestioned hockey hotbed, the team appeared to be profitable. Gate receipts at the Met Center in Bloomington, a Twin Cities suburb, increased from $8.4 million in 1991–92 to $11.2 million the next year. Revenue from corporate sponsorships doubled, and *Financial World* magazine valued the franchise at $42 million, $8 million more than the year before.

Green, a Calgary real estate baron and minority owner of the Flames, had been hailed as a saviour when he bought the Stars for $31 million in 1990. The Byzantine transaction—which saw the previous owners, George and Gordon Gund, swap the club for a new expansion franchise in San Jose—seemed to secure hockey's Minnesota future. (The Gund brothers, once the owners of the failed California Golden Seals, who moved to Cleveland in 1976 and became the woeful Barons, then merged with the North Stars two seasons later, had wanted to reverse the process and head back to the west coast.) And during the '91 Cup run, Minny fans had taken to chanting Norm's name to show their appreciation. But the love affair didn't last. When Bloomington officials refused to let him develop land around the aging Met Center and piggyback on the success of the nearby mega Mall of America—the largest consumer terrarium in the country at 4.2 million square feet—he tried unsuccessfully to move the club to downtown Minneapolis, then St. Paul. And with each setback, Green's claims about his losses since buying the team escalated, eventually surpassing $24 million.

Behind the scenes, he had worked out a deal to move the Stars to Anaheim, but Disney's brand power, and the company's willingness to pay a $50-million expansion fee, guaranteed it would be the Mighty Ducks that shared Los Angeles, not him. As a consolation prize, Green's fellow owners let him have his pick of open US markets for relocation. He chose Dallas, and soon the crowds in Minnesota were bellowing "Norm sucks!" After a while, he stopped attending games for fear he might get beaten up. (Three years later, Green, facing his own financial troubles, was forced to sell the Stars to Tom Hicks for US$84 million.)

The lesson was pretty clear: In the new NHL, money and the attendant happiness of owners trumped the desires of fans and communities. And if the league hadn't fought very hard to keep hockey in far-flung Minnesota, what hope was there for an even smaller market 750 kilometres farther north?

Standing in front of the media in Winnipeg, Bettman hammered home the point. His job wasn't to get all misty and sentimental about the Jets, or the Oilers, or the Nordiques. "Canada, if nothing else, is a natural resource for the NHL in terms of where we get most of our players," he said. "I don't want to do anything that we don't have to, to diminish our role up here. But, like it or not, the NHL has a huge business component to it that has to be addressed." Hewers of wood, drawers of water, exporters of skaters.

On May 3, the day after the Jets closed out their season with a 2–1 loss to Wayne Gretzky and the LA Kings, MEC officially threw in the towel. Shenkarow let it be known that he had received a US$65 million—nearly $100 million Canadian—offer for the team from a pair of Minneapolis businessmen. So on May 6, there was an emotional funeral ceremony at the Winnipeg Arena, where the players said teary goodbyes to the fans. Don Cherry, dressed in a Herb Tarlek–approved plaid sports coat, gave a blustering eulogy. "Now I hear they're going to go down to the United States to a place where they've already failed once," he said as the crowd of more than 15,000 booed. "I guess we in Canada only get one chance. Down in the States they get two or three." Centre Ed Olczyk promised that he and his teammates would be back someday soon for a visit—with the Stanley Cup in tow. And Thomas Steen, the steady Swede who played his whole fourteen-year NHL career with the Jets, saw his number 25 hoisted to the rafters.

But it wasn't the last gasp. The first phone call Loewen received after announcing the deal's demise—if you put aside the obscene and threatening ones—was from the thirty-five-year-old president of a group of local auto dealerships. He didn't know Mark Chipman very well, but he was relieved to hear that someone else was willing to make an attempt to keep the team in town. The Spirit of Manitoba group came together quickly, uniting most of the city's young entrepreneurs, the key MEC money folks, and a grizzled dealmaker, Izzy Asper, the chain-smoking, martini-slurping founder of CanWest Communications. Although Asper, whose passion was jazz, not hockey, wasn't exactly rah-rah about their prospects. At Spirit's first press conference, he introduced his co-conspirators, including his "bastard son Leonard, who got me into this mess."

But there was no question of the public just giving up. A Save Our Jets rally at the Forks on May 16 drew 35,000 people and saw kids emptying the contents of their piggybanks into the fund-raising buckets. Troy Bodie—then an eleven year old from nearby Portage la Prairie, now a hulking twenty-seven-year-old left winger in Anaheim's minor-league system—was among them, instructing his mother Shirley to give the team everything he had. "It was about 100 bucks. Gold at the time," he recalls. She demurred, and made a family contribution instead. (Bodie eventually repaid the debt, getting the Ducks' Teemu Selanne, her all-time favourite Jet, to autograph one of his sweaters for her.) Two days later, Spirit had the $10-million down payment for the franchise, and $50 million more in commitments toward the purchase and an endowment they hoped to create to cover the club's operating losses.

In the end, it was the Nordiques who left first, abandoning Quebec City for Denver, Colorado, with far less fuss. Marcel Aubut and his ownership group had also been engaged in a high-stakes game of chicken with the city and province since the end of the lockout, seeking to replace the ramshackle Colisée, built in 1949 when another generation of fans were flocking to watch a teenaged Jean Béliveau star for the Quebec Aces. Not only did he want the public to pay for the new building, he was asking the government to cover the team's losses before, during, and after construction. Aubut, a big man with an ego to match, was as connected as anyone in the province and was used to getting his way. He had helped pilot the WHA's merger with the NHL in 1979 and had been the driving force behind the Rendez-vous '87 series that pitted the league's all-stars, including Gretzky and Lemieux, against the Soviet national team. (They split the two games, but the Russians scored more goals, winning 8–7 on aggre-gate.) And he had been among the first to raid the talent trapped behind the Iron Curtain, personally flying to Austria to help Czechoslovakian stars Peter and Anton Stastny defect to the West during a 1980 European Champions Cup tournament. It turned out to be worth the cost of the plane ticket. In their first season with the Nordiques, Anton tallied 85 points and Peter scored 39 goals and added 79 assists, capturing the Calder Trophy as rookie of the year. Older brother Marian joined them a year later, and the trio contributed 107 goals and 193 assists during the 1981–82 season. Then they added 40 more during a playoff run that saw Quebec beat the Habs and then the Bruins before falling to the Islanders—who went on to win their third of four consecutive Stanley Cups—in the conference finals.

There had been some pretty lean times since. Starting in 1987–88, the Nords missed the playoffs for five consecutive seasons, finishing at the very bottom of the table three years in a row. Although the compensatory draft picks, which netted them young guns like Joe Sakic, Owen Nolan, and Mats Sundin, as well as the fruits of the Lindros trade, had them on the upswing again. In 1994–95, under rookie coach Marc Crawford, they finished first in the Northeast Division, going 19–1–4 at home, with the one loss to the Penguins coming on a late goal. Expectations were high for the playoffs, but they fell to the Rangers in the first round, bowing out in six games on the same day the masses in Winnipeg were rallying to save the Jets.

With another referendum on Quebec sovereignty on the horizon, it seemed inconceivable that the new premier, Jacques Parizeau, and his Parti Québécois would just let the team—a source of considerable francophone pride—walk. But Aubut didn't get everything he wanted, and on May 24, less than a day after receiving the government's "best" offer, he concluded a deal to sell the Nords to the Comcast Entertainment Group for US$75 million, pocketing

$15 million for his own shares. The players and coaches didn't see it coming, and it all happened so fast that local opposition never really got off the ground—a protest rally organized by the official booster club drew just 300 people. Even Aubut seemed stunned by what he'd done. "I was there when he told the people in the office [about the sale] and those tears were real," recalls Crawford. "He was crying like a little baby. You can't fake that."

Or maybe you can. As Bettman would later reveal in testimony during the 2009 court battle for control of the Phoenix Coyotes, it had taken months of hard work to pull the Denver deal together. "We knew very early on, in the middle of that season at the latest, that this franchise was likely to be moved," said the commissioner. Aubut "spent something like two or three months living in my office. He actually had an office in the office, where he was working on the sale."

Either way, the NHL was back in Denver, a market it had abandoned when the Rockies moved to the swamps of New Jersey thirteen years before. And the next season, bolstered by Montreal's impetuous decision to trade goalie Patrick Roy, the Nordiques-cum-Avalanche won the Stanley Cup.

Quebec City's loss should have invigorated the fight to save the Jets, but somehow it just made the team's departure seem inevitable. Efforts stumbled on all summer, and tentative deals were twice announced but never consummated. In mid-August, faced with the reality that the pledges they had been collecting were more expressions of goodwill than actual promises to lay down money, Asper informed Premier Filmon that he couldn't work a miracle, and the Spirit group officially surrendered. With the opening of training camp only a few weeks away, an immediate move wasn't in the cards, but Shenkarow announced that 1995–96 would be the team's final season in Winnipeg.

Canada, the birthplace of hockey, would soon have just six teams in the sport's biggest pro league. And all indications were that a further winnowing was in the cards, as Edmonton, Ottawa, and Calgary continued to struggle with the game's new economics. The public and pundits were practically tearing their hair out. A TSN *For the Love of the Game* documentary from that spring captured the growing national hysteria about whether the sport was being led southward and the NHL "de-Canadianized." Over footage of the Jets "final" game against the Kings, and an ominous musical soundtrack, the narrator sadly wonders about the strain on the country's emotional fabric: "The damage assessment is hard to quantify. Some people say it tears all the way down to the roots of the game." Bettman appears, sitting behind a massive and otherwise empty conference table—probably the one Ivan Boesky left behind in the old NHL offices—to mouth some bromides about the importance of fan and government support. For part of the interview, the camera operator shoots him from below, from the far end of the room, like an outtake from *Dr. Strangelove*. And just in case that was too subtle, TSN includes a quick cut to protestors in Winnipeg. "Bettman sucks! Bettman sucks," they chant.

The Canadian public and media may have once liked the sound of a commissioner who promised to bring NBA-style global exposure to their national sport. But one lockout and two lost franchises later, they had sure as hell changed their opinion.

THERE'S MORE THAN A LITTLE HOSER in Mark Chipman. Forget the fact that his athletic scholarship to the University of North Dakota, a seven-time NCAA national hockey champ, was to play on the gridiron, not the ice. (The lanky wide receiver eventually earned a brief tryout with his hometown Winnipeg Blue Bombers, playing in a single CFL exhibition game.) Or that his first job post–law school, in the mid-1980s, was as a prosecutor in crime-ridden Florida. He drinks beer, not wine. And he loves Canada's game almost beyond reason. Take, for example, his trip to the 2002 Salt Lake City Winter Olympics. On impulse, he and his buddy Brent, an accountant, got in the car and drove all day and night from Manitoba's capital to Utah—2100 kilometres away—to try and catch some of the hockey tournament. Arriving at 11 A.M., they thought about a shower and a sleep, but decided instead to go out and score tickets to the Belarus/Sweden quarterfinal.

Most people remember that game for Vladimir Kopat's seventy-foot slapper that bounced off Swedish goalie Tommy Salo's head and into the back of the net with only 2:24 remaining, handing Belarus a 4–3 victory. There was nothing mild about the upset: One Stockholm newspaper designed a fake stamp of Salo ducking at the moment of impact with the title "Salt Lake City 2002—Fiasco." Another tabloid published pictures of all the *Tre Kronor* players alongside their pro salaries under the headline "Guilty: They betrayed their country."

But what Chipman most remembers it for was an opportunity. Gary Bettman was at the game. So during one of the intermissions, he and his friend sweet-talked their way past two security check-points and into his suite. Chipman was intent on reminding the NHL commissioner of something he'd brought up the first time their paths crossed a couple of years before: Winnipeg wanted back into the big league.

Chipman had been disappointed by Spirit's failure, but not discouraged. In his heart, he knew the Peg was a hockey town, and he was willing to use his family money to prove it. Even before the Jets' final home game in April 1996, he was hard at work on a plan. Jim Ludlow, one of his pals from St. Paul's High School, was a junior lawyer at Aikins, the firm that had been representing

Barry Shenkarow in the sale and transfer of the team to the States. So Chipman dropped by the offices in the Commodity Exchange Tower, high above Portage and Main, to propose another transaction: buying the Minnesota Moose, a struggling International Hockey League franchise that was playing in St. Paul, and relocating them to the Winnipeg Arena. Redubbed the Manitoba Moose, using the same logo and a barely altered colour scheme, they played their first home game six months after the Jets flew off to Phoenix, losing 1–0 to the Las Vegas Thunder.

The Moose were hardly an instant success. Winnipeg fans, who for close to twenty-five years had enjoyed a string of star players like Bobby Hull, Anders Hedberg, Ulf Nilsson, Dale Hawerchuk, and Teemu Selanne, found little to excite them in a minor-league franchise, two rungs below hockey's show, whose biggest name was Randy Gilhen, a defensive centre who played his final three NHL seasons for the Jets. The first year was a disaster. By February, the Moose were sitting dead last in their division, and the players were in open revolt against Jean Perron, the twitchy coach who had guided the Montreal Canadiens to the Stanley Cup in 1986. Chipman replaced him with former Jets stalwart Randy Carlyle a couple of days after Perron cut a player at six in the morning at the Kalamazoo Airport.

Things got better, on and off the ice. By 1998, Chipman was optimistic that he could succeed where so many others had failed and build a modern, luxury-suite-filled concert and hockey venue in downtown Winnipeg. He set up a company, True North Sports & Entertainment (Ludlow became its first employee) and quietly approached the new premier, Gary Doer, and Glen Murray, who had replaced Susan Thompson as mayor, to gauge their enthusiasm. Murray remembers a meeting at a downtown coffee shop where he and Chipman sketched out possible locations on a napkin. But there was still the niggling question of how to pay for it all. Initially, Chipman asked Doer for $60 million, an on-site casino to cover his operating costs, as well as a guarantee that the provincial government would take care of any losses. He was almost laughed out of the room.

It was Murray, now Ontario's minister of innovation, who came up with a more practical solution: a very deep-pocketed partner. Osmington, one of the holding companies belonging to Toronto's billionaire Thomson family, had recently acquired the Canadian assets of a troubled Dutch pension fund, which included the vacant Eaton's building on Portage Avenue, formerly the hub of Winnipeg's downtown. They were eager to do something—anything really—with the historic white elephant, including ripping it down and replacing it with a rink. The $170-million project was officially announced in May 2001, with Ottawa, the province, and the city eventually agreeing to pick up 30 percent of the construction costs.

Even before the sod-turning, Chipman was busy talking up the dream to Bettman. (At the time, he was also helping the IHL merge with the American Hockey League, which happily necessitated the odd phone call to the NHL commissioner just to keep him in the minor-league loop.) Bettman told him how much he genuinely regretted Winnipeg losing its team back in 1996. And Chipman believed him. At the game that day in Salt Lake City, they talked a bit more about its progress. The door cracked open.

It was November 2004 when True North finally cut the ribbon on its slick new arena. The MTS Centre was tiny by the standards of the new NHL—just 15,000 seats—but it was also designed to be a top-flight venue for concerts and events and to be a year-round cash box. If pro hockey was ever going to work in Winnipeg, Chipman figured the venue would need to stand on its own. Soon the MTS was one of the busiest facilities in North America, with more than 200 bookings a year. The first time David Thomson, ranked seventeenth on *Forbes* magazine's list of the world's richest people with a fortune pegged at US$23 billion, visited his family's new investment was for an Elton John show.

With his dark side-parted hair, toothy smile, and wire-rimmed glasses, the fifty-one-year-old Chipman bears a passing resemblance to Clark Kent. But if he possesses a super power, it's an otherworldly ability to keep his mouth shut. He is a sealed vault. Sphinx-like. Cat got his tongue and buried it in an undisclosed location.

So while he was open about his ambitions with Bettman, Chipman was keeping it on a strictly need-to-know basis with everyone else. Part of it was a fear of raising, and then perhaps having to dash, public expectations in the Peg. The rest was a well-founded sense that the NHL is a league that likes to conduct its business behind closed—and preferably barred—doors. After the 2005 lockout won a cap on player salaries and changed the economics of the game, he quietly reached out to the Oilers and Senators and asked for advice. Both teams opened their books, imparting the lessons they had learned about operating in small Canadian markets, and respected Chipman's request for absolute confidentiality. Ludlow started crafting the business case, filling big blue binders with potential operating and financing models. Around the True North offices, it was called "Project X," and only a handful of staff knew what it was all about—an exercise in quiet patience.

In January 2007, Bettman called out of the blue and asked them to come to New York and sell the league's executive committee on the idea of returning to the Prairies. No promises, no timeline, just a twenty-minute PowerPoint briefing for the commissioner and the NHL's six most powerful owners. On his way out of the league offices, Chipman stole a look at the guest book: suitors from Houston, Las Vegas, Kansas City, and Seattle had all been there before him. Maybe they weren't the first choice, but he and his camp were at least proving themselves the deferential opposites of Jim Balsillie, the brash Canadian high-tech billionaire who was sniffing around for a franchise to buy and relocate to southern Ontario during the same period. The *Winnipeg Free Press* didn't find out about Chipman and Ludlow's presentation until July. And they didn't get it from True North.

Soon it became clear that Bettman and the NHL weren't just listening to be polite. First the president of the struggling Pittsburgh Penguins stopped by to take the measure of the MTS Centre. Then Craig Leipold, looking for a way out of Nashville after his $220-million deal to sell the Predators to Balsillie was quashed by the league, called to ask if they would be interested in owning— and keeping—a team in the home of country music. (By the time Chipman and Ludlow flew down to take a look at the operation, a local group of buyers was coming into the picture.) In the spring of 2009, with the BlackBerry maven again threatening to move a team, Bettman called and asked True North to consider buying the Phoenix Coyotes out of bankruptcy and making one last go of it in Arizona. The timeline to get a deal done—the commissioner wanted new ownership in place for the beginning of the coming season—was too tight, Chipman determined. But by US Thanksgiving, Bettman was calling about Phoenix again. This time the league—now the official owners and operators of the club— was asking True North to be their backup plan and to get ready to repatriate the once-Jets if they couldn't find someone else to take the team off their hands and keep it in place.

A non-disclosure agreement was signed, and the due diligence process began. Working with its partners in Toronto, True North lined up financing for the purchase. And in mid-May, with no other buyers in sight, Chipman flew down to New York to hammer out a deal. Maybe a dozen people, including his immediate family, knew why he was there. Only one thing stood between Winnipeg and a return to the NHL. Under the terms of its "rescue" agreement with the NHL, the City of Glendale—home of the Coyotes—had an option to keep the dogs in the desert for another year by plopping down US$25 million to help cover the club's losses. The deadline was 5 P.M. EST, May 21, 2010. As the hour approached, Chipman and his team sat in a boardroom at the league offices high above the Avenue of the Americas, pens at the ready. Back in Winnipeg, chairs, risers, and backdrops had already been set up inside the MTS Centre for a triumphant press conference. It was the Friday of the May long weekend, and Jim Ludlow was pacing in the loading dock with his cell phone in hand waiting to hear whether he was going to spend it in his office preparing for the onslaught or at the cottage with his wife and kids.

The mayor of Glendale, Elaine Scruggs, rang Bettman at ten-to-five to inform him that her city council had voted to fork over the dough. A half-hour later the millions showed up in the league's bank account, and Chipman called Ludlow to give the order to tear down the stage.

It was another blow, but one that had been preemptively softened when Bettman had stopped by the boardroom that morning to deliver the message that Winnipeg was "likely" to get a team one way or another in the not-too-distant future. Flying home, Chipman was drained, yet content. "We just went through something that was extraordinary and we learned a great deal and we did a lot of the work that would be necessary for another one— for the next one," he says. "Now we had a year to really get ready."

A decision over the summer to expand the MTS Centre press box provoked some excited media speculation, but True North stayed the course and said nothing. Behind the scenes, they worked out the how-tos of launching a lightning season ticket drive. (Not that they had much to worry about: a promise to give Moose ticket holders priority if an NHL team ever came to town already had the phones ringing.) And by the beginning of 2011, they were again deep in discussions with the NHL about acquiring a team for the next season. The only new wrinkle was that there were now two possible salvage operations: Phoenix and Atlanta.

The Atlanta Spirit group, which owned both the Thrashers and the NBA's Hawks, was busy setting the international standard for front office dysfunction. When they purchased the money-losing teams in March 2004, it was with an eye to making a quick buck. Anticipating the NHL lockout and an eventual salary cap, Atlanta Spirit figured the value of the Thrashers in particular was set to soar after cost certainty was imposed and planned to flip the franchise as soon as possible. But in 2005, an internal struggle between Steve Belkin, the largest single investor with a 30-percent interest, and his seven partners over the basketball team derailed all such designs. First there was a tiff about complimentary tickets to the league's All-Star Game—Belkin, the designated NBA governor, had to buy his own because his co-owners used or gave away all the freebies. Then there was a more serious difference of opinion about efforts to pry Joe Johnson away from the Phoenix Suns. Belkin wanted to wait until the summer, when the shooting guard was due to become a free agent, and lure him with a big contract. The other owners wanted to work a "sign and trade," where the Suns would lock Johnson into a new, slightly cheaper extension and then ship him to the Hawks for a bunch of future draft picks. Under the partnership agreement, it was supposed to be majority rules. But when management worked out the trade, Belkin refused to sign off. Furious, the other investors scheduled a board meeting to remove him as team governor, and he went to court to seek a protective injunction.

At the NBA's insistence, a deal was quickly brokered to buy out Belkin's shares. But that, too, dissolved into acrimony and legal challenges. And in December 2010, after close to five years of litigation, a Maryland judge essentially voided the transaction. A settlement with Belkin was reached a couple of weeks later, and the remaining members of Atlanta Spirit later went on to file a US$200-million malpractice action against the law firm that had drafted the original partnership agreement, claiming the murky ownership situation had kept them from selling the Thrashers. According to that suit, the value of the team had dropped by $50 million since 2005, and their cumulative losses in the puck business had topped $130 million. The matter was settled out of court, for an undisclosed amount, in September 2011.

Even before the internecine owner wars, hockey had a long and troubled history in Atlanta. The city's original NHL franchise, the Flames, decamped to Calgary in 1980 after eight unspectacular seasons. Playing in a league that bounced between seventeen and twenty-one teams, they made the playoffs six times but never won a series. And while the fans who did show up were enthusiastic, Atlanta was hardly a dream market, recalls Cliff Fletcher, the team's first and only general manager. The club's radio rights brought in more money than did TV. The Omni, their 15,000-seat rink, boasted great sightlines, but had no luxury boxes or room to expand. Attendance sagged with each passing season, and when the war with the WHA started to rapidly push up player salaries, the original Flames ownership looked for the exit. Nelson Skalbania and his Calgary group were a godsend, willing to pay US$16 million—a then record price for an NHL team and significantly more than the only other bidders in Houston.

The Thrashers, who joined the league as an expansion franchise in 1999–2000, had the Philips Arena, a new barn with all the bells and whistles, but severely tempted fate by building it on the exact same site as The Omni. And even by the standards of a city with exactly one championship title—the Braves' 1995 World Series—in 151 seasons of the four major pro sports, they sucked. Over a decade in a thirty-team NHL, the Thrashers made the post-season only once, winning their division in 2006–7 and then getting swept by the New York Rangers in the first round. Some of that futility surely had to do with their chintzy and battling owners—by the time the team left town, it had the second-lowest payroll in the league, right down near the $43.4-million floor. But even obscene amounts of money—a reported $101 million over twelve years—couldn't entice star winger Ilya Kovalchuk to keep playing there. (After a February 2010 trade to New Jersey, he signed with the Devils at the discounted rate of $100 million over fifteen seasons.)

The suspense over which franchise—Phoenix or Atlanta—was going to implode first continued until the spring of 2011. In early May, Bettman called Chipman to say he was confident that Glendale was going to pony up yet another $25 million to keep the Coyotes playing at the civic-owned Jobing.com Arena for 2011–12. True North turned its focus exclusively to the Thrashers, and started making final preparations to welcome the NHL back to Winnipeg after a fifteen-year separation, all the while maintaining its customary silence.

On the evening of May 19, a Thursday, Chipman took the night off to attend a celebratory dinner for his friend Gary Doer, the outgoing premier, at the Manitoba Museum. As the cocktail hour wound down, he and his wife, Patti, took their seats at the head table, and Chipman turned his thoughts to the speech he was set to give. It was then that another guest walked up, thrust out his hand, and offered his congratulations. Figuring the man was confused, or drunk, the True North honcho asked why. "For getting the Thrashers," was the response. Chipman looked around. Practically everyone in the room was looking at their phones. Soon he was beset by well-wishers. "I had turned my BlackBerry off because we were at this event," he says. "So I turned it on and it just about started on fire." Dozens of calls, emails, and texts were flooding in, wondering if the story then *Globe and Mail* columnist Stephen Brunt had just posted on the paper's website was true. Was Winnipeg back in the bigs?

But the message that concerned him most was a terse text from the commissioner of the NHL. Bettman was in a box at the Tampa Bay Times Forum in Florida watching the Lightning and Boston Bruins battle it out in Game 3 of the Eastern Conference Final. His iPhone was melting, too, and he wasn't happy. The TV cameras even caught him scowling and typing when he should have been watching the action.

Chipman wrote back, explaining that he wasn't in a position to talk and would call as soon as he could. Then he grimly waited out the dinner and the tributes. It was a couple of hours later when he and Patti finally made it to the privacy of their car. He called Bettman back and got an earful: "I don't know if he was yelling, but he was firm. He was understandably concerned." Chipman put the car in drive and turned down Main Street. When he got to Portage Avenue, he found his way blocked by thousands of celebrating hockey fans—high-fiving, waving flags, and gleefully chugging beers. There was no actual deal yet, but it didn't matter to them. On the phone, Bettman was demanding to know where the leak had come from. (Since the Thomson family also owns the *Globe*, one can be fairly certain it was inside dope.) Chipman pleaded ignorance. Finding it difficult to get a word in edgewise, the True North chairman eventually rolled down the car window and stuck out his phone so Bettman could hear the "Go Jets Go!" chants and honking horns. "I was trying to convey to him that my situation wasn't any better than his." Soon they were both laughing.

It took almost two weeks for the official announcement to come. During the interim, all the parties carried on the charade that it was business as usual. In Atlanta, the Thrashers even held their annual select-a-seat event for fans, blaring rock music through the iceless Philips Arena as pictures of the players flashed across the overhead scoreboard. Out in the parking lot, a group of 250 fans convened for one last tailgate. Some wag—undoubtedly a wandering Manitoban—had hung a Go Jets Go! banner from the rink's covered garage. The Thrashers fans cut it down and set it on fire. It was their only protest.

The local press worked itself into medium dudgeon about the league's desultory efforts to find new ownership for the team, with Bettman drawing flak for not flying in to twist arms and beat bushes, like he had done so many times in Phoenix. His explanation for letting the Thrashers bolt sounded eerily familiar to fans in Quebec and Winnipeg. "In this case, the franchise wasn't economically viable," he told the *Atlanta Journal-Constitution*. "The litmus test is: Does someone want to own the franchise?"

Certainly there is room to debate whether Atlanta really was the worst US hockey market. In their final season, the Thrashers ranked twenty-eighth in the league in attendance with an average of 13,469 fans a night, only 200 fewer than Columbus, but more than 1000 ahead of the Coyotes, and positively robust compared to the thirtieth ranked New York Islanders, who drew just 11,059.

But the hard-to-escape reality was that pro hockey had twice come and gone and left nary a mark on the Deep South. The Georgia Sports Hall of Fame in Macon, 120 kilometres southeast of Atlanta, boasts 14,000 square feet of display space and some 3000 artifacts. Just four of them relate to the two defunct NHL teams: a stick from the Thrashers' first game, signed by all the players; a souvenir jersey from the same night; a vintage red Flames sweater adorned with the burning "A," donated by a fan; and a goalie mask autographed by their backstop, Dan Bouchard, who finished his career with the Winnipeg Jets in 1985–86. And none of the hall of fame's 377 inductees have anything to do with hockey. "It's open to anyone who brings honour to Georgia through sports," Benjamin Baughman, the senior curator, explained. "I guess no players have been deemed worthy enough in the eyes of the voters."

On the morning of May 31, True North called a press conference at the MTS Centre for 11 A.M. For a while, it hadn't been clear just what they were going to announce—the dotting of i's, crossings of t's, and chasing of signatures had gone on throughout the night, and the deal still wasn't done when Bettman boarded a private jet in New Jersey shortly after dawn. But things had worked themselves out by the time he arrived—his first trip back to the Peg in sixteen years. Chipman and Ludlow gave him a tour of the Thrashers' new home. "Nice building. I like it. This will do," was the commissioner's reaction. David Thomson and his deep pockets were there, too, having flown in on an Air Canada flight from Toronto, economy class. As they all stood gathered in the directors' lounge, waiting for their cue to march before the cameras, they could hear the sound of stamping feet and cheering above their heads. The lobby of the MTS Centre was packed with delirious fans, just like the intersection of Portage and Main and the official party site at the Forks.

Once things started, it took a few minutes before Chipman finally got around to setting the city's fandom free: "I am excited beyond words to announce our purchase of the Atlanta Thrashers. We received the call we've long been waiting for." Winnipeg's civic pride restored at the cost of US$170 million—$110 million for the fractious Atlanta Spirit group and a $60-million "relocation fee" for the NHL, just $20 million less than the expansion fee the league had collected for the franchise in 1997.

Bettman, dressed in a dark suit, blue shirt, and natty red tie, stepped to the podium and smiled. Moving a club for the first time since the Whalers left Hartford fourteen years before wasn't an easy choice, he said, but he was happy all the same to return a team to Canada, "which we know is the heart and soul of our game." Better still, the NHL was back in a place that it never really wanted to leave. "To be able to come back to right a wrong, if you will, is an extraordinary thing," said the commissioner.

Winnipeg's future had finally caught up with its past.

THE MESSAGE WAS UNCHARACTERISTICALLY BLUNT. None of the equivocating or lawyerly subclauses that the public had become so used to. Just an unmistakable warning that ended up scaring him as much as the fans. "If this team continues to draw 9000 people a night, this team isn't going to be here long-term," Gary Bettman told the *Edmonton Journal* in January 1996. "At 9000 people, there's a wall coming and we're going to run into it head on."

The glory days of the Oilers—five Cups in seven seasons—were a fading memory, as were the sellout crowds at Northlands Coliseum. In the lockout-shortened 1995 season, Edmonton's pride had finished twenty-second in a twenty-six team league, barely ahead of the most recent expansion franchises. Gretzky,

Kurri, and Messier had given way to players like Scott Thornton and Louie DeBrusk. And the only remaining on-ice links to the dynasty were goalie Bill Ranford and captain Kelly Buchberger. The fans had been bitter after the 103 days of labour strife and indifferent to an outclassed club of cast-off veterans and raw rookies. But by the time the next season rolled around, they were just angry—they'd finally had enough of Peter Pocklington. The self-promoting swashbuckler was born for a boomtown winner; a sugar daddy in a tight three-piece suit, the kind of guy who bought a pro-hockey club in exchange for a Renoir painting, a vintage Rolls-Royce that had been used in the film version of *The Great Gatsby*, and a fifteen-karat diamond ring plucked right off his wife's finger. Once the celebrations ended, however, it became impossible to ignore the fact that he was kind of a prick. He'd been the catalyst for one of the bitterest strikes in Canadian history, freezing wages, cutting benefits, and then once the workers walked out, busing in replacements to his Gainers meat-packing plant, dividing the city and the province. He was the man who sold a national icon to Bruce McNall's LA Kings for $15 million, and then had the gall to cry crocodile tears. And he was an owner who never seemed to tire of threatening to move the team to greener hockey pastures if his demands weren't met.

The NHL commissioner had stepped in before the lockout, when Pocklington was musing aloud about Minnesota, and helped broker a deal that got him a break on rent and a bigger cut of concessions and parking revenue, in exchange for renovating the twenty-year-old rink. But his gratitude was fleeting. The Edmonton entrepreneur had been among the most militant owners around the bargaining table and a vocal critic of the new compromise CBA. And now, just a year after settling with the players, Bettman was back in Alberta to try and again save the Oilers.

The precarious state of the Canadian franchises could no longer be downplayed or ignored. The Nordiques were already gone, while Winnipeg was playing out the string on its final season. And Calgary, Edmonton, and Ottawa were all strong candidates to be the next failure. Salaries, always due in US dollars, were skyrocketing, but the loonie was heading in the other direction, trading at just 74 cents US. Even the board of governors, who had firmly rejected all talk of revenue sharing during the labour negotiations, were forced to acknowledge that the game was in deep trouble in its heartland. And in December 1995, they finally gave the commissioner permission to intervene. The initial response was an assistance package that would skim as much as US$15 million a year off the top of the new $155-million Fox TV deal, provided that the three remaining small-market Canadian clubs met certain conditions. The teams had to flog all their rink-board advertising and luxury boxes, and establish a season ticket base of at least 13,000. It was an all-or-nothing proposition—hit the targets by the end of May and you got the cash. Fail, and live with the consequences. Edmonton, where Pocklington had been trying to back up the moving vans for almost five years, was the diciest proposition. "My intention isn't to be provocative or inflammatory," Bettman told the local paper. "But at some point, the economics of this isn't going to work." He was leaving it up to the fans and local businesses to make the team stay.

Hockey's place at the centre of Canadian life is painfully obvious, says the commissioner: "All you have to do is spend time there and you feel it. How the game brings the people and the community together in the coldest, harshest time of the year. It's palpable. I mean, hockey's on the back of the $5 bill." Nonetheless, he'd been shaken at the intensity of the grief and anger over the departure of the Nordiques and the Jets. And it was clear to him that having another franchise head south was the kind of blow the league might never recover from. The new league imperative was to do whatever it took to keep the remaining teams in place. "Lots of other people gave up before we did," he says.

Heeding some unsolicited advice from Bill Smith, the mayor of Edmonton—to make it about the team rather than its spot-light-loving owner—the drive to keep the Oilers slowly picked up momentum through the winter and spring. But the Oilers made it over the top only right at the final deadline, thanks to a local grocery chain's purchase of 1000 season tickets at a cost of more than $800,000 to bring the total to 13,482. Less dramatic efforts in Calgary and Ottawa secured emergency funding for the Flames and Senators, too. The full amount per team worked out to $7 million Canadian, or a quarter of the average league payroll. It was, however, just a temporary fix.

By the beginning of 1998, with the dollar having sunk to a new 60-cent low against the US greenback, only the Toronto Maple Leafs, forever selling out their games, were on solid ground. In Vancouver, where the basement-dwelling Canucks were often playing to crowds of 11,000 or 12,000 a night, the club was on track to lose $36 million for the year. And their owner, John McCaw, a Seattle cell phone billionaire, was looking to get out. In Ottawa, where the Senators were drawing more than 16,000 fans and had the third-lowest payroll in the league, the team still reported losses of more than $5 million. And even in Montreal, where the Habs were filling the Molson Centre—the NHL's biggest building—their slim $5.6-million profit was in danger of turning into a substantial loss once contracts for star players like Saku Koivu, Vince Damphousse, and Mark Recchi came up for nego-tiation in the off-season. "Every time the Canadian dollar drops one cent we lose $300,000," Ronald Corey, the team president, complained to the *Montreal Gazette*. "The question is, how are we going to compete with the American teams?"

Bettman had an answer, but it wasn't one Canadians were particularly receptive to. For months, the NHL commissioner had been quietly lobbying Ottawa and the provinces for tax breaks or direct subsidies, like a share of the money wagered on sports lotteries, to help shore up the northern teams. The US clubs enjoyed strong government support—tax holidays, sweetheart lease deals for state-of-the-art rinks that had been built with public money—and the best way to level the playing field was to extend the same type of special treatment above the forty-ninth parallel, he argued. The owners of the Habs, for example, were paying $11 million a year in property taxes for their new arena—more than all twenty-one US teams combined. Flanked by the presidents of all six Canadian clubs, Bettman appeared before a House of Commons subcommittee that spring to press the case. "This is an international commerce problem," he argued.

Rod Bryden, the owner of the Senators and a major fundraiser for the governing Liberal Party, had helped lay the groundwork. Economists were brought on board to marshal favourable statistics—NHL hockey was responsible for 8000 jobs, $250 million in tax revenue, and tens of millions of dollars more in spinoffs—and lobbyists were engaged to work the backrooms. Prime Minister Jean Chrétien was sympathetic, but his caucus was leery: handing out money to multimillionaire owners and players didn't sound like smart storefront politics.

The issue wasn't fading away, however. In Edmonton, Pocklington was under stress from his bankers and had again tried to sell the team to an American—Les Alexander, a billionaire stockbroker who owned the Houston Rockets. The deal fell apart when it became clear that the city, which had a ten-year lease agreement for Northlands, wasn't going to let the Oilers walk away without a fight. And then the Alberta Treasury Board, which had extended $120 million worth of loans to various Pocklington enterprises, stepped in and took control of the club. After several months of scrambling, Bettman managed to cobble together a new local ownership group, but the solution just illustrated the problem: Even to fetch the discount asking price of $70 million for the money-losing club, he had to enlist thirty-six different local investors. In Ottawa, where Bryden was also facing debt pressure, the Senators owner started a countdown on his franchise's move south, giving the government eighteen months to act. He was particularly incensed that 5 percent of the club's TV revenues were being diverted into a government fund for Canadian content, like the CBC's depression-era family drama *Wind at My Back*. The public better enjoy it, he warned, because soon it would be the only thing to watch on Saturday nights.

The debate dragged on through 1999. There was a high-level hockey summit that summer, bringing together the league, teams, politicians, and business leaders to brainstorm solutions. Bettman officially registered himself as a lobbyist, listing a variety of "formal and informal communications" with a half-dozen federal departments, including Canadian Heritage and Revenue Canada. He even trekked to Parliament Hill on a couple of occasions to brief MPs and for tête-à-têtes with the prime minister, although Chrétien was a cagey enough political operator to keep the meetings quiet. Bryden, who was busy entertaining ministers and backroom operatives in his box at Senators games, kept up the pressure as well, officially putting the team on the block for outside bidders in early December. It was at a New Year's Eve soiree at 24 Sussex Drive to celebrate the new millennium that the prime minister finally caved and told his cabinet to go ahead and offer government help.

It was left to John Manley, the minister of industry, to try and sell the "temporary, modest" package: up to $20 million in annual aid for the six northern teams, provided that municipalities, the provinces, and the league kicked in equal shares. "The federal government's willingness to participate in a shared solution for Canadian NHL teams is not about giving money to rich hockey players and team owners," he gamely ventured. "It is about ensuring that Canadians will have the opportunity to enjoy and support their Canadian NHL teams for many years in the future." The government had anticipated a backlash, but not the cascade of derision that met the announcement. Provincial premiers wondered why the money wasn't going to health care. "Maybe the solution is to put a rink in every hospital," snarked Nova Scotia's John Hamm. The opposition asked about the homeless crisis. The Canadian Taxpayers Federation hatched a protest dubbed "The Great Canadian Puck-Off," urging voters to deluge Liberal MPs with rubber discs. And when Manley visited Halifax, unemployed shipbuilders peppered him with questions about the deal. Three days later, the minister was back before reporters in Ottawa to announce that the proposal was utterly and irreversibly dead.

If the NHL commissioner had been as indifferent to the fate of hockey in Canada as fans liked to pretend, he now had the perfect excuse to cull some weak markets from the game. But Bettman didn't give up. If anything, he worked harder to keep the teams in place. He helped convince the Alberta government to set up a lottery to benefit the Flames and Oilers. (The three-year experiment was a bust, with the two clubs netting a total of just $2.8 million and barely making back their promotion costs in the final months.) And in 2001, when a local buyer couldn't be found for the Montreal Canadiens—despite a seven-month-long search that canvassed pretty much every big name in the province, including Celine Dion—the NHL head convinced George Gillett, a Colorado billionaire, to pay $275 million for the team and the Molson Centre. The outgoing owners had made the deal contingent on a commitment to keep the Habs in place, although Bettman made it clear that the league's most iconic franchise wasn't going anywhere on his watch. "To say they might move because they are sold to an American, that's like saying that because somebody from Ohio buys the Yankees that they're going to move to Columbus," he chided reporters. Similarly in 2003, when Rod Bryden was forced out by his lenders and the Senators were placed in bankruptcy, Bettman was waiting in the wings with Eugene Melnyk. The Ontario pharmaceutical billionaire, who now lives in Barbados, ended up getting the team for $100 million and its rink for just $27 million more (it had cost $220 million to build a decade before), but he brought deep pockets and stability to a franchise with a long history of turmoil. And after the dust settled from the 2005 lockout, the commissioner helped orchestrate Daryl Katz' purchase of the Oilers. The Edmonton Investors Group wasn't keen to give up the team, but the unsolicited bids from the owner of the Rexall drugstore chain, which started at $145 million in the spring of 2007 and eventually climbed to $220 million by the summer of 2008, became impossible to resist. And the thirty-six voices that the NHL had been dealing with were conveniently reduced to one.

Bettman's not the type to admit to epiphanies, but if his attitude about the worth of the Canadian franchises did change, it surely started with a single man. Harley Hotchkiss was part of the original group that brought the Atlanta Flames to Calgary in 1980. The son of a tobacco farmer from Tillsonburg, Ontario, he had grown up playing the game on ponds and outdoor rinks during the Great Depression, idolizing Syl Apps and the Toronto

Maple Leafs. After studying geology at Michigan State, he was recruited to work in Alberta in the early boom days following the Leduc oil strike. In the mid-1950s, he moved from exploration to finance, working first for the Canadian Imperial Bank of Commerce then starting his own petroleum company. The Texas oil tycoon T. Boone Pickens was a friend and early investor. And by the time Hotchkiss sold out in 1976, he was a multimillionaire and probably the richest minor hockey coach in Canada.

The Flames had plenty of success under his leadership, building a new rink for the 1988 Winter Olympics, and then winning the Cup in a six-game triumph over Montreal the next season. And after Bruce McNall's 1994 implosion, Hotchkiss was named his replacement as chair of the NHL board of governors. A steady, gentlemanly type, he soon formed a close friendship with Bettman. They spoke three or four times a week, including every Sunday afternoon, when Hotchkiss would call the house and chat with Shelli and the children before getting down to the business of hockey. The Calgary oilman was a passionate defender of the Canadian franchises and the need to keep the smaller markets healthy even as the sport tried to move on to the larger American stage. "He always thought about the league, as opposed to his team," says Bettman. "He was a constructive force."

The pair were so tight that the commissioner tried to convince Hotchkiss to serve a third six-year term when his time as chair expired in 2007, but the Flames owner, then nearing his eightieth birthday, was determined to step aside. And even after he sold his 22-percent stake in the club in 2010, they continued to talk on a weekly basis. Bettman stopped in Calgary on his way to the Game 7 showdown in Vancouver between the Canucks and the Bruins for the 2011 Stanley Cup. He was supposed to be the surprise speaker at a dinner feting Hotchkiss for his charitable endeavours, but the guest of honour, suffering through the final stages of cancer, was too ill to attend. So he went to his house instead and spent three hours talking about the game.

A week later, the day after the board of governors met in New York to approve Atlanta's transfer to Winnipeg, Hotchkiss died at the age of eighty-three. At the NHL Awards in Las Vegas that night, the commissioner took to the stage in a dark suit and tie to deliver a tribute. Red-eyed, his voice breaking, he barely made his way through it: "He was a dear friend and counsellor to me, and his loss leaves a giant void." Canada had finally regained a seventh team, and the man who runs the game had lost a friend.

The work in Edmonton still continues, though. For more than a year, Bettman has been lobbying hard for a new rink to replace the almost forty-year-old Northlands, now known as Rexall Place, the second-smallest building in the league. On a swing through the Alberta capital to catch a game, he reprised an old warning about the team needing a proper home, saying he didn't want to go through yet another campaign to save the Oilers. But in the fall of 2011, Bettman invited Katz and Stephen Mandel, the mayor of Edmonton, to his New York offices to try and broker a deal. A week later, city council approved a $125-million contribution to a snazzy, oil-drop-shaped arena that they hope will revitalize the downtown. So far, Katz' contribution to the municipally owned building would be $100 million of its estimated $450-million construction costs—spread out over thirty years—and another $100-million investment in a surrounding entertainment district. The province has yet to come through with the $100 million that the city and NHL have decided should be its share, but Bettman hasn't given up. One of the ideas being floated is a new lottery, or maybe even the legalization of online sports betting in Canada, with part of the proceeds flowing to the club. A new twist on a familiar proposal to solve the same old problem.

HE WAS THE ONE who turned out the lights. That April night, after the Winnipeg Jets had been knocked out of the 1996 playoffs, losing 4–1 at home to Detroit and bidding adieu to the NHL, it was Craig Heisinger who stood by himself in the dressing room, long after the last fan and player had disappeared. As the team's equipment manager, it was his job to wash the sweaters, air out the gear, vacuum the rug, and lock the door behind him. By then, he had decided he wasn't going to follow the franchise to Phoenix. Uprooting his wife and four young kids—three still in diapers— from their hometown and extended family simply didn't feel right. So "Zinger" did the only thing he could: He shed a few tears and moved on.

Now fifteen years, four months, and twenty-two days later, in the hours before the reborn Jets' first preseason game, the forty-eight year old is sitting in his office in the bowels of the MTS Centre trying to put his emotions into words. "I never really bought in. I knew all the work going on behind the scenes, but I never thought it would come to fruition," he says. "I couldn't convince myself that they wanted another team in Canada. I just couldn't see it." A brand-spanking-new official NHL ID card with his picture sits on his blotter. In three hours, the puck will drop and both his cell and desk phone are ringing incessantly. He's still wearing shorts and a Jets hoodie, but his dress pants and sports coat are carefully laid over the back of a nearby chair.

The son of a Canadian National Railway pipefitter, Heisinger had dreams of becoming a pro goalie, but eagerness couldn't make up for his small stature, and he never made it beyond the Fort Garry Blues, a local Junior A team. Just twenty, and in search of a new career, he tried his hand as an apprentice mechanic for a small airline, although he could barely start a lawn mower, let alone keep a plane in the air. When his former junior coach offered him a job as a part-time equipment manager with his old team, he gladly put down his tools in favour of filling water bottles.

Two years later, Heisinger moved up to a full-time position with the Winnipeg Warriors of the Western Hockey League, and then on to the Brandon Wheat Kings. For eight seasons, he plied his trade in major junior, earning recognition as one of the best trainers in the game. In 1988, he was behind the bench when Canada won the World Junior Championship in Moscow; the fading tattoo of a penguin on his calf is a souvenir of a night on the town celebrating that victory with a young Joe Sakic and Theoren Fleury.

When he got the call up to the bigs, joining the Winnipeg Jets as their assistant equipment manager in the fall of 1989, he thought he had reached the pinnacle: "I aspired to be an NHL equipment guy in my hometown, and I made it." The players used to tease, telling him that he didn't want to spend his life hanging up their underwear, but they were wrong. He loved all aspects of the job—from unpacking the equipment bags at 3 A.M. in the old Montreal Forum, to handing out pucks and sticks to star-struck kids, to being the coach's eyes and ears in the room. And he was good at what he did—so adept at fixing broken and worn-out gear that even players from visiting teams sought out Zinger to extend the lifespan of favourite skates and goalie gloves. Within a couple of years, he was named the team's head trainer.

People thought he was nuts when he refused to follow the Jets to Phoenix, but he was sure there would be other opportunities closer to home. And it only took a couple of months before he got the job offer from the soon-to-arrive Manitoba Moose. Mark Chipman remembers people coming at him from all directions when he bought the team and advising him to make Zinger its "caretaker."

After Jean Perron was fired that first season and Randy Carlyle took over as both coach and GM, Heisinger found himself pitching in to help with travel arrangements and player paperwork. Soon the administrative duties were taking up the bulk of his time. Still, he left the trainer's room only under duress. When True North promoted Heisinger to assistant GM in 1999, he made them add a clause to the contract allowing him to go back to being equipment manager if he hated the job. In 2002, when Carlyle became an assistant coach with the Washington Capitals, Heisinger took over the Moose. In his nine seasons as GM the team had eight playoff appearances, made a trip to the Calder Cup Final (losing in six games to the Hershey Bears), and posted an overall .588 winning percentage.

In early June, shortly after the announcement that the Thrashers were moving to Winnipeg, Heisinger was named the club's senior vice-president and director of hockey operations/ assistant general manager—a title so unwieldy he jokes about getting a fold-out business card. Although the more apt job description might be "team conscience." But not in a preachy, Jiminy Cricket sort of way. Zinger's just the guy who never gave up on hockey, even when it gave up on his hometown. "It's really all I know," he shrugs.

The fervour that greeted the NHL's return to Winnipeg caught everyone off guard. The day before season tickets went on general sale, Jim Ludlow chaired an anxious meeting to work out contingency plans in case the club—which was asking for a steep five-year commitment—didn't make it to its 13,000-seats-sold goal. But when the website went live and the phones opened, it took just one minute and forty-five seconds before all the ducats were spoken for. (Chipman, more bullish than Ludlow, made a side bet with Gary Bettman that it would take two days to sell out. The NHL commissioner, who took the under, won himself a free dinner.) Within forty-five minutes, they had an additional 8000 names on their waiting list. More than 50,000 people have since signed up for the random draw that allocates the few hundred tickets made available each game day.

But it went far deeper than that. When Kevin Chevaldayoff, the team's new general manager, drove up from Chicago to take the job, his immigration interview at the Manitoba–Minnesota border turned into an in-depth interrogation about the roster and the prospects for a Stanley Cup. Andrew Ladd, who as Thrashers captain enjoyed deep-cover anonymity in Atlanta, travelled to Winnipeg to check things out early in the summer and people kept stopping him in the street to shake his hand. At lunch, he asked for the cheque and was told a stranger had paid the bill. And once training camp began in September, he and his teammates found they were no longer a sporting afterthought. The day of the first exhibition game there were twenty-six reporters on hand, representing outlets from all across the country. In Atlanta, the media scrums could almost always be conducted in a phone booth.

Jets merchandise, featuring the team's über-patriotic logo—a silver CF-18 fighter jet atop a red maple leaf—quickly became one of the league's top-five sellers, rivalling the Leafs and Canadiens. (Some of that is surely the novelty, but True North are no dummies: Over the summer, they quietly bought back the original Jets trademarks from the NHL and put a moratorium on their use. When the logo returns, probably as a third sweater a couple of years hence, demand will be sky-high.) TSN and Bell signed a ten-year deal for the club's regional TV and radio rights. And at the MTS Centre, in-house sponsorship and advertising opportunities—everything from beer pouring rights to the rink boards to the side of the Zamboni—sold out before the puck ever dropped. With the shortest of those agreements not up for renewal until 2016, True North converted its entire sales staff to account agents. Once all the numbers from the Jets' first comeback season are crunched, Ludlow is confident that Winnipeg will be among the league's top ten teams in terms of revenue.

So how does a city that was once the least desirable market in the NHL come to rank among its elite? Inhabitants of the Peg will tell you that it's a far different place than it was in 1996. There's a new airport terminal, the soaring (architecturally and cost-wise) Canadian Museum for Human Rights that's taking shape down at the Forks, and a $70-million "Journey to Churchill" polar bear exhibit—complete with tundra buggies—under construction at the Assiniboine Park Zoo. There are also plans for a new CFL stadium and a supersized IKEA, "the second biggest in Canada," trumpeted the *Free Press*, slated to open in late 2012. However, with a metro population of around 750,000—65,000 more than when the Jets left in 1996—it remains a very small market, about a third the size of Edmonton. Household incomes and net worth are below the national average, and the city has one-eighteenth as many high-income residents as the Toronto area. Winnipeg does boast twice as many head offices as Quebec City—thirty-three—but True North still has fifty-five luxury boxes to fill at the MTS Centre.

A Canadian dollar trading at par, or even above the US one, makes the math a lot more favourable. So does a salary cap that keeps player costs at 57 percent of league-wide revenues, with the prospective of further clawbacks in this fall's labour negotiations.

The simplest truth, however, is that Winnipeg is back in the NHL because of the one thing that didn't change: its fans. In an increasingly fragmented entertainment marketplace, the league has found a new respect for its loyal consumers—"avids" in brand speak—the kind of ticket buyers and TV viewers who stick with a franchise through good times and bad. The faithful can be monetized, at the local and league level, a lot more easily than casual devotees. And Manitoba is full of people like Craig Heisinger.

It's the kind of financial equation that makes perfect sense to one of the world's richest men. David Thomson, like his late father Ken, is a bit of an odd duck—a shy fifty-three-year-old art lover who tends toward the mystical in his public pronouncements. The NHL's return "fortifies your persona as a city," he told the media the day the Thrashers deal was unveiled. "And we'll find it will be another segue into the psyche of Winnipeggers and Manitobans and one that emits pride and attachment." He is a hockey fan— the basement of his Rosedale mansion houses a vast collection of memorabilia from his childhood idol Bobby Orr—but is not blinded by his sentimentality. Thomson's company Osmington not only holds a 50-percent interest in True North, it owns a considerable amount of land in Winnipeg's depressed downtown. When the Jets came back, the value of its holdings soared—more than offsetting the price it paid for the team, according to some estimates. And with plans afoot to create a US-style sports, hospitality, and entertainment district to revitalize the area around the arena, there is much more money to be made.

On the day of the Jets' regular season home opener against Montreal, October 9, 2011—Thanksgiving Sunday, appropriately enough—the lineup to enter the official Jets store in the MTS Centre stretched around the block. The crowd on the patio of the adjoining Moxie's restaurant is lustily booing anyone brave enough to walk by in a Habs sweater. "Twenty-six Stanley Cups," says a guy in a porkpie hat, gesturing at the CH on his *Sainte-Flanelle*. "Twenty-six Cups." The heckling only gets louder. "Dancing

Gabe" Langlois, a simple soul who found notoriety jiving in the stands of the old Winnipeg Arena as a chubby, curly-haired youth, is on hand in his new team gear, older, greyer, and still gyrating for all he's worth. The nostalgia is palpable, but there's something more underpinning the party: relief. "Fifteen years ago, it was like someone stuck a fist between your ribs and pulled your heart out," says Sam Katz, Winnipeg's current mayor.

What was once lost has been found. And the city—and the country—is celebrating. Proof, finally, that bigger isn't necessarily better. That passion can count for more than dollars. That the game we claim still belongs to us. A win, even if it is by default.

Prime Minister Stephen Harper, who seems to spend as much time in NHL rinks as the House of Commons, has flown in to take it all in. So has Gary Bettman.

It's easier to be magnanimous in victory than in defeat. And time and distance have even mellowed the appraisals of some of those who felt the most betrayed by the commissioner in the spring of 1995. "I think to a certain degree at the time we all misunderstood Bettman's role," says John Loewen. "I sort of arrived at the conclusion that really what he was doing was speaking for the owners. This is what the owners wanted."

Still there is trepidation about how he will be welcomed. Chipman has publicly asked fans to be on their best behaviour and not spoil the occasion. Although the odds of the commissioner being booed at centre ice have been handily reduced by combining the ceremonial faceoff with a heartfelt tribute to Rick Rypien, a Jets forward who committed suicide over the summer.

Little is being left to chance. An hour before game time, Bettman is scheduled to appear on the pre-game radio show. The day is special, so hosts Gary Lawless, the *Free Press* beat writer, and Andrew "Hustler" Patterson have set up a remote broadcast in the lobby of the MTS Centre. A few minutes before airtime, John Morris, the coordinator of the league's security department and Bettman's head bodyguard, arrives to check out the scene. Jets fans are crowding the floor in front of the riser and packing the balcony above. Morris, a former New York City cop, doesn't like it and warns the hosts that he will be ushering his boss off the stage and out the door at the first sign of trouble.

The chanting starts as Bettman makes his way through the crowd. By the time he takes his seat, the lobby is reverberating. Not with curses, but his name: "Gar-ee. Gar-ee. Gar-ee." While the interview goes on, people jostle to take his picture. He mugs obligingly, flashing thumbs-up, and putting his arms around the hosts. Things have changed in Winnipeg. And the man who has made a career out of being dispassionate about passion can't wipe the wide smile off his face.

5 The Promised Land

The fluffy snow is cotton batten, stapled to two-by-fours so it won't drift away in the breeze. The ice, crisp and white thanks only to the application of 350 cans of paint. And since the weather can no longer be trusted to cooperate—even at the beginning of January—there's a fifty-three-foot-long refrigeration truck parked outside Philadelphia's Citizens Bank Park pumping 1500 gallons of glycol a minute underneath the rink just to keep it from melting away in the late afternoon sun. The devil is in the details at the NHL's Winter Classic. Creating the illusion of an old-timey outdoor hockey game in a baseball stadium before 47,000 fans requires months of preparation. There are prosaic concerns: Are the toilets still going to work if there's a cold snap? And esoteric questions of protocol, like which direction the players face during the national anthem—toward the big American flag fluttering over the centre-field fence, or the smaller one the Marine honour guard is hoisting at home plate? (Never turn your back on a solider is the advice from the U.S. State Department.) A small army of workers has been preparing the grounds for weeks, laying down vinyl mats to protect the turf, erecting temporary grandstands and broadcast positions, and building a regulation-sized rink, complete with boards and glass, that looks like a postage stamp to those who paid as much as US$300 for scalped tickets to sit in the upper decks.

The total cost to the league for this single regular season game, including the compensation paid to the Flyers for handing over a home date against the Rangers, approaches US$10 million. And it's worth every penny to the man obsessing away in one of the luxury boxes along the third base line. Gary Bettman pulls his iPhone, with its homescreen picture of his grandchildren, from his pocket and dials up Colin Campbell, the league's director of hockey operations, who's standing down next to the rink. The score is 3–2 for New York with less than ten minutes left, but the commissioner is thinking ahead to his post-game press conference. "I just wanted to know, are you hearing anything about the ice, or the officiating?" he asks. There can be no surprises on the one day of the year that America gives hockey more than a passing glance. Since its 2008 inception, the Winter Classic has averaged just over 4 million viewers, and each of its five editions now ranks among the top-rated regular season NHL games in US television history. The 2011 matchup, which pitted Sidney Crosby's Penguins against Alex Ovechkin and the Washington Capitals—in prime time, thanks to a rain delay—drew 4.5 million pairs of eyeballs. Still less than the college football bowl games it went up against on New Year's Day, but sufficient to justify NBC's counter-programming gamble. And enough to offer Bettman hope that his sport may finally be breaking through to the wider audience that the league has so long coveted.

Returning the game to its outdoor roots wasn't an original idea. Gordie Howe and the Detroit Red Wings played an exhibition game against a team of inmates at the Marquette Branch Prison in Michigan's Upper Peninsula on a frigid Groundhog Day back in 1954. Jack Adams, the team's GM, arranged it as a favour for a couple of mobster friends who were missing the pros while serving their time. But it wasn't that entertaining; they stopped keeping score at the end of the first period with the Wings leading 18–0. In September 1991, Bruce McNall's LA Kings, on a preseason barn-storming tour, played the Rangers on a pad set up in the parking lot at Caesars Palace in Las Vegas. It was still 30°C at game time, and most of the 13,000 spectators were wearing shorts and T-shirts. Wayne Gretzky, the main attraction, had a goal in a 5–2 victory, although the game is mostly remembered for the biblical-style plague of grasshoppers attracted by the lights. When the insects landed, they froze to the sticky ice, and on the benches between shifts, players were kept busy wiping the remains off their skate blades. And in November 2003, the Oilers faced off against the Canadiens at Edmonton's Commonwealth Stadium in a regular season tilt broadcast across Canada by the CBC. The viewers at home loved it, but with the temperature dipping down to −18°C (−30°C with the wind chill), it was an experiment that not everyone was keen to repeat. When NBC pitched the idea of having the Rangers play under the lights at Yankee Stadium the following season, they were politely rebuffed. While Bettman was enthusi-astic, the Blueshirts owners weren't, and there were real worries about Manhattan's capricious winter weather.

So the concept that was to become the NHL's television salva-tion remained on the back burner until John Collins dropped in on the commissioner for a cup of coffee in the fall of 2006. The former vice-president of marketing for the National Football League was between gigs, having lost a power struggle and his job as president of the Cleveland Browns earlier in the year. A native New Yorker, but with the tall, tanned look and natural ease of a California power broker, he'd been offered a senior position with a sports media organization and was seeking some advice from a professional acquaintance. What he found instead was a business soulmate. It took just five minutes for Bettman to convince Collins that the opportunity he was considering wasn't right for him. Then the conversation turned to the problems the NHL was facing coming out of a lockout that had killed an entire season. The league needed to find a new identity and better ways to connect with both fans and advertisers. Collins, who had been behind some of the NFL's biggest marketing alliances, including a ten-year, $1.2-billion deal with Pepsi, made some off-the-cuff suggestions. The blue-sky session lasted about an hour, then Bettman had to leave for a lunch meeting.

Collins had barely made it downstairs when his phone rang. The NHL commissioner was offering him a job. Hockey was about the only sport that Collins hadn't played growing up, but he was warming to both Bettman and the challenge his league presented. So that afternoon the pair met up again and spent another couple of hours excitedly batting around some potential strategies for the business. "I didn't really know what the position was, and I don't think he did either," says the fifty-year-old Collins, now the NHL's chief operating officer. "But we shook hands on it." On his way out the door, Bettman took Collins by a conference room and showed off his prize catch to several senior NBC executives who were gathering for a meeting about the coming season's broadcast schedule. The next day Jon Miller, NBC's vice-president of sports, called Collins at home with a suggestion. The network had a hole to fill in its New Year's Day schedule, having lost the Gator Bowl to rival CBS. And they still liked the idea of an outdoor hockey game. "I said, shit, if NBC is willing to give us a national window to do a big event, then this is exactly what we're talking about," says Collins. "We had a shot."

It took more than a year to organize. Initially there was little enthusiasm among the league's sponsors, or its teams, and it was finally the small-market Buffalo Sabres who volunteered to sacrifice a home date against the Penguins for the good of the collective. But the January 1, 2008, game ended up being something magical. A gentle snowstorm swept in just before the puck dropped, creating a Christmas card atmosphere at Ralph Wilson Stadium in suburban Orchard Park, New York. And the 71,000 fans who had snapped up the tickets to sit in the cold were electric, cheering and singing even as crews cleared the ice with shovels during stoppages in play. The game itself—with the two teams dressed in throwback uniforms—also lived up to the hype, going to overtime and then a shootout. It was Sidney Crosby who scored the winning goal, slowly dangling the puck around the piles of snow and tucking it past Buffalo's Ryan Miller. His Penguins teammates mobbed him at centre ice like they had just won the Cup. The snow-globe tableau created instinctive good feelings, *The New York Times* would later gush: "If hockey fans ten years from now are following an NHL that is healthy and prosperous, they can look back at that snowy afternoon outside Buffalo as the day the league saved itself."

It was certainly a fair distance from where Bettman had found himself when he became commissioner a decade and a half earlier. In 1993, NBC was coming to the end of a four-year deal to broadcast the All-Star Game—and that was the only appearance hockey made on US network television throughout the entire season, including the playoffs. Even then, the league's talent showcase was hardly a valued commodity. During its broadcast of the Super Bowl the week before the Montreal All-Star Game, NBC didn't bother to promo the upcoming hockey game. And its affiliate in Syracuse, New York, less than an hour's drive from the Canadian border, chose to show the 1957 Marlon Brando film *Sayonara* instead.

The last time the NHL had a significant presence in America's living rooms was during the 1974–75 season, when the Flyers pummelled their way to a second straight Stanley Cup. The Broad Street Bullies' violent style filled seats in Philadelphia, but it repelled a national audience; and when NBC dropped the sport from its schedule, no other broadcaster stepped forward. The lack of country-wide exposure didn't much matter to the league's owners. The NHL's first network deal—a game-of-the-week package with CBS in 1967—had been worth less than $2 million, a twelfth of what the NFL was then getting, and the price hadn't really increased since. Split between eighteen franchises it was a pittance. Teams made more money from their local or regional broadcasting contracts.

During his tenure, John Ziegler felt little pressure to change the status quo. In 1982, the USA Network, a minor cable player that had just started broadcasting twenty-four hours a day, signed an $8-million, three-season deal for the national rights. (In comparison, the NBA was getting $92 million over four years from CBS at that point, as well as an additional $5.5 million a year from cable channels.) By 1985, when the NHL jumped to ESPN, the asking price was $24 million for three years. The next go-around got the league a lofty $17 million a season when Ziegler signed a three-year agreement with SportsChannel America in 1988. But the deal, made just prior to Gretzky's trade to Los Angeles, turned out to be a disaster for everyone involved. The channel, with a reach of only 16 million households (compared with ESPN's then 60 million subscribers) was ill-positioned to capitalize on hockey's new-found popularity and went on to lose $10 million on the games each season. As a sop, the league agreed to a one-year extension in 1991 at the bargain-basement price of $5.5 million. It was not long after Gary Bettman had finalized the NBA's new deal with NBC—four years at $150 million a season, or twenty-seven times what pro hockey was getting for its US TV rights. And even that was chump change compared to the NFL's $900-million-a-year take—which worked out to $32 million for each of its then twenty-eight teams.

Gil Stein's brief time in office saw the league return to ESPN with a five-year contract worth $125 million for twenty-five regular season games, some of the playoffs, and all of the Stanley Cup Final. Part of the deal required the sports channel to pay a mainstream network to carry at least five playoff games every season. And so, on April 18, 1993, meaningful NHL hockey returned to big-time television for the first time in almost two decades. The three first-round playoff matches broadcast by ABC—owned by the same parent company as ESPN—were available in 91 percent of US homes, but that didn't guarantee an audience. Chicago versus St. Louis was the best of the bunch, drawing just over 2.5 million viewers. Hockey still trailed all other athletic events that weekend, including a kitschy Battle of the Superstars competition—pro athletes facing off on an obstacle course—on *Wide World of Sports*.

When Bettman took over, he made it clear that finding a major broadcaster who was willing to actually shell out money for the product was a top priority. "Our not being on television for so long has caused a learning deficit," he told *New York* magazine. The game wasn't just alien to American sports fans, they were no longer even trying to understand it. Luckily for him, the TV landscape was about to undergo a radical shift. Rupert Murdoch's upstart Fox network had decided that sports was the fastest way to build its brand, and in December 1993 the company stunned the industry by handing the NFL $1.6 billion over four years for the rights to Sunday NFC games and the Super Bowl. CBS, which had bid $100 million a year less, suddenly found itself without pro football for the first time in thirty-eight years. The new NHL commissioner swiftly volunteered to fill their weekend void, and negotiations carried on through the spring and summer of 1994. But just as a deal was about to be finalized that September, Fox surprised everyone again by stepping in to scoop up hockey, too, with a $155-million, five-year offer—$5 million more than CBS. The agreement would see up to twenty games a season broadcast on the network, including three Stanley Cup Final matches in prime time. The remaining years of the ESPN deal had to be discounted, but the bottom line was that the NHL would receive a total of $220 million in American TV revenues through the end of the 1998–99 season. Perhaps it didn't matter if Bettman thought that icing came in a can.

David Hill, the longtime head of Fox Sports, is an unapologetic, take-no-prisoners Aussie, just like his boss, and he felt that "ice hockey" was a perfect fit for the brash young network. His first experience with the game was in the run-up to the 1988 Calgary Olympics when Ralph Mellanby, the executive producer of *Hockey Night in Canada*, took him to see the Flames play at the Saddledome. "I was blown away," he says. "I'd never, ever experienced anything like it. It was the most insane feeling in that stadium. I became an instant devotee." Hill had seen games on television before, but somehow the excitement, speed, and energy that were so present in the rink didn't translate to the small screen. Now he was in a position to alter that, and in the NHL he had a partner that was end-of-the-night desperate and open to almost anything. "We never made any secret of the fact that we were opportunistic," says Hill. "We felt that this game could be developed."

Fox had given football a facelift, experimenting with new camera angles, adding the first on-screen "bug" to constantly remind viewers of the score and remaining time, and miking the field so thoroughly that tackles sounded like freeway crashes. Away from the action, there were good ol' boy hosts, jazzy graphics, and plenty of highlight videos set to thumping rock music. It was sports for the ADD generation.

Hockey was to get the same treatment. Once the lockout was settled in January 1995, Fox got to work shooting promos that were meant to entertain and educate. Rob Blake, the LA Kings defenceman, appeared in one, standing in front of the net. "The crease is an area bordered by a red semi-circle, six feet in front of the goal," he intoned with all the vigour of a hostage in a Hezbollah-scripted tape. The camera then panned back to reveal an ironing board. "I like to keep my creases nice and neat," he added as he pressed a hockey sweater. "The trick is to lay it out and flatten anything that doesn't belong there." It was as if Felix Unger had been a serial killer. His teammate Gretzky was conscripted to do the spots for local affiliates: "Get ready for the fastest, wildest sport on TV. Catch the NHL on Fox starting April 2, right here on Fox 49 KPDX." A request that he slap his forehead and say "D'oh!" each time, like the network's biggest star Homer Simpson, was politely declined.

The telecasts themselves drew mixed reviews. The league praised the production values—multiple camera angles, plentiful graphics, and documentary-style profiles of players between periods. But the hockey media heaped scorn on some of the more fanciful enhancements, like the animated Transformer-style battle-bots that appeared on screen after every goal to punch each other silly. The cyborgs "might mildly entertain a 6-year-old boy," wrote the Minneapolis *Star Tribune*, but adults "will find them stupid and obtrusive." The next season, Fox found another way to enrage purists, introducing its infamous glowing puck. Officially called FoxTrax, the idea came from Hill, who was always bothered by something that is barely noticed by those who grow up watching the game—the puck's frequent disappearance from view as the action moves along the boards closest to the camera. He enlisted the help of Stan Honey, a California engineer who designed high-tech navigation systems for yachts and pioneered digital map displays for automobiles. Hill makes the surely apocryphal claim that Honey's first proposal involved the use of plutonium. "I didn't want to be the one who had to explain a small nuclear explosion at the LA Forum to the press," says Hill. "So I sent him back to the drawing board."

The eventual, and far less actionable, solution was infrared technology. A transmitter was embedded inside the puck, and special sensors were placed around the rink to capture its movements in real time. That information was then relayed to a powerful computer that matched the data with the images being recorded by the TV cameras. The system, which cost $3 million, was as sophisticated as anything then being used by the US military. (The pucks, which had to be made by hand, were so expensive that league representatives were dispatched to try and retrieve them from fans when they went into the stands. Vancouver goalie Corey Hirsch had the misfortune to record his first NHL shutout against Boston in a game where FoxTrax was being tested, and even he didn't get to keep the puck.) What viewers saw at home was a blue glow that hovered around the puck wherever it went. When the disc was shot, the haze stretched out like a comet tail. And if the puck was moving faster than 55 miles per hour, the streak turned red.

The press loathed it. "The puck sucks," declared the *Toronto Star*. In Pittsburgh, the *Post-Gazette* said it made players look like they were stick-handling a neon beach ball. "Why Fox failed to carry this banal exercise to its logical conclusion is unclear. Or did network brains think it too hazardous to have the goalie's glove emit a puff of green smoke upon contact with the rubber disk?" Hill, who had received death threats over the football score bug, was ecstatic at all the free publicity. Ratings for the hockey telecasts went up.

For the conspiracy-minded, it was more proof that Bettman's real agenda was to remake the game for US audiences. The playoff schedule had already been tweaked to accommodate Fox's time slots—turning *Hockey Night in Canada* into an afternoon affair. And there were dark mutterings that the American network had a hand in the Nordiques' move to Denver and the Jets' relocation to Phoenix. Jerry Colangelo, one of the Coyotes' initial owners, was certainly surprised when Bettman called out of the blue and offered him Winnipeg's franchise. A few years earlier, when he was building a new home for his Phoenix Suns basketball team, he had reached out to the NHL only to be told that "hockey would never work in the desert." Now the commissioner was begging him to join the party.

Hill dismisses such conjecture as "total bullshit." But Brian Burke, then the NHL director of hockey operations, says Fox did shape expansion plans. "There was considerable pressure. Fox said, 'You need to add more US markets, you're not in enough top thirty markets. You need a team in Atlanta.'" At Bettman's direction, Burke and his assistant, Dave Nonis, prepared a rush study of how many junior hockey franchises, European clubs, and NCAA teams had been established since the Panthers and Ducks joined the league in the 1993–94 season. "We concluded that there were more than enough players to add four more teams," says Burke. "And only then did Gary say, 'OK. We'll have the discussion.' He put the game first. He put the game ahead of TV." Or at least searched for a way to balance the demands of the network and his cash-hungry owners while maintaining a halfway decent on-ice product.

Whatever influence the $155 million did buy Fox, it wasn't nearly as much as they had anticipated. Their efforts to convince the league to move to two halves instead of three periods and to add more and longer timeouts for commercials never gained traction. Not that they were alone in wanting to remake the game. Michael Eisner had found success in Anaheim with a show biz approach to selling hockey. At The Pond, there were nightly fan giveaways, laser light shows, cheerleaders, and Wild Wing, the first NHL mascot to rappel from the rafters to the ice. But the Disney honcho also had a lot of ideas about how to make the sport itself more appealing to an American audience. Banning fighting was at the top of the list he presented to the board of governors, which also featured bigger nets, players being forced to remove their helmets while on the bench (so that viewers would get to know their faces), and shootouts to settle tie games. Bettman, who once joked to a reporter that he was going to sell Eisner on the idea of a see-through helmet, wasn't that enthusiastic: "I knew that coming in as the new guy that this was the place where I needed to move a little more slowly and establish my credibility. I didn't want to be like the bull in the china shop." In the end, it didn't matter. The other NHL owners, still singed from McNall's flame-out, were hardly ready to let another Hollywood type try and remake the business.

They were, however, happy to take more of Disney's cash. In 1995, Eisner had paid $19 billion for Capital Cities/ABC Inc., acquiring not just a broadcast network, but the growing ESPN cable empire as well. The merger created the world's largest entertainment company, and the CEO's hockey obsession was to again pay off for the NHL. In August 1998, with a full season still remaining on the Fox contract, Eisner's hand was apparent when the league signed a new five-year deal with ABC and extended their cable package with ESPN through 2004. The agreements were worth a total of $600 million, and the reaction from Murdoch's network alternated between flabbergasted and royally pissed. Despite the high-tech tricks, Fox's ratings for the late-season games and playoffs had been spiralling downwards—four consecutive Stanley Cup Final sweeps were a big part of the problem—and had ultimately struck bottom, trailing pro wrestling and even women's soccer. "There are people who think Disney will make money in it, but then again there are people around the country who believe the president didn't have sex with Monica Lewinsky," sniped Ed Goren, executive producer of Fox Sports. Knowing that Fox had lost $40 million and counting on their deal, many industry watchers wondered why ABC would pay $250 million—2.6 times more—for the network rights. And rather than basking in the glow of his accomplishment, Bettman instead found himself fielding questions about the sanity of his new partners. "I didn't attend the negotiations with a mask and a gun, and they weren't in a trance," was the commissioner's peevish response.

But once the deal kicked in during the 1999–2000 season, it quickly became clear that Disney's primary interest was in bulking up its fledgling ESPN2 operation rather than growing the game. In the first year, ABC broadcast regular season matchups on just four occasions—the absolute minimum under the agreement. Shoehorned in on Saturday afternoons, they drew even smaller audiences than Fox's final telecasts, and when the network insisted on the same time slot for the playoffs they managed to tank ratings in Canada as well. (CBC, which was paying $66 million a year—half the value of the US deals—complained to no avail.) ABC carried three games of the 2000 Stanley Cup Final between New Jersey and Dallas, but when the Devils clinched in double overtime in Game 6, only 5.8 million Americans were watching—20 million fewer viewers than the network was getting for *Who Wants to Be a Millionaire?*

In the second year of the deal, the ratings were even lower, tumbling 15 percent on both ABC and ESPN2. An effort to carve out a regular Wednesday night slot for the NHL on the main ESPN channel starting in the 2001–2 season did little to reverse the trend—year after year, the US audience for hockey was shrinking, no matter what outlet it was broadcast on. In the spring of 2003, ABC's playoff numbers plunged a further 27 percent, and in most markets nationally televised NHL contests attracted fewer viewers than arena football. All of the cable games were shifted over to "The Deuce," as ESPN2 was nicknamed, where they drew an average national audience of around 210,000. (In comparison, games on the Canadian cable rights holder, TSN, were attracting 311,000 viewers.) And even the hockey highlights were getting hard to find on ESPN's flagship program *SportsCenter*.

When the agreement expired in the spring of 2004, ABC made it clear that it wasn't interested in re-upping, period. Fox and CBS, both still nursing hurt feelings, also took a pass. And with a lockout looming, Bettman had to practically beg to get a meeting with NBC. "The truth of the matter is that there was nobody in the United States, no American television network that really wanted a deal. Including us," says Ken Schanzer, then president of NBC Sports.

The NHL commissioner had a history with the Peacock Network, and good feelings still lingered from the 1990 deal he had negotiated for the NBA, which ended up being highly lucrative for all involved. He set about pestering Schanzer, and his boss Dick Ebersol, the NBC Sports chair. "Gary's like a bulldog. He was on us constantly," Schanzer recalls. The answer was "no," but that didn't matter to Bettman … he just kept coming back and asking again. NBC's bottom line was that it was unwilling to assume any risk: There were lots of sports the network could broadcast on weekend afternoons and easily make money on, but hockey wasn't among them. The deal that the NHL ultimately got was the same one NBC had extended to arena football in 2002—no rights fee, but an equal share of any profits after the production costs were paid for. The agreement to broadcast seven regular season and six playoff matches, as well as Game 3 through Game 7 of the final, was for two years, with an option to extend it to four. And Schanzer is blunt about why it happened—it was a favour for a friend in a time of need: "We have great affection for Gary. Great respect. A piece of this was a function of the fact that we knew it was important to him. So, if we could do it, we wanted to."

There was no way to spin a deal that saw the league go from $50 million a year for its US network rights to nothing, but the timing was in a way felicitous, adding heft to the commissioner's claim that the NHL's spiralling salaries were unsustainable. However, when the game returned after the cancelled 2004–5 season, now supposedly on a new economic footing, there was a far nastier surprise waiting. ESPN, which had been paying $70 million a year for the cable rights, was now offering only $30 million. The sports channel was in the midst of concluding an eight-year agreement with Major League Baseball at a cost of almost $2.4 billion, and it was looking to cut corners elsewhere. Bettman tried to negotiate, but Mark Shapiro, the network's executive vice-president, told him it was strictly a take-it-or-leave-it proposition. Their meeting ended acrimoniously, and years later it's still a sore spot for the commissioner. ESPN2 was built on hockey, he says, his voice rising, and yet the company saw fit to kick the NHL when it was down. "I think they thought they could do it. They took us for granted, or either they didn't value us the same way we thought we should be valued."

Left with no good options, Bettman chose the available one. Cable giant Comcast, part owner of the Philadelphia Flyers, was looking to expand the profile of its Outdoor Life Network (OLN)—an almost sports channel that was home to hunting and fishing shows, rodeo, cycling's Tour de France, and reruns of *Survivor*. It was available in 64 million households, almost 30 million fewer than ESPN, but they were willing to pay $69 million a season to become the American home of the NHL. The three-year deal was signed in August 2005, although few around the league were happy about it. OLN, rebranded as Versus the next season, occupied space way up in the digital ether. Most of the hotels that NHL clubs stayed in while on the road didn't even subscribe to the channel, making it impossible for players and management to watch games or catch the highlights. And the initial audience for their hockey broadcasts was half of ESPN2's already anemic number—little more than 100,000. Infomercials drew more people.

The deal was a necessity that Bettman now casts as a virtue. "The biggest reason I couldn't go back to ESPN after the lockout was that I knew that if they weren't paying us enough they wouldn't have any incentive to grow us," he says. "They wouldn't have any incentive to promote us the way they promote the more expensive properties. We wouldn't be treated the way we should be." Occupying the limelight at Versus was never a problem—in winter, there was little else to showcase. And the channel's puck ratings have slowly grown. During the 2008–9 season, it averaged 318,000 viewers for its fifty-plus exclusive games, and renewed its deal for three more years at $77.5 million per season. By 2010–11, the average grew to 353,000, with a top audience of 750,000. And during the playoffs, the number of Americans watching on any given night was closer to 800,000. But even today, Versus (rebranded yet again at the beginning of 2012 as NBC Sports Network) continues to find itself far down the pecking order, in 25 million fewer homes than ESPN or ESPN2 and 9 million fewer than the somniferous Golf Channel. Most subscribers pay 28 cents a month for its service, compared to a fee of more than $5 for the slate of basic ESPN channels.

The national network audience for hockey in the United States also remains stubbornly small. A first-round playoff matchup on NBC regularly draws about a quarter of the viewers for a similar basketball playoff on ABC or a NASCAR race on Fox. And even if Game 7 of the 2011 Stanley Cup Final between the Bruins and the Canucks was, as the league trumpeted in a press release, "the most-watched NHL game in thirty-eight years," its 8.54 million viewers in the States was still 200,000 less than CBC got for its coverage in Canada, a country with one-tenth the population. The 2010 World Series between the San Francisco Giants and the Texas Rangers—the lowest rated in baseball history—drew an average of 14.3 million viewers. The 2012 Super Bowl, pitting the New York Giants against the New England Patriots, drew 111 million viewers, with 3 million more tuning in at halftime just to watch Madonna, a performer whose age is now greater than most football jersey numbers.

But in a fragmented entertainment marketplace, any event that can entice people to sit in front of their televisions and watch live programming, rather than skimming through the commercials later on a PVR, is valuable. "Hockey has always appealed to its audience," says Schanzer. "Its baseline is a very intense, relatively targeted, decent demographic. And as overall network ratings diminish, hockey has performed better relatively." NBC made money on the profit-sharing deal; so did the league.

When the US rights came up for bidding again in the spring of 2011, Bettman had multiple suitors for the first time in more than a decade. Fox took a look then passed. And there were serious negotiations with Turner Broadcasting, which was looking to add more sports to its truTV cable channel, already a big part of the NCAA's March Madness coverage. ESPN made an offer that was far in excess of the $30 million a season that Bettman walked away from in a huff in 2005. It was NBC, however, that stepped up to the table and gave the NHL the most lucrative television deal in league history—$2 billion over ten years. At a press conference in New York, Dick Ebersol paid tribute to his friend Gary and the "incredible deal" he had driven. "Our wonderful—for us—run of not paying anything is over."

There was again an element of luck at play. Earlier in the year, Comcast had completed a $13.75-billion merger with NBC Universal. Versus was now part of the empire, and securing content that could be promoted across the company's vast new field of TV and internet platforms was a top priority. With six years already invested in selling hockey to its basic and cable audiences it didn't seem like the time to change horses. So, NBC simply went bigger. All told, the network and its cable outlets are now committed to broadcasting 100 regular season games a year and every single playoff match nationally on a "major" channel. (The company now owns twenty different basic ones and forty of the digital variety.) The new arrangement was a key point for Bettman and the NHL—hockey had too often been treated as disposable programming under the past deal, like when the network cut away from a Buffalo–Ottawa overtime playoff game in May 2007 to show lead-up coverage of the Preakness Stakes horse race.

In exchange, NBC and Versus got a lot more "exclusive" games. Weekend and weeknight slots where no other NHL teams are playing in the United States, and more special events like a mid-afternoon Thanksgiving Day "Showdown" match. (The initial 2011 game between Boston and Detroit was promoted via an

NHL float in the annual Macy's parade featuring toque-wearing kids firing pucks through the five-hole of a giant wooden turkey.) But Ebersol, who parted ways with the network—as did his deputy Schanzer—shortly after concluding the deal, said the impetus for really buying into hockey was the Winter Classic, "the single most successful new venture on the American pro sports landscape in the past decade." A national audience discovered by playing up hockey's northern past rather than its Sunbelt present.

As the seconds tick down on the 2012 Classic in Philadelphia, the drama and tension that NBC is pinning its hopes on are in abundant supply. Still down 3–2 in the game's final minute, the Flyers pull their goalie for an extra attacker and pin the Rangers in their own end. The fans are on their feet as the pressure grows around the net. After a prolonged scramble, New York captain Ryan Callahan is called for covering the puck in the crease—an automatic penalty shot—with just 19.6 seconds remaining. It's veteran winger Danny Briere, a shootout specialist, who gets the call. He glides in slowly, dips a shoulder and tries to go five-hole, but Henrik Lundqvist quickly closes his pads and then pops to his feet waving his glove in celebration. The Rangers hang on for the win.

A few minutes later a smiling Bettman, as casually dressed as he is ever seen in public, button-necked Ralph Lauren cashmere sweater over a dress shirt, takes the podium to declare the day a grand success. "A rivalry outdoors is as good as one indoors," he says. "It's not every day that an event can equal or exceed the hype." It's an uncommonly cheery session with the press, and the commissioner is gone within minutes. By the time Rangers coach John Tortorella enters the room, he's already in his black Mercedes (the big SUV provided by official NHL sponsor Honda has been parked for the day), driving himself back home, two hours up the turnpike in New Jersey.

It's just as well. Tortorella, who looks like Fonzie from *Happy Days* but has a chronic problem keeping his cool, is furious in victory. "I'm not sure if NBC got together with the refs or what to turn this into an overtime game," he says. "Everything starts going against us. There are two good referees, but I thought that game was reffed horribly." The third period in particular, he says, was "disgusting."

The Rangers coach later issues an apology for his "tongue-in-cheek" comments about the broadcaster, but the damage is done. Two days after the Classic he is assessed a $30,000 fine by the NHL for conduct unbecoming. It's never a good idea to rain on Gary Bettman's parade.

ANYONE WHO HAS EVER SPENT an evening watching hockey at Toronto's Air Canada Centre (ACC) can attest that the Bay Street cashbox is about as far as one can get from hockey's rough-and-tumble roots. The crowd is mostly suit-clad business people who come late, leave early, and rarely get excited about anything. The rink's most expensive seats—the so-called "platinums" with a face value of $458.50 each—sit empty for large portions of the game, as the best-heeled patrons slowly make their way back from the canapés and Chardonnay served in the below-ice luxury suites. A large beer costs $15. A plain hot dog will run you $7. Park anywhere within ten blocks and the flat rate is $25. Ties aren't required at the games, but they might as well be. And despite a record of futility that now dates back almost forty-five years, the waiting list for Leafs season tickets is two decades long. (Although most of the people who can afford them simply jump the line and buy them on the private market, where the "personal seat licences" that Maple Leafs Sports and Entertainment (MLSE)—the parent company of the NHL club as well as the Toronto Raptors—attaches to its prime seats, trade for as much as $30,000 apiece.)

So in early December 2011, the ACC was an entirely appropriate place for a press conference about obscene amounts of money. George Cope, the Chara-sized president and CEO of Bell Canada, was there with his greatest telecom rival, Nadir Mohamed, the CEO of Rogers Communications, to announce their companies' joint purchase of the NHL's most valuable franchise. The $1.32-billion deal for a 75-percent stake of MLSE also gave the two phone companies control over the rink, the bottom-dwelling NBA team, the Leafs' minor-league affiliate, and Major League Soccer's Toronto FC, but there was no denying what they were really paying for—an original-six team with a national following. A few days before, *Forbes* magazine's annual survey of NHL clubs had ranked the Leafs as the league's most valuable at $521 million. This transaction, which pegged the total value of MLSE at $2.1 billion, suggested they were worth even more to motivated buyers.

The big winner on the day was the Ontario Teachers' Pension Plan, which had started buying into the company—then just the lowly Leafs playing at the old Gardens—back in 1994, and gradually increased its stake to 80 percent. Over the next decade and a half, MLSE built a state-of-the-art arena on Toronto's waterfront, took over an NBA expansion franchise, started its own digital TV channel, branched out into condo development, and became the country's biggest sporting empire. And even though the Leafs never went further than the third round of the playoffs over that whole period, their value kept escalating, in no small measure due to the undying—and unrewarded—loyalty of their fans. Teachers' was now recouping more than seven times its cumulative $180-million investment.

Television was the key. The same distracted viewing habits that drive network sports contracts in the States were also influencing deals on the Canadian side of the border. By 2010, the

Leafs were commanding $750,000 a game for their regional TV rights—the most expensive in the league—split between Rogers-owned Sportsnet and Bell-controlled TSN. With those agreements set to expire in 2015, MLSE, under the direction of its chair, Larry Tanenbaum, a minority shareholder, was looking to double the going rate. And if the networks wouldn't pay, the Leafs were threatening to set up a sports channel of their own, like baseball's New York Yankees.

When Teachers' let it be known that it was ready to get out of the hockey business, both Rogers and Bell took hard looks at buying MLSE on their own, but balked at the asking price. What ultimately drove them to band together was fear that somebody with even deeper pockets would swoop in and take control of the club and its TV contracts. The centrepiece of the deal was a ten-year extension of the regional rights for both networks at the "discount" price of $1 million a game—providing Toronto with $52 million a season in broadcast revenue that it doesn't have to share with anyone else. (The Leafs' remaining thirty games are the linchpin of CBC and TSN's national TV deals.) It was a very expensive way to guarantee access to the country's premium hockey brand, but Rogers and Bell didn't have much choice. In Canada, a sports channel without the Buds—the biggest team in the country's biggest market—doesn't have much of a future.

In this case, content wasn't just king, it was more like galactic emperor. But the MLSE deal also served a secondary purpose—keeping Gary Bettman in check. If the NHL commissioner has had a tough slog finding willing TV partners in the United States, he's barely broken a sweat north of the border. The competition between those who want to showcase pro hockey in Canada is almost as fierce as among those who play it. And Bettman had taken full advantage.

For decades, Molson Brewery had a virtual monopoly on NHL hockey in the Great White North. Not only did the beer maker own the Montreal Canadiens, it had also sewn up the regional rights to the Leafs and Vancouver Canucks, and was the producer and title sponsor of CBC and Radio-Canada's national *Hockey Night in Canada/La Soirée du Hockey* broadcasts. The company was protective of its turf. In March 1979, when it looked like a merger would finally be completed with the World Hockey Association, Toronto, Vancouver, and Montreal all voted against the deal, assuring that it wouldn't receive the required support of three-quarters of the league's teams (Boston and Los Angeles were also opposed). Fans of the Edmonton Oilers, Winnipeg Jets, and Quebec Nordiques—owned by rival brewer Carling O'Keefe—went nuts, starting boycotts of Molson products as well as making bomb threats and firing the odd bullet at the company's plants. The beer maker claimed it had nothing to do with the merger's defeat, but two weeks later when the matter again came before the NHL's board of governors, the Habs and Canucks reversed their position.

The change of heart had a lot to do with a last-minute condition that league president John Ziegler imposed on the incoming Canadian clubs. Part of the price of entry would be the surrender of their TV rights to three other Molson-backed franchises for a period of five years for zero compensation. The WHA teams were given the limited capacity to show their games on home turf, but *Hockey Night in Canada* had the power to take them away at any time and put them on the English or French CBC—where the only beer commercials would be for Molson brands.

It was Marcel Aubut, the president of the Nordiques, who devised a way to open the TV market. Molson also had deals with the NHL's fourteen US-based clubs, paying them $150,000 each for the Canadian rights to their games—not that important during the regular season, but crucial once the playoffs began. The trans-border agreements were set to expire at the end of the 1983–84 season, and Aubut convinced Carling O'Keefe to acquire the foreign rights of five American teams by offering them $300,000 each. The idea was to set up a rival hockey broadcast on CTV and trade the US games for some of the Canadian ones that Molson controlled. When the league tried to block the transactions Aubut went a step further, offering the NHL an unprecedented $7 million annually for five years for the non-exclusive rights to all of the regular season and playoff games between US teams. When the proposal was put to the board of governors at the 1984 All-Star Game in New Jersey, they broke out the champagne at 10:30 in the morning. Molson never even got a chance to make a counterproposal. The brewery sued, but just before the matter was scheduled to go to trial they settled, signing the same deal as their rival at the same price. The American teams, getting just $125,000 each from the league's national deal with the USA Network, were now receiving an additional $650,000 a year from the two foreign broadcasters.

The Carling O'Keefe network was a costly flop, barely nudging beer sales, and after three years, the company approached the league about getting out of its commitment. Molson stepped into the breach and offered to double its payout for the return of exclusive Canadian rights to nationally broadcast all the NHL's games. Two years later, they took over Carling and forever cut their hockey rival out of the picture. But the competition in sports television only grew stronger.

Another competitor, Labatt Breweries, then owners of the Toronto Blue Jays, launched its own cable sports network, TSN, in 1984. The channel struck a deal with the NHL for a secondary package of weeknight national games starting in the 1987–88 season. And by the mid-1990s, they were paying the league almost

$10 million a year to broadcast a couple of regular season games each week and opening-round playoff matchups between US clubs.

Bettman's first real kick at the Canadian can came at the end of the 1996–97 season when both the *Hockey Night* package and the TSN deal were up for renewal. Molson, the longtime producer of the Saturday night telecasts, offered to sign a five-year, $60-million-a-season extension, but the commissioner turned them down flat. (The league's counterproposal was $80 million a season.) It was the CBC that ended up taking control of the rights, paying $265 million over four years, with Labatt underwriting part of the cost as the new title sponsor. It was only $6 million a season more—"an increase, but not a windfall," said Bettman—but the precedent had been set. Money trumped tradition as far as the NHL was concerned.

The commissioner engineered a similar power play with TSN. When the network, then owned by a consortium of investors, offered $13 million a year for the cable rights and refused to go any higher, Bettman approached CTV to see if they might be interested in starting up a rival sports channel. They struck a deal to pay $15 million annually for five years, and CTV Sportsnet launched on the night of October 9, 1998, with a game between the Flyers and the Rangers. (The channel was sold to Rogers, a minority partner, in 2001 after CTV purchased the company that owned TSN and several other specialty stations.)

And the price Canadians were willing to pay for hockey just kept getting higher. When TSN reacquired a share of the national rights in the fall of 2001 by teaming up with the CBC—sixty regular season games a year for the cable outlet, five more years of *Hockey Night in Canada* for the public broadcaster, and shared playoff coverage—the two networks signed on the dotted line for a combined annual fee of close to $80 million.

In 2006, with the CBC agreement drawing to a close, TSN and its parent company, CTV, reportedly sought out Bettman with a $1.4-billion, ten-year bid to become the exclusive Canadian home of the NHL. What saved *HNIC*—at least temporarily—was the commissioner's belief that the league could make more money over that period by playing the two big networks against each other.

Richard Stursberg, then the head of CBC's English services, describes the process of negotiating the last deal with the NHL as both painful and off-putting. An initial meeting between himself, network head Robert Rabinovitch, and Bettman and Daly, held at the famed Manhattan sushi joint Nobu, was like a bad date. The NHL commissioner and his deputy spent most of their time ogling the various celebrities in the room. And when the talk turned to business—specifically the CBC's desire to get a deal done quickly, lest the new Tory government in Ottawa slash their funding—the commissioner gave the distinct impression that he didn't give a damn. "'Hmmm,' Bettman replied noncommittally. 'Hmmm,' he said again, his voice almost lost in the cacophony of the celebrity crowd," Stursberg wrote in his 2012 tell-all, *The Tower of Babble*. "Billy Daly passed us more sushi. He stared at me balefully. Sugar Ray Leonard wandered by, shadow boxing, throwing little lefts and rights into the expensive restaurant air. 'Hmmm,' Bettman said once more. He ordered the cheque, smiled menacingly and promised to get back to us."

The process dragged on for months. When the CBC made a formal offer, Bettman informed them that he was going to "sniff around" for a better deal. Canadians might be sentimental about a broadcasting relationship that stretches all the way back to 1952, but the commissioner wasn't, coldly informing Stursberg that the Mother Corp. could afford to pay more if it had better salespeople. The two sides were tens of millions of dollars apart.

Fearing that its rival was going to snatch away the one thing that distinguished it from a bad digital channel, the CBC dug deep and found more money. Another dinner meeting was convened in Manhattan, at the even more exclusive Rao's—a tiny Italian eatery with a distinct *Goodfellas* vibe. The crowd "looked like businessmen with a penchant for weightlifting, diamond rings and hearty arm punching," Stursberg recounted. "I wondered why Bettman had brought us to this particular restaurant. Was there a subtext?" As it turned out, he did have a deal that the CBC couldn't refuse: The NHL would take their money, but wanted the network to hand over more Leafs games and playoff coverage to TSN. It was part of a larger pattern: Every time an agreement seemed within reach, Bettman would come back with a new demand and the explicit threat that the NHL would move to CTV unless it got what it wanted. It was a bluff. When an excerpt from Stursberg's book appeared in *Maclean's*, Ivan Fecan, the former CEO of the rival network wrote a letter to correct the record. CTV/TSN had dropped out of the running by that point: "Stursberg bid against himself."

The final contract, concluded in the spring of 2007 after a year of to and fro, was close to an unconditional CBC surrender. In exchange for keeping *Hockey Night in Canada* through 2014, the network agreed to rights fees that started at $87 million a season, quickly ramped up to a $95 million, then finished with payment of $100 million and $105 million over the final two years. The total price for the six-year package, all taxpayer funded, was $569 million—80 percent of them destined to end up on the balance sheets of American clubs. Despite the enormous price tag, the network has actually made money on the deal—commercial sales for the games brought in about $120 million in 2011–12, leaving a slim $5-million profit after production costs. But the trend will be hard to sustain. The current CBC leadership, spooked yet again by Bettman's flirtations with the competition, is already on record saying they will pay whatever it takes to keep NHL hockey after the end of the 2013–14 season. And the price this time could include a rebranding of the flagship show itself. Bettman has often complained that it should be the more-specific NHL Night in Canada.

TSN's deal, which also expires in 2014, began at $60 million and will finish at $75 million a season. Throw in the modest millions that the Canadian highlight channel The Score is paying the league, and the NHL's take out of Canada is already nudging up against the $200 million a season it receives from NBC. And heading into the next round of negotiations, it seems certain that the smaller nation will soon again account for the lion's share of TV revenues. "For him to get that much out of this country is incredible," says another Canadian broadcast executive who regularly sits across the table from Bettman. "He would have been a great poker player. There's no tell. When he's playing you, he's pleasant, almost warm. It's weird." What the commissioner understands, says the exec, is that there really isn't a ceiling for broadcasters north of the border. They will pay whatever they need to in order to secure hockey, and simply pass the cost on to advertisers and consumers. CBC, for example, is receiving $7.5 million a season from Scotiabank, just for the naming rights to its pre-game show. And if not for the MLSE deal, the next round of national negotiations would have likely been a three-way battle between CTV/TSN, the CBC, and Sportsnet, which would have driven the price up even further.

But for all that TV money flowing south, the relationship between the NHL commissioner and his Canadian broadcast partners is surprisingly rocky. For instance, Bettman has been quietly boycotting *Hockey Night in Canada* since 2010, in a fit of pique. His main complaint is the way he regularly gets grilled when he goes before their cameras—a sharp contrast to the kid-glove treatment his compatriots in the other major leagues receive from their rights holders. The last interview he gave to host Ron MacLean during the 2010 Stanley Cup Final between the Blackhawks and Flyers was a classic of the genre. It was the night of Bettman's fifty-eighth birthday, and MacLean began by singing his best wishes—then things went rapidly downhill. The *HNIC* host took issue with a statement the commissioner had made a couple of days before, assuring the press that all thirty of the league's clubs were on a stable financial footing and that "no owner is giving back the keys," embarking on a series of pointed inquiries about the sale of the Florida Panthers, the real price paid for the Tampa Bay Lightning, and the soon-to-be-bankrupt Dallas Stars. Bettman's lips pressed together and his shoulders visibly tightened as he shot a murderous glance at the camera. "Ron, Ron, Ron. We're coming through a recession with five years of record revenues," he said in a tone usually reserved for small children or recalcitrant animals. "It's not an issue." And when MacLean continued on in the same vein, asking about the health of the St. Louis Blues and Carolina Hurricanes, Bettman made it clear he had had enough. "We've had a great season, the hockey has been terrific, these playoffs are great, we're watching a wonderful game, and you just want to tick off franchise after franchise?" he asked, his voice rising in anger. "What inside of you compels you to want to go in that direction?" By the end of the eight-minute interview, when MacLean apologized for its confrontational tone, the commissioner looked like he might be ready to draw on some of the mob management lessons he wrote about in his Cornell thesis.

In his 2011 memoir, *Cornered*, MacLean writes extensively about his testy relationship with Bettman, whom he likens to Dustin Hoffman's autistic savant character in the movie *Rain Man*. (MacLean swears it's a compliment: Gary is great with numbers.) CBC brass have long been demanding that he and Don Cherry tone down their criticism of the league, he says, going as far as trying to add a clause to his contract that would forbid him from expressing opinions on the air. And executives have regularly expressed fears that the network—which hwas for many decades the league's largest corporate partner—will see the sixty-plus-year relationship severed in the next go-around unless it becomes friendlier.

Since his book climbed the list of Canadian bestsellers, MacLean says the situation has only worsened. *Hockey Night in Canada's* access to other senior NHL figures, like discipline czar Brendan Shanahan, has been totally shut down. "The pressure on me to back off, toe the company line and be the good marketing arm of the NHL is incredible," he says. "The way it gets presented to me is that 'Gary wants to hear you say that the new NHL is fantastic, and he's upset that you won't do that.'" When the *Coach's Corner* host encounters the commissioner off-camera it's cordial, but the message is unmistakably the same: "After Scotiabank came on as a sponsor, he walked right up to me and said, 'You know, I'm the only reason you have a job.' And he gave me a crocodile smile." But the anger doesn't just emanate from league headquarters. At the 2012 All-Star Game in Ottawa, when senior CBC executives made a presentation to owners and their GMs, they received an earful from six of the seven Canadian franchises, complaining about bias on the Saturday night broadcasts. There were calls to usher Cherry—closing in on his eightieth birthday and more erratic than ever—out the door. And once he goes, MacLean, now in his twenty-fifth year with the show, may not be far behind.

Bob McCown, a veteran sports talk radio host in Toronto, whose show is simulcast nationally on Sportsnet, is another of the commissioner's *bêtes noires*. A few years ago, he started calling Bettman "The Count" on-air, suggesting he resembles the plush *Sesame Street* Muppet vampire. Then, after a tense in-studio interview in which he basically accused Bettman of lying about the Phoenix Coyotes' prospects for success in the Arizona desert, he unilaterally banned the NHL honcho from ever returning. McCown says it had more to do with his "asshole" radio persona than any personal beef, but his opinion has since hardened. The league, he claims, has orchestrated a whisper campaign against him, trying to undermine his credibility, all the while dissembling about the health of the game, especially in the Sunbelt. "Gary tells you what he believes the truth is in his world, and my job is to be skeptical," says McCown. "But his ego is beyond anything I have ever met in my life. He absolutely refuses to acknowledge that there's anybody in the world who is as smart as he is."

And despite almost twenty years in the job, the commissioner in some ways remains a hockey outsider. Taking over from Ziegler, he immediately grasped some of his predecessor's shortcomings, instituting a personal policy of never leaving his seat at the rink until the game is over. But other Bettman diktats, like his refusal to cheer or applaud the action, lest he be perceived as biased, feed the widely held belief that he doesn't really know or care about the game. Then there are the inevitable missteps. In the spring of 2008, Bettman went on New York's WFAN radio to talk about the NHL playoffs. One of the hosts, Chris "Mad Dog" Russo, mentioned that he had been fascinated by a vignette showing on the NHL Network about "Ace" Bailey, Eddie Shore, and the origin of the All-Star Game. The first such exhibition in Toronto in 1934, he explained, was a benefit for Bailey, a Leafs forward who had almost died after Shore, a Boston defenceman who defined truculence, hit him from behind, sending him to the ice and fracturing his skull. Bailey never played again. That was the point at which Bettman jumped in and added his two cents: "And the tragic end to that story is he, Ace Bailey, was on one of the planes on 9/11." Mad Dog and his co-host marvelled at that tidbit, wondering what a man that old was doing flying that day. And back at NHL headquarters, staffers who were listening to the broadcast picked their jaws up off of the floor. Garnet "Ace" Bailey, a winner of two Stanley Cups as a player with the Bruins in the early 1970s and the director of pro scouting for the LA Kings, was one of the unfortunates aboard United Airlines Flight 175 when it crashed into the South Tower of the World Trade Center, but he wasn't the same guy. Shore's victim Irvine "Ace" Bailey, who went on to work as a timekeeper at Maple Leaf Gardens for more than forty-five years, died of natural causes at the age of eighty-eight in 1992.

The gaffe became the subject of much merriment around the league, but received surprisingly little coverage in the press. Perhaps that's because many hockey reporters have learned discretion is the better part of valour when it comes to Bettman and his NHL lieutenants. According to one former league executive, NHL head office began officially "keeping score" during the first lockout, following a suggestion made by some outside consultants who had previously helped Bill Clinton win the White House. Since then, the doling out of inside dope and juicy gossip from New York has been tightly controlled, directed only toward sympathetic ears. And media members who habitually refuse to play nicely can sometimes find themselves totally frozen out. Russ Conway, the longtime Boston Bruins beat writer for the Lawrence, Massachusetts, *Eagle Tribune*, was almost single-handedly responsible for the downfall and eventual prosecution of Alan Eagleson. His investigative work,

TOP: *A young and very enthusiastic Gary Bettman dons an NHL sweater for the first—and probably last—time at his December 1992 unveiling as commissioner. Bruce McNall (L), the chairman of the board of governors, and Gil Stein (R), the outgoing league president, were almost as giddy.* (Bruce Bennet/The Associated Press)

LEFT: *Bettman looking a lot less thrilled to be the centre of attention prior to the 2010 Hockey Hall of Fame induction ceremony.* (Matthew Manor/ HHOF Images)

RIGHT: *It pays to have friends in high places, at least for Prime Minister Stephen Harper, who seems to spend as much time at NHL rinks as in the House of Commons.* (Courtesy of the NHL)

BELOW: *Pressing the flesh—and the NHL's bid for tax breaks and government subsidies—during a 1999 meeting with John Manley, then Canada's minister of industry.* (Kevin Frayer/The Canadian Press)

LEFT: *Wayne Gretzky, still the only hockey player most Americans have ever heard of, did his part to hype the debut of the NHL on the Fox network back in 1995.* (Ron Tom/Courtesy of Fox Sports)

MIDDLE: *Hockey got the full football treatment, including animated robots duking it out before commercial breaks.* (Courtesy of Fox Sports)

BELOW: *American viewers liked the comet tails produced by Fox Trax, but to hockey purists the electronic puck was proof that Bettman was out to ruin the game.* (Donald Waller/ Courtesy of Fox Sports)

TOP: *The relationship between Bettman and Bob Goodenow (R), the executive director of the NHLPA, went from bad to worse over the course of two lockouts. The settlement in July 2005 barely merited a handshake.* (Tibor Kolley/ *The Globe and Mail*)

ABOVE: *Players such as Trevor Linden, the president of the NHLPA, and Brendan Shanahan, a member of the bargaining committee, weren't exactly overjoyed with the salary cap.* (Tobin Grimshaw/The Canadian Press)

TOP: *The outdoor Winter Classic games have been a hit with fans and viewers, especially the 2010 edition that pitted Sidney Crosby (L) and the Penguins against the Washington Capitals and Alex Ovechkin.* (Keith Srakocic/The Associated Press)

ABOVE: *But the memory of lost franchises still rankles Canadians, like Nordiques fans who travelled en masse to a December 2010 game between the Islanders and Atlanta Thrashers to press the case for a return to Quebec City.* (Kathy Kmonicek/The Associated Press)

TOP: *Donald Fehr kept the baseball owners at bay for close to thirty years. Now in charge of the NHLPA, he may prove to be Bettman's toughest foe.* (Darryl Dyck/The Canadian Press)

ABOVE: *As deputy commissioner, Bill Daly seems to have a hand in everything, but he says it's Bettman who sets the tone and agenda.* (Nathan Denette/The Canadian Press)

TOP: *Mark Chipman (R) figured out how to bring the Jets back to Winnipeg and make Gary Bettman happy: keep your mouth shut and do what you're told.* (David Lipnowski/The Canadian Press)

ABOVE: *The commissioner said that returning one of Canada's lost teams was an opportunity to right a wrong. And for once, grateful fans embraced him.* (John Woods/The Canadian Press)

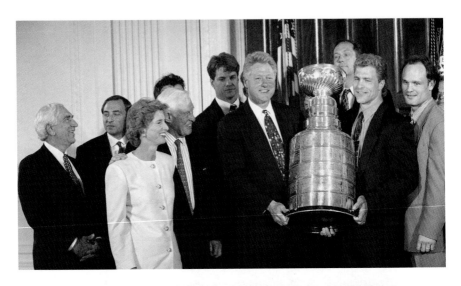

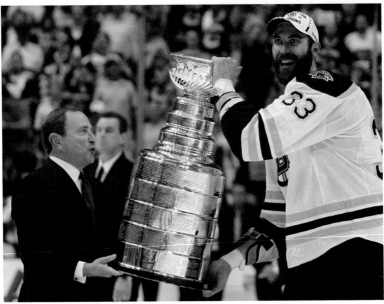

TOP: *A tradition was born when fans booed Bettman as he presented the Cup to the New Jersey Devils in June 1995. But things were a little cheerier the next month at the White House with Bill Clinton and a young Scott Stevens.* (J. Scott Applewhite/The Associated Press)

ABOVE: *If the Boston Bruins and captain Zdeno Chara ever capture Stanley again, the commissioner might want to bring along a stepladder.* (Jonathan Hayward/The Canadian Press)

which culminated in the 1995 book *Gross Misconduct*, earned him not only the accolades of his peers but also the 1999 Elmer Ferguson Memorial Award for bringing honour to his profession and the game, and automatic enshrinement in the Hockey Hall of Fame. Still, later that same season, he found himself without credentials for the Stanley Cup Final after writing a series of articles criticizing the quick, and effectively career-ending, suspension Bettman handed Marty McSorley after his attack on Vancouver's Donald Brashear. "The implication was quite clear," says Conway, now retired and living in Florida. "I had been covering the Final since 1970 and suddenly they didn't have room for me." After a couple of nasty go-arounds with a junior PR staffer, Conway called Bill Daly and mused aloud about writing a book on the inner workings of the NHL. Bettman himself soon phoned and apologized, suggesting there had been a mix-up. But when the league eventually found him a spot in the press box for the matchup between the New Jersey Devils and the Dallas Stars, Conway was so angry that he refused to take it: "I stuck up for Marty and they tried to punish me. I just thought it was wrong."

With the advent of the internet and the devolution of the scoop to 140-character tweets, today's reporters, tasked to be fast rather than thorough, might even be more vulnerable to coercion. Or blandishments—a good pipeline to the league is the easiest path to a fat TV contract. "Not only is there pressure, there is an absolute temptation to sell your ability to think for yourself for the ability to be told," says the CBC's MacLean. "You'll live the high life, you'll be travelling, staying in five-star hotels, and be famous and making good money."

But the NHL's control of the message obviously falls well short of absolute. "I've never minded critical press as long as it's accurate," says Bettman. "Just don't make up things I said to fit your needs."

And while the commissioner allows he has no problem getting Canada's prime minister or senior US legislators on the phone, he can't stop fans from going online to blog or tweet about how big an idiot he is.

Bettman is undeniably powerful, but sadly for him and the NHL owners, mostly in the place where hockey requires no help and can hardly grow bigger. As a recent study by the University of Toronto's Mowat Centre pointed out, the NHL's record ratings in the United States during the opening round of the 2010 Stanley Cup playoffs not only paled numerically to the viewing figures in Canada, they neatly underlined the gulf between a fringe sport and a national pastime. "Given the difference in population between the two countries, the results suggest that Canadians outside of Quebec were roughly 40 times as likely as Americans to have been watching a national broadcast of NHL hockey during the first week of April. And the French-language hockey audience was proportionally even bigger: A Quebecer was as much as 90 times as likely as an American to have been watching a hockey game."

In the United States, hockey has historically been, and largely remains, a regional game. In the 2010–11 season, the league's five largest local TV audiences were found in Pittsburgh, Chicago, Detroit, Boston, and Philadelphia. While the five smallest were in Tampa Bay, Columbus, Phoenix, Atlanta, and Miami, where on an average night just 3000 households tuned into a Panthers game. According to the Fan Cost Index, a ranking produced by an Illinois sports-marketing firm, a night at the rink for a family of four in Dallas—including tickets, parking, hot dogs, souvenirs, and a couple of beers—cost US$223.78. In Manhattan, it cost $393.80. The three most expensive NHL cities are, in ascending order, Winnipeg, Montreal, and Toronto, where the same evening out would set a family back $626.45. And the law of supply and demand remains painfully evident even in the post-season. During the second round of the 2011 playoffs, tickets to home games for the Lightning could be purchased from StubHub, a resale site, for as little as $33. In Philadelphia, the lowest asking price was $75. In Boston, it was $120, and in Vancouver, $189.

The major American TV networks, resigned to the fate of having to chase after ever-shrinking audiences, no longer seem to care if the game plays in Peoria anyway, just so long as it plays somewhere. As negotiations for the NBC deal progressed in the spring of 2011, it became clear that the NHL was preparing to leave the country's eighth largest media market, Atlanta, and perhaps its twelfth largest, Phoenix, as well. But Ken Schanzer says the issue never came up at the table: "Would we rather have an American city than a Canadian one? Sure, but neither of those markets had embraced hockey."

And these days, the NHL seems more intent on mining its existing fan base than expanding it. When John Collins joined the league, he arranged for the advertising firm Young & Rubicam to assess the strengths and weaknesses of hockey's brand with the same eye they usually turn on dish soap or toothpaste. Their key finding was that followers of hockey were far more tribal than fans of pro baseball, football, or basketball. If their team wasn't playing, they rarely paid attention to the games, even in the post-season. It was a mindset that mirrored the sport's geography, and Collins set about trying to change it. "What we wanted to do was create a halo over the top of the whole business that would get our fans not to trade their passion for a team, but at least watch more hockey," he says. The Winter Classic was the first step in that plan to build scale in the United States by creating an event that felt special regardless of who was playing. The second step was to make highlights and games as widely available as possible on digital platforms. "They weren't getting it on *SportsCenter*, so we thought if we were able to give our fans the kind of content they wanted, we'd be able to change their behaviour," says Collins. Make them watch more TV, buy more things, and therefore be more attractive to advertisers, bettering the bottom line even if the game doesn't grow. The ultimate goal is to make people fans of the league, rather than its teams. "That's the reason the NFL is the NFL. Nobody ever cancelled their Super Bowl party because they didn't like who was playing." The dream at the beginning of Bettman's tenure—to transplant hockey to the sunny climes where so many Americans cluster—isn't dead, but it has been deferred.

Las Vegas, Nevada, is really the last large US market without a major-league sports team. And for a number of years it figured prominently in rumours about the NHL's expansion plans. Hollywood producer Jerry Bruckheimer and the Maloof family, owners of the NBA's Sacramento Kings, were among those supposedly vying to bring puck to Sin City. And when the league struck a deal in 2009 to move its annual end-of-season awards show from Toronto to the Maloof-controlled Palms Casino, it seemed like a prelude to something far bigger.

The Palms is well off the strip, but not the beaten track. It's where Charlie Sheen staged one of his forty-eight-hour-long hooker and blow bacchanalias just before his career implosion in the fall of 2010, renting the $40,000-a-night Playboy suite, atop the aptly named Fantasy Tower (featuring an eight-foot circular bed, a Jacuzzi that seats forty, and, presumably, complimentary penicillin in the mini-bar). And for the two days a year the NHL is in town, it only gets weirder.

At the 2011 edition of the NHL Awards, the league had all of its most hallowed hardware on display just inside the front doors of the casino, a stone's throw away from the Wheel of Fortune slot machines. Grouped together in a tight circle atop tables covered in black fabric, the trophies—relics of simpler and cheaper times—didn't just look out of place, they seemed downright ugly. The Vezina, with its black-and-white reliquary photo of Georges, cheap wood base, and what appears to be a faithful silver replica of the altar at St. Peter's in Rome, excepting the puck and beaver, might have been taken from the display case of a small-town Legion. The Art Ross, with its peeling varnish and winners' names affixed to cheesy miniature hockey pucks, screams garage sale. And the Rocket Richard Trophy, which captures the Flying Frenchman hatching from some sort of silver space egg, suggests the involvement of a cult. The league's one truly elegant award—the Stanley Cup—sat at the centre of the mess, identified by two placards and largely ignored by the gamblers.

Bettman wandered through the casino, deep in conversation on his cell phone. The NHL's biggest stars, many of them still sporting cuts, shiners, and beards from the playoffs, drifted in, attracting little attention. And despite the presence of one certifiable celebrity—Jon Hamm, the star of *Mad Men* and a diehard fan of the St. Louis Blues—there weren't many fans willing to stand outside in the 39°C heat to seek autographs. Donny Osmond, still boyish and making thirty-five-year-old jokes about his sister Marie, presented the Jack Adams Award for coach of the year. Illusionist Criss Angel, dressed in a leather jacket with no shirt, gave out the Selke Trophy for the most defensive-minded forward. And two highly tanned women from a reality TV show about wives in Beverly Hills handed out the Lady Byng. It was all entertaining, but perhaps not for the right reasons.

A couple of weeks before the show, the latest efforts in Vegas to build an arena came to a screeching halt when the state legislature declined to endorse a bill that would have allowed three competing developers to begin the process of accessing public funding. Nevada, with an unemployment rate of close to 15 percent and 40,000 personal bankruptcies in 2011, was the last state in the union to officially climb out of the recession. And analysts predict that it will be 2015 before the job market rebounds. In Vegas itself, where housing values declined more than 60 percent, the recovery may take even longer. The day before the awards gala, the Maloofs, facing their own financial difficulties, lost control of the Palms. And Mayor Oscar Goodman, a longtime champion of an NHL team, didn't bother to turn up for the ceremony.

The next day's *Las Vegas Sun* carried a few photos and a column by ancient gossip maven Robin Leach. But by 11 A.M., all traces of pro hockey—banners, souvenir stands, trophies, and players—had disappeared from the hotel. And workers had changed the marquee outside in favour of the next attraction, Deep Purple in concert. The letters were twice as big as the ones they used for the NHL Awards.

The hard-won NBC deal gives the NHL more visibility than it has ever enjoyed on US television, and enough money that the league can now credibly claim to have separated itself from competitors like beach volleyball and arena football. But in many ways, hockey is still wandering in the desert—passionately followed by millions and largely ignored by everyone else. Will $200 million a season seem like an enormous bargain in ten years, or will it be another high-water mark for a sport that has often been on the cusp but never quite broken through? It took twenty years for Bettman to reach the mountaintop. But the land of milk and honey is still a good distance away.

6 Selling Hope

It wasn't just the sight that sickened, it was the sound; a percussive ring like a sledgehammer driving a spike that carried all the way up to the rafters of Montreal's Bell Centre. And now Max Pacioretty was lying face down on the ice, twitching.

The play had started innocently enough. A draw in the Habs' end that was won a little too cleanly by Boston's Gregory Campbell, with the puck flying back through his legs and skittering all the way to the far boards. Pacioretty, a fleet twenty-two-year-old Canadiens winger, got his stick on it first, chipping it past the oncoming defenceman Zdeno Chara. But when he tried to step around the Bruins captain the big man rode him into the boards and gave him an extra shove for good measure, propelling him helmet first into the glass partition between the players benches. Chara was looking down the rink when Pacioretty's head met a thinly padded stanchion at speed, stopping for the briefest of moments, then reversing directions like something out of an old Looney Tunes short. The 6-foot-9, 255-pound Slovak was given a five-minute major for interference and a game misconduct. Pacioretty, who remained unconscious for long minutes while the crowd at the rink and viewers at home anxiously held their breath, was taken to hospital where he was diagnosed with a severe concussion and a nondisplaced fracture in his neck. Had his head hit the stanchion faster, or at a slightly different angle, he could have easily been left paralyzed, or worse.

The NHL had trouble divining intent. The day after the March 8, 2011, incident, the league issued a press release saying it would levy no further discipline on Chara, a player who had never been suspended in the course of a thirteen-year career. Gary Bettman shrugged the hit off as a hazard of the trade. "It was a horrific injury, we're sorry that it happened in our fast-paced physical game, but I don't think whether or not supplemental discipline was imposed would change what happened," he told reporters, somehow working a marketing pitch into the middle of an expression of regret. As far as he was concerned the subject was closed, and the whole league was "extraordinarily comfortable" with the decision. But supporters of the Canadiens were not. At the behest of a local sports radio show, they flooded Montreal's 9-1-1 network with thousands of calls reporting that a crime had been committed at the Bell Centre (it got so bad that the authorities pleaded for people to stop, voicing fears that the system would collapse). The papers asked whether the commissioner had been the one who received a blow to the head, and demanded justice. Within a day, the provincial director of criminal prosecutions instructed the Montreal Police to open an official investigation. Public opinion was running solidly against the league. A poll for *Maclean's* magazine found that 91 percent of Quebecers were dissatisfied with Chara's punishment; nationally, 60 percent of Canadians said that they believed pro hockey had become more violent in recent years.

And it wasn't just the fans that were enraged. Geoff Molson, who along with his brothers Andrew, Justin, and some other partners had returned the Habs to the family fold in 2009, paying American businessman George Gillett more than $500 million for the team and the rink, posted a message on the club website. The NHL's decision "was a hard blow for both the players and fans of the Montreal Canadiens," he wrote. "It was one which shook the faith that we, as a community, have in this sport that we hold in such high regard." The franchise would lead the charge to clean up the game, he vowed, so that no other family would have to go through what Pacioretty's parents were then experiencing.

Calin Rovinescu, the CEO of Air Canada, went a step further. He had been watching his favourite team from the comfort of his Montreal living room that night and was soon on the phone to his marketing department, running white hot. The result was a strident letter to Bettman, copied to presidents of the other Canadian franchises, in which the airline threatened to sever its commercial relationship with the game. "While we support count-less sports, arts and community events, we are having difficulty rationalizing our sponsorship of hockey," it read. "Unless the NHL takes immediate actions with serious suspensions to the players in question to curtail these life threatening injuries, Air Canada will withdraw its sponsorship."

With its focus on punishment, the missive was perhaps more a product of the boss's unbridled love for the Canadiens than any deep commitment to corporate social responsibility, but it garnered a lot of attention. Other NHL sponsors in Canada were soon drawn into the fray about player safety. In that same national *Maclean's* poll, 70 percent of respondents said they supported the airline's position. And just 6 percent said they believed the league was doing a "very good" job of protecting its players. Michael Ignatieff, the leader of the federal opposition, urged Bettman to take action to clean up the sport before Parliament had to. Mario Lemieux, the former Pittsburgh Penguin star-turned-owner—still smarting from the loss of Sidney Crosby to a concussion three months before—weighed in, proposing a system of escalating fines for teams to go along with player suspensions. Several agents called for a total ban on blows to the head, whether deliberate or accidental. "Everybody acts like everything is OK. Well, it's not OK," said Ritch Winter, the Edmonton-based representative who counts Marian Hossa (who joined the ranks of head-shot victims during the 2012 playoffs) and Ryan Getzlaf as part of his stable. "I'm speaking as a father and a husband who doesn't want to attend a client's funeral. I don't want to be there."

For the briefest of moments, it seemed like a movement might be building—even within the game's more conservative constituencies—to eliminate on-ice thuggery. Then Bettman turned his guns on his critics and shut it down. The first target was Air Canada, whose public letter was greeted with a public warning. When he was buttonholed on the issue, Bettman flashed a cold smile and allowed that the airline had every right to direct its sponsorship dollars—local agreements with the six Canadian franchises plus $1.5 million a year for the naming rights to the home of the Maple Leafs—anywhere it wished. "Just like it's the prerogative of our clubs that fly on Air Canada to make other arrangements if they don't think Air Canada is giving them the appropriate level of service," he said, neatly calling $20-million-a-year worth of business with eleven different teams into question. From that point on, the airline refused to comment on the affair, abandoning its charge to fix the game for the good of its bottom line. And when the 2011–12 season opened, all its sponsorship deals were still in effect.

Geoff Molson, who had been canny enough to at least share his screed with NHL headquarters in New York before releasing it to the public—but then rashly failed to make all of the editorial changes that were suggested—won himself a blistering phone call from the commissioner. Eugene Melnyk, the owner of the Ottawa Senators, who had gone on a Toronto radio station espousing zero tolerance for goons, received a similarly pointed reminder of the need to keep ranks. And at a regularly scheduled meeting of general managers in Florida, Brian Burke, Bettman's old friend and defender, took on his colleagues from Montreal and Pittsburgh, suggesting that their respective owners needed to learn to keep their yaps shut. "It was typical Brian Burke," the Leafs executive later joked to reporters. "It had no impact but it was entertaining."

The commissioner then went into proactive mode, introducing a five-point plan to reduce head injuries. There would be a joint player and league committee to look at changes to equipment as well as a "blue ribbon" panel to look at the larger issue of concussions. Lemieux's suggested fines for teams and coaches were given the thumbs-up. Safety engineers would be dispatched to all thirty NHL rinks to assess the boards and glass. And a new protocol was put in place requiring players who had had their bell rung to at least leave the ice and be evaluated by a doctor.

It all fell far short of what many fans and observers had been demanding, but it was enough to dampen the fires. Ten days after the Chara incident, Montreal coach Jacques Martin reported that Pacioretty—already at home and apparently symptom free—might be back in the Habs lineup for the playoffs. (He returned to the ice in early April, but didn't receive medical clearance to play before the Canadiens bowed out in the first round to Boston.) The regular season drew to a close and the hunt for the Stanley Cup began. Despite a near tragedy, and the continuing absence of the game's biggest young star, Sidney Crosby, Bettman had managed to change the channel. Just like he had done so many times before.

SOME TRUTHS ARE SELF-EVIDENT, but it's still nice to see them in *The New York Times.* "Hockey and beer go together," Andy England, the executive vice-president and chief marketing officer of MillerCoors told the paper in February 2011. "Hockey fans are big beer drinkers. In fact, we have data that shows hockey fans are the biggest beer drinkers of any major sports league." The occasion was the announcement of the largest sponsorship in NHL history, a seven-year, US$375-million deal to make MillerCoors and its Canadian partner, Molson Coors, hockey's official brewers. The agreement, which was to begin after the playoffs ended in June, was worth more than twice as much as Anheuser-Busch and its corporate subsidiary Labatt were currently paying for the North American beer rights. And it nicely capped a record business cycle for the league.

In the 2009–10 season, the NHL had performed better than any of the other big four sports, with sponsorship spending on the league and individual teams up 20 percent and advertising buys increasing by 37 percent. In the United States, Bridgestone had signed a five-year extension to be hockey's official tire and the presenting sponsor of the Winter Classic. Honda and Gatorade also both re-upped on their deals. And Discover came aboard as the official credit card. The trend continued into the next season, with the insurer GEICO and McDonald's restaurants extending their deals. In Canada, Tim Hortons took over the Heritage Classic game. And Canadian Tire—which claims that 40 percent of the population shops at one of its 480 outlets every week—was on board to sell NHL gear and promote young stars like Jonathan Toews. A league that used to have to go begging for partners now had companies fighting to get a piece of the action ... literally.

A week after the Molson deal was announced, Labatt filed suit in Toronto asking the Ontario Superior Court to tear up the NHL's record-setting agreement with its rival. The company, which had held hockey's Canadian beer rights for almost thirteen years, accused the league of bad-faith dealings and breach of contract, claiming they had struck a deal to renew their sponsorship for another three years in the fall of 2010—at a much cheaper price. The legal challenge, which in contrast to the vast majority of commercial litigation in Canada sped through the courts in a matter of weeks, produced a small mountain of pleadings and affidavits. And much to the NHL's chagrin, it pulled back the veil on some of the league's most sensitive business dealings.

Labatt had been a league sponsor since 1998, when it paired with the CBC to put its name on the *Hockey Night in Canada* telecasts. But its past deals were a far cry from the big-dollar contract the company was now contesting. The five-year agreement signed in July 2002, for example, had the brewer paying annual rights fees that started at just $2.1 million Canadian and ramped up to $2.9 million (payments that would be reduced if one or more Canadian teams relocated to the States under a complicated formula that valued the Leafs and Habs far more than the Senators and Oilers). In addition, the company committed to spending $1.5 million a season on "NHL themed television and radio spots," print ads, and point-of-sale materials. The NHL Alumni Association got about $100,000 a year, and the league received 475 cases of beer annually to slake VIP thirst at special events like the All-Star Game, NHL Awards, and board of governors' meetings. The total value of the deal was just over $20 million, but only $12.5 million actually made it into league coffers.

When the sponsorship was renewed in 2008 (the first agreement was extended by a year because of the lockout), the rights fees increased to $3.75 million annually. Labatt also hiked the amount it would spend promoting both its beer and pro hockey to $4 million a season. And there was a new wrinkle—a commitment to buy at least $3.5 million more in advertising spots from the Canadian broadcast rights holders CBC, TSN, RDS, and XM Satellite Radio. The three-year package was worth $33.75 million, but this time just a third of the money was actually going to the league and its teams.

Neither deal was particularly easy to close. Kyle McMann, the NHL's lead negotiator in both cases, provided an affidavit outlining the endless frustrations he and his colleagues experienced as they tried to pin down the brewer. In 2008, the league had initially been looking for $8.7 million in annual rights fees and a five-year span. Labatt's counterproposal was $3 million annually over three years. Talks broke off, and the NHL sounded out Molson about the beer rights but found little enthusiasm for a big new commitment in the midst of the worst recession in a generation. They returned to the table with Labatt. It took several months more to agree on the final numbers and terms for the contract, and some outstanding points, like the language of the renewal clause, never did get sorted out.

With this experience in mind, the NHL started negotiations for a new agreement almost a year before the suds package was set to expire at the end of the 2010–11 season. Their initial pitch asked for a five-year deal with an average annual rights fee of $5 million, broadcast "spends" of $3 million each on CBC and TSN, and a further $4 million for other ads and promotions. Per the terms of the original 2002 agreement, once talks began Labatt had an exclusive sixty-day window to strike a bargain before the league could shop itself around to other brewers. Although neither side seemed to be in a particular hurry, and instead concentrated on side deals for the beer rights to the upcoming season's opening "Faceoff" festival and the 2011 outdoor Heritage Classic game in Calgary.

It was late September when Labatt made its first counterproposal, a three-year deal offering about $1 million less a season in rights fees and $2 million less in broadcast buys. The NHL, busy with the start of the season, agreed to extend the negotiating window and finally responded in mid-October. The two sides were working toward the middle ground on the money, but were hung up on a much smaller detail—freebie promotional items. As part of its sponsorship agreements, the league usually requires its partners to promote the brand by giving away team-themed merchandise. The T-shirts or toques rarely cost more than a couple of dollars each to produce, including a cut of 10 to 15 percent that flows back to the league. The NHL wanted to be able to count on a minimum $300,000 a year in such royalty revenues from its beer deal, but Labatt was now offering at least $1 million, and that was setting off alarms back in New York. "Labatt's proposal to raise the minimum so greatly caused us serious concern that Labatt would flood the market with NHL branded merchandise," said McMann's affidavit. "Thus, the NHL had to be sure that it protected its retail business." Why buy a T-shirt when they come for free with a two-four?

All the same, the talks remained friendly and seemed to be moving forward. In one of the emails submitted to the court, McMann invited his Labatt counterparts to watch a mid-October Leafs–Rangers game at the Air Canada Centre and "toast our new partnership ... or at least continue to negotiate while holding steak knives." His boss, Keith Wachtel, the NHL's senior vice-president of sales, wrote to tell them that the league was committed to getting the deal done with its valued partner. And after a November 12 meeting, when a handshake agreement was reached on the freebies issue, congratulatory messages flowed back and forth. Letters of intent were drafted, and work began on the formal contract for a three-year sponsorship worth a total of $37.8 million: $11.7 million in rights fees to the NHL and the remainder in promotion and advertising. The increase was modest, although the league would have been happy to trumpet the sponsorship as yet another business victory. Then somebody came along offering a lot more money.

Wachtel had started negotiations to renew the US beer deal with Anheuser-Busch in mid-November, but it wasn't going well. It took the giant brewer more than two months to respond to the league's first proposal—three years with an annual rights fee of $4.3 million, about the same as the NHL was getting for the much smaller Canadian market. And their counteroffer of $2.55 million a year was downright insulting. Sensing that things were heading sideways, the league put out feelers to MillerCoors, the country's second-largest beer maker, just after New Year's via a discreet John Collins call to Genesco, a Dallas-based sports marketing firm that arranges marriages between big business and pro sports. In an email to Miller's Andy England, John Tatum, the head of Genesco, recapped the conversation: the NHL was disappointed in Anheuser-Busch's support of its key events like the Winter Classic, and worried that hockey was becoming a distant priority for the brewer, behind the NFL, Major League Baseball, and even Ultimate Fighting. Their sixty-day exclusive negotiating period ended on January 17, and Collins was eager to meet with MillerCoors immediately thereafter.

A couple of weeks later, England wrote back to Tatum: "This still a live topic? I've got an idea ..." A meeting was quickly arranged to coincide with a global sales and marketing summit that the beer maker was holding in Chicago at the end of the month. Some top Molson Coors executives were asked to sit in, since they actually knew something about hockey.

On January 26, over lunch at the Westin Hotel, Collins and Wachtel pitched the brewer on the virtues of sponsoring hockey in the United States. England's response took their breath away—MillerCoors was interested, and so was Molson Coors, but only in the North American–wide rights. The companies had done some homework, and through sources with the Edmonton Oilers, Ottawa Senators, and league headquarters in New York they had learned that a deal was done with Labatt tying up the Canadian market until 2014. They thought they were engaging in some long-range planning. But Collins indicated that there might be wiggle room and asked for twenty-four hours to check things out.

At 2:32 P.M. that afternoon, Wachtel sent an email to Kyle McMann in Toronto. "Which lawyer drafted Labatt? Will call you shortly," was all it said. Collins got on the phone to Bettman. The commissioner must have shared his excitement, because the next day Collins informed England that there was no impediment to immediately starting talks on a deal for both countries. Miller and Molson didn't exactly take his word, asking instead for a legal indemnity in which the NHL would confirm that the rights really were available and agree to cover their legal costs if Labatt sued. MillerCoors was particularly suspicious of the league's motives. In the summer of 2010, when Major League Baseball said its deal with Anheuser-Busch was dead, MillerCoors entered into some heavy negotiations only to see its rival sue, claiming breach of contract. Commissioner Bud Selig quickly capitulated and signed an extension with the makers of Bud. A similar thing happened with the Boston Red Sox, who claimed that they, too, were looking to change beer sponsors, and then jumped back into bed with Anheuser. In both cases, MillerCoors felt that it had been used as a stalking horse to drive up the price. And they were afraid the NHL might be engaged in the same game. But the promise of legal protection convinced them that the hockey opportunity was legit, and everyone reconvened in Chicago on January 28.

It only took four days to flesh out the deal. The two brewers agreed to pay $13 million a year for the North American rights through the 2017–18 season—giving the league a total of $91 million—and committed to a further $283.5 million in promotional "spends." The majority of the rights money— $56 million—would be coming from the Canadian company. Ditto with the broadcast and activation amounts. But it hardly mattered to the NHL. Any way you sliced it, the $375-million sponsorship was the most lucrative one the league had ever landed. A contract was signed on February 8, and that afternoon Wachtel called his counterpart at Labatt's Toronto offices and told him that the NHL was no longer interested in their $38 million.

To say that the news was a shock is an understatement. Lawyers for Labatt were busy reviewing the contract to extend the sponsorship arrangement, and the brewer was in daily contact with the league about a variety of promotional activities and commercials for the current season and beyond. The company was also in the midst of changing its hockey beer from Bud Light to Budweiser, a rebranding exercise that cost more than $5 million. The biggest blow, however, would be the one to the beer maker's future sales. "The importance of the NHL to beer marketing in Canada cannot be overstated," Kyle Norrington, a national marketing director for Labatt, reported in his affidavit. "Canada has a deep psychological connection to hockey. The loyalty of the fans to Canada's game is deep. It is a lifelong passion." Piggybacking on the national game enabled the brewer to wrap itself in the flag and reach millions of thirsty young men. The NHL sponsorship was "the single greatest opportunity to grow Labatt's share in Canada," he said. "There is no other substitute for this national access to these consumers."

The NHL's position was that Labatt got what it deserved for dragging its feet on the renewal and that there had been plenty of sneakiness on the brewer's side of the table, too. During the first couple months of negotiations, the company hid its plans from the NHL to switch its hockey brand to Bud for fear the league would ask for more money. (Budweiser is the best-selling beer in Canada, with about 13 percent of the market, two-and-a-half times Bud Light's share.) Labatt negotiators had also tried to speed up the process at one point by suggesting they were being pressured to quickly conclude a deal by the parent company's "global procurement" guys in New York, which was a lie since no such office actually existed.

The initial court ruling, handed down at the beginning of the Stanley Cup Final in June, found that Labatt had indeed struck an agreement back in the fall and ordered the league to live up to its handshake. But the matter was quickly appealed, and at the NHL Awards in Las Vegas—a week before the old beer agreement officially expired—it was Molson Canadian that was being served at the after-party around the Palms Casino pool. The show of confidence wasn't misplaced. In mid-July, the Ontario Court of Appeal overturned the decision on the grounds that the judge had gone further than even the plaintiff had asked (Labatt hadn't actually argued that its deal was binding). And just before the puck dropped on the 2011–12 season, the brewer's attempt to advance that theory was quashed. The NHL did have the legal right to open talks with Molson, said the ruling, although the presiding judge showed little sympathy for any of the parties. Knowing that the matter was destined to end up in court, the league and its new partners had taken a calculated risk to burn Labatt and won, he wrote, while the beer maker fell victim to its own negotiating strategy. There is no honour among thieves, and the same rule might apply to marketers.

As it turned out, the February 2011 Heritage Classic outdoor game in Calgary was the last big collaboration between the league and its sponsor of thirteen years. The rights for the event didn't cost Labatt much—just $225,000 plus $15,000 worth of beer for the NHL's "internal hosting" needs, and the use of a Budweiser sound stage according to an agreement filed as part of the court challenge. And in return they received plentiful promotion: two camera-visible ads on the rink boards, four thirty-second spots on the CBC telecast, and a "live look-in" during the telecast to a bar filled with people drinking their beer—a product placement valued at $30,000. The company also got banner ads on NHL.com and team websites and pouring rights and signs within McMahon Stadium. And there were perks, including a hundred tickets and ten VIP passes to the game, and an hour of ice time so that Labatt executives and key clients could play some shinny and soak up the atmosphere.

The deal also required the brewer to produce a new NHL-themed commercial to debut during the game. On January 26, the day that Collins was in Chicago talking to Miller and Molson, there were a number of phone calls and emails about its proposed script. Like most pro sports, hockey exercises rigid control over its brand and image, and even longtime sponsors have to navigate an approval process for their ads and promotions that covers everything from the colour quality of team logos to "NHL senior management exposure." Getting the thumbs-up on the new spot to introduce Bud as a hockey brand was proving to be complicated. The idea of portraying fans watching games in three different bars—one in a small town, another in a big city, and the third at a local rink—was fine, but the league had a lot of concerns about the finer details. The TVs on the walls should be made by LG, another NHL sponsor, or completely generic. Sticks being carried by the rec players would have to be Easton, Sher-Wood, or Reebok brand, and a helmet placed on a stuffed deer's head should also come from an official supplier. A bubble hockey game would also have to be NHL approved. The crowds cheering in the bars shouldn't be wearing the jersey of any Canadian franchises—lest rival fans get turned off. And the game footage should be of US clubs and shot from a high angle so that no players were identifiable (unless Labatt wanted to get additional rights from the NHLPA). The league suggested including a shot of a wood plaque with pucks from all thirty teams to help with "collective use." It even wanted a say over the team-themed bottles of Bud in the bar fridge—a shot that lasted no more than a second—to ensure an appropriate mix of US and Canadian clubs. They also warned that use of the Habs logo was "very unlikely based on ownership."

The version that went to air less than a month later incorporated almost all of the suggestions. Starting with bar staff wiping down tables and setting up chairs to the sounds of a slow guitar riff, it keys on a theme of Saturday night anticipation as fans flood in and exchange manly slaps on the shoulder while glasses fill with beer. The music builds to a crescendo, the Chicago Blackhawks score, and the party begins, all high-fives and clinking bottles. "Great games are waiting. Why not grab some Buds," reads the tag line. The commercial didn't seem that remarkable. But a few months after it started airing, it gained some notoriety on the internet. With the return of an NHL franchise to Winnipeg, fans began to marvel at how prescient the spot seemed, with a shot of a framed Jets sweater on a wall, another team logo appearing on the deer's helmet, and one of the rec players carrying a Manitoba Moose hockey bag. Had pissed-off Labatt insiders been trying to spoil Gary Bettman's surprise?

In June, the brewer snatched up the rights to become the local sponsor of the reborn Winnipeg Jets and sell its products at the MTS Centre. Similar agreements were also quickly reached with the

Vancouver Canucks and Calgary Flames. All told, Anheuser-Busch now has direct deals with twenty-four of the league's thirty clubs, able to flog its suds at their games and advertise its puck connections within each team's 75-kilometre territory. Molson refuses to comment on whether its sales in either the United States or Canada have actually increased since making the deal. But they've had plenty to say about a Bud "Playoff Payoff" contest that debuted during the 2012 Stanley Cup run, promising "tickets for life" to one lucky Canadian hockey fan, calling it an ambush. The NHL even issued an official statement saying it could offer no assurance that the winner will ever be attending its games. As it turns out, the fine print in the contest disclaimer never explicitly promised tickets to major-league hockey games, and it reserved the right to pay out the prize in cash—$250,000—rather than seats. It's all part of a new marketing strategy for the brewer that taps into the good feelings surrounding the sport, without ever mentioning Bettman's league. There is no marketing substitute for hockey in Canada, but there are plenty of ways to stick it to the NHL.

THE SCOREBOARD IS FLASHING and the arena rock music is thumping inside the Air Canada Centre, but the stands are empty. And unlike most nights when the Leafs play, there's actually something happening down between the boards. More than 100 display booths crowd the rink floor, all of them stuffed with officially licensed pro-hockey merchandise. The NHL Exchange is an annual summer trade show that gives clubs and retailers a chance to assess what kind of hockey tchotchkes they want to flog to fans in the coming season. There are team-themed baby soothers, sippy cups, and onesies. Toys, T-shirts, and plush likenesses of stars like Sidney Crosby, Jonathan Toews, and Henrik Sedin. One company offers a complete array of birthday party supplies for every NHL franchise. Another has official team garden gnomes. Club ties, cuff-links, airplane pillows, cell phone covers, and office furniture are all available. There is even a line of toasters that will scorch the logo of your favourite team onto your favourite bread. All that is missing are coffins, though surely not for long—Eternal Image, a Michigan funeral-products firm, already offers MLB-endorsed team caskets and has expressed interest in branching out to hockey.

The big boys like Reebok and New Era are present with their sweaters and hats, but many of the exhibitors are mom-and-pop operations—or at least started out that way. Angela Sparling and her husband, Brad, originally ran Mustang Drinkware—purveyors of team mugs, glasses, and hundred-ounce beer tubes attached to goalie masks—out of their garage in London, Ontario. A licence with Hockey Canada led to a deal with the NHL, then a contract with Vancouver 2010 saw them produce all of the giveaway Olympic glasses for Petro-Canada's gas stations. Now they have a 30,000-square-foot warehouse and agreements to supply NHL souvenirs to chains like Walmart and Shoppers Drug Mart. Old Time Sports, which makes throwback-style hoodies, jackets, and weathered-looking ball caps, was started in a Boston-area basement by Eric Magnuson, a former New York Rangers draft pick, and his two brothers. (Hall of Famer Adam Oates, his college teammate at Rensselaer Polytechnic Institute in upstate New York, is also a partner.) Their original concept—shirts with cartoons of brawling players, think Andy Capp without the rugby ball or wife beating—was spiked by the league. But they came up with some subtler tough-guy designs, and in the 2010–11 season did close to $20 million of business in the United States and Canada. "If somebody gets traded, we'll have product with their new team and number the next day," says brother Bob, the company president. "Hockey is 99 percent of our business. It's all we're focused on."

Such tales fit nicely with the plucky and tradition-heavy image the league has worked so hard to create for itself in recent years; hockey is a sport that hopes to get bigger by pretending to be small. In a luxury box overlooking the rink floor, Brian Jennings, NHL executive vice-president of marketing, reads aloud with gusto the entirety of the framed league creed that hangs on the wall:

> We don't own the game of hockey—we serve it.
> We protect it, we guide it, we bring it to the
>   world.
> We are the proud stewards of a 90 plus year
>   heritage on ice.
> It's a game we play like champions,
> be it on the backyard rink in Red Deer, or in a
>   place we call "The Gardens".
> It's a game that gives meaning to the word *team*,
> where a star player can be just as famous for his
>   assists
> as he is for his goals.
> It's a game we get up at 4 A.M. to play,
> and where we mourn for months when we lose.
>
> To serve the game means to hoist it high, as if it
>   were The Cup itself.
> We clear the ice for hometown heroes, future stars
>   and living legends.
> And we reserve a place in the rafters for those
>   who have made their mark.
>
> This is a league with a respect for the past that
>   propels us into a great future.
>
> It's a league full of legends that have bred a whole
>   new crop of players, hungrier, and more deter-
>   mined, than ever.

The best in the world, who were born to play,
    who live for the game,
live every shift, and have us all wondering:

Is this the year a team records only 7 losses all
    season?
Is this the year a defenseman scores 140 points?
Is this the year someone scores 50 in 38? In 37?
    In 36?

Watch. See what happens. Be there to cheer when
    history is made.
Whose fate will change when The Cup changes
    hands?
The players, the fans, entire cities.
Why? Because The Cup changes everything.

We've gone back to the rule book. Made things
    tougher.
Playing in the NHL now demands more skill
    than ever before.
You're going to see things you've never seen
    before.

And we've got the players who can do it.

This is the NHL. This is hockey.

It's stirring stuff, even without the accompanying strains of
Guns N' Roses wailing over the Air Canada Centre sound system.
And every heartfelt word of the NHL's mission statement was
written by one of the world's biggest advertising agencies. Coming
out of the lost 2004–5 season, the league desperately needed to
reconnect with its disgruntled fans and reintroduce the game to an

American sporting culture that had got on just fine in its absence. On the ice, the transformation was accomplished via the changes that Red Wings forward Brendan Shanahan had brainstormed with other players, coaches, GMs, and television executives in the midst of the labour dispute—a crackdown on hooking and holding, limits to the size of goalie equipment, allowing the two-line pass, and the introduction of the shootout—a bunch of rule tweaks that promised more and better action. Off the ice, the redemption was to come through rebranding. Bettman had obsessed about the issue during the lockout, charting the league's comeback as meticulously as he had planned for its labour war. The meetings were endless. "We wanted to put our players in a heroic position, to celebrate the past and make that connection to the future," says Jennings, a chatty New Yorker who tends to refer to people in hockey nickname fashion, adding "er" or "y" to their last names, even if they never played. "We were going to be doing things differently and bigger and bolder than before."

The makeover started with the league's look. The shield was updated, and the orange-and-black colour scheme was replaced with white and silver to evoke ice and the Stanley Cup. The letters *N-H-L*, which had slanted downwards since 1917, were reoriented in the other direction. "Ninety-five percent of the world's successful brands have the words in their logos in ascension," says Jennings. (A stat which might be true, but ignores the examples of the NFL, NBA, Major League Baseball, and English Premier League Soccer, which all display their names horizontally.)

But striking the right tone with consumers wasn't so easy. The league's first attempt at reinvention was downright laughable; a series of commercials produced by the Los Angeles agency Conductor—used to promoting Hollywood blockbusters like *Spiderman 2*—that sought to paint hockey players as mystical gladiators. The initial "My NHL" spot opened with a quote from Sun Tzu, the ancient Chinese general: "A clever warrior is one who not only wins, but excels at winning with ease." Then it cut to a shirtless man meditating in a dressing room filled with candles. Before long, a buxom woman arrives to drape shoulder pads and a sweater over his head while he stares Zenlike into the middle distance. Ready for battle, he takes the ice in a darkened arena, and then does a lot of vaguely hockey-like things in slow motion to swelling *Lord of the Rings*–style music. The tag lines referenced "The Sound" and "The Fury" of the game, with no apparent knowledge of Faulkner, or Act 5, Scene 5 of Shakespeare's *Macbeth*: "It is a tale told by an idiot, full of sound and fury. Signifying nothing."

Bettman defends the trial-and-error approach as being all he could do at the time. The NHL he inherited was still in many ways stuck in the 1970s; a corporate entity that organized the schedule, assigned the game officials, and didn't do much else. The other majors had evolved quickly through the 1980s, but hockey, run by a few highly opinionated old-school owners, hadn't kept pace. And it took a long time to change that. "You couldn't do it by throwing a light switch," says the commissioner. "There were a series of small steps that you had to take to build the foundation before you could get bigger steps. It required changing the culture of the business, and the business of the game." And getting the right people in the right places.

When John Collins joined the league in late 2006, he immediately ordered a rethinking of the promotional strategy. As a starting point, Young & Rubicam (Y&R), whom he had dealt with extensively during his time at the NFL, were brought in to map out the negatives and positives associated with the NHL brand. Once those results came back, the firm suggested using the findings as the basis for an inspirational creed, like the one they had recently crafted for the struggling auto giant Ford. The manifesto so pleased Bettman that he ordered up copies to be placed in every NHL rink. And from that moment on, the marketing emphasis for the game has been on hockey's power to unify rather than divide and its links to tradition, even in nontraditional markets. "It's the classic definition of a brand," enthuses Jennings. "It's a trust, it's a pledge. It's a promise that you are going to meet or exceed your customers' expectations."

Chris Jordan, the president of Y&R Canada and a former marketing executive with the CBC and Coca-Cola, helped oversee the process. His first impression was that the NHL, run out of Manhattan but doing well over half of its business in Canada, sorely needed to trade American-style hubris for a more humble brand of confidence. (A notion echoed by Collins, who for his first few months on the job used to delight the league's northern sponsors and partners by introducing himself as "the latest New York asshole here to tell Canadians how they feel about hockey.") The NHL brand scored highly as fun, traditional, and authentic with consumers on both sides of the border, but it was also seen as arrogant and somewhat distant. And even a couple of years after the lockout, there was plenty of lingering resentment toward Bettman and the league among hardcore fans. Not enough to make them stop watching, but sufficient antipathy to dull their enthusiasm. Those were the people the NHL needed to worry about most. "Until you satisfy your core, you don't go after new users," says Jordan. Taking the focus off the business of hockey—and the commissioner, who had come to symbolize the money and strife—and trying to turn it back toward the game and its heritage was the first step. So Y&R's initial campaign featured a host of past and present stars asking a simple question pulled right from the creed: Is this the year? It pleased sponsors and consumers enough that the league has since returned to the well two more times for spots that focus on how "history will be made" and "the Cup changes everything."

It's a simple and straightforward approach that celebrates the things that make hockey different, rather than trying to suggest that it's the icy equivalent of football or basketball. Or some trendy gravity-defying extension of the X Games. Collins likes to describe it as a constant search for authenticity. The relationship between hockey fans and their sport is very different from the NFL and football fans he says: "In hockey, there's this idea of *The Game*. Respect for the game, the love of the game. It's a deeper connection." And in Canada, where the sport crosses from passion to obsession, it's even more fraught. Not only is the audience exponentially larger—26.5 million people, or 80 percent of the country's population, tuned in to watch the gold-medal game in men's hockey at the 2010 Vancouver Games—it is highly demanding and perpetually on guard against all slights, real or perceived. "It's something that Gary educated me about on the first day," says Collins. "He said, 'You have to watch it, you have to feel it. You're going to get burned by it, and you're just going to have to live with it.'" A lesson the commissioner had learned through bitter experience, but still sometimes finds difficult to put into practice.

But as it turns out, avid fans do have their advantages, and chief among them is that they spend a lot more money. Per the league's reckoning, its most dedicated followers—roughly 13 million Americans and 6 million Canadians, overwhelmingly male—each attend a minimum of four or five a games a season and watch the NHL on TV at least once every week. What's more, compared to other sports fans they tend to be more affluent (average household income is over $100,000), better educated (70 percent attended college or university), and more tech savvy. Factor in hockey's unusually high number of "displaced" partisans—nearly 40 percent live outside the home market, state, or province of the team they support and must therefore plunk down more cash to keep up with their team—and it all adds up to an enticing demographic for advertisers. A smart, well-off, and in many cases captive bunch of eighteen to forty-nine year olds.

Even the so-called casual NHL fans—27 million of them in the States and 7 million more in Canada by the league's numbers—tend to rate hockey above all other sports that they follow. And marketing research suggests the game's appeal to those less knowledgeable consumers is even more directly related to its rugged and tough "warrior" aspects than among its hardcore fans. In other words, not only are the casual fans not turned off by on-ice thuggery, it's what attracted them in the first place. Which perhaps explains why the NHL is so reluctant to heed calls from the media—or even the occasional sponsor—to clean up its act. Violence is the league's gateway drug. And once fans are in the rink, that blood lust only deepens. A recent poll for *The Globe and Mail* asked 1000 Canadians whether they agreed or disagreed with the statement that "fighting is an acceptable part of hockey." Among those identifying themselves as hardcore watchers, 70 percent said "Yes" (in comparison to an 82 percent "No" from those who don't follow the game at all). Simply put, the NHL sells the rough stuff because that is what appeals to its audience. Not even Detroit, widely recognized as the NHL's classiest organization, is immune. An ad in the *Windsor Star* promoting a series of games in January 2012 featured Jonathan Ericsson landing a haymaker on the temple of a Columbus Blue Jacket. "More than Matchups ... Battles," it promised. Although, given that the Swedish defenceman has amassed a grand total of forty-four penalty minutes in five NHL seasons, perhaps it was an attempt at satire.

Bettman knows that he has to tread a fine line when it comes to the on-ice mayhem. NHL fans love it (until it happens to a player on their team), but when incidents like Chara's hit on Pacioretty, or Todd Bertuzzi's 2004 attack on Steve Moore, migrate from the sports pages to the front of the news section, it's no good for the game. He argues that progress is being made: "There's far less fighting than there was fifteen, or twenty, or thirty years ago. And in terms of the stuff you really don't want to see, there's far less crap in the game." At the same time, Bettman says the increase in bodychecking proves that hockey can be cleaner, yet remain a rugged sport: "You take something that has an almost hundred-year history and tradition and you evolve it, you don't knee-jerk it." The kind way to describe it is as an incrementalist approach to the problem. Although glacial works, too.

Either way, Bettman, Collins, and their associates at NHL headquarters are now convinced that the NHL is finally on the right track when it comes to marketing, engaging both the fans and the advertisers. The proof in the pudding is the 350-percent growth in sponsorships since the 2007–8 season. Never mind that the actual dollar value remains modest—the first time centrally generated league revenues, which includes all national corporate partnerships and broadcast agreements as well as web profits and a portion of the merchandise royalties, topped US$300 million was the 2010–11 season, thanks to the new NBC deal. It's the appearance of momentum that draws business. Collins's plan to "build scale" by packing the league's calendar with flashy events, from season-opening festivals in October through the draft and NHL Awards in late June, was all about making the landscape more inviting for big corporations. "When we talked to advertisers and agencies and corporate marketers, what became clear was that they just didn't know how to spend money on hockey—particularly in the US where the approach was so fragmented," he explains. "So we had to create a path that led the advertiser directly to this very attractive fan demo."

Sponsorships, with their contractual requirements for media buys that promote both the game and the league, are also the NHL's most efficient way to market itself. Someone else foots the bill to tell consumers that hockey is important and exciting. Make enough noise in the marketplace, goes the theory, and the sport starts to take on a new sheen. Casual fans are converted to avid ones, and therefore become better consumers. It's nice to have people in the stands and watching on TV, but what the league really wants them to do is spend money, on its products as well as those of its sponsors. That's the true business of hockey, and it's something that Bettman has never lost sight of from the moment he took the job.

And even if you can't attract new eyeballs to the game, there's still plenty of room to expand—the league claims 40 million US followers, yet NBC's audience for Game 7 of the 2011 Stanley Cup Final was only 8.54 million. Becoming more efficient can often be a far easier way to make money than getting bigger.

This new inward focus at least tacitly acknowledges the cold hard truth for the NHL in the United States: It is so far behind the other major-league sports, not to mention pro golf and NASCAR, in audience size, TV money, and ad dollars, that it will likely never catch up. Barring the emergence of a superstar with global appeal, hockey will remain on the periphery for most American sports fans. It's not so much Bettman's failure to market the game to his fellow countrymen as the luck of the draw. The NBA, which was on the verge of imploding in the early 1980s, started rising with Larry Bird and Magic Johnson, but entered the stratosphere almost exclusively thanks to Michael Jordan, and has been slowly coming back down to earth since he retired in 2003. The same can be said for the PGA and Tiger Woods. Hockey had its chance with Wayne Gretzky after his 1988 trade to Los Angeles but failed to fully capitalize. At the zenith of his US fame in the early 1990s, the Great One—a ubiquitous shill for everyone from Nike to Domino's Pizza to Coke to Zurich Insurance—was earning more than $12 million a year in endorsement fees, eclipsing his salary from the Kings. And he was a big enough presence to be part of the Official All-Star Café chain of "stadium food" restaurants, along with Shaquille O'Neal, Joe Montana, and Andre Agassi. Even today, close to fifteen years after his final game, he remains the only hockey player most Americans can name. A vestigial memory of a time when they paid attention, like their widespread belief that Pierre Trudeau is still Canada's prime minister.

If you take the cover choices of *Sports Illustrated* editors as a barometer, hockey's relative appeal in the United States has been in decline for decades. In the 1970s, the magazine put the NHL up front on twenty-three occasions, featuring stars like Bobby Orr, the Esposito brothers, Guy Lafleur, and Denis Potvin. In the 1980s, there were sixteen covers—half of them devoted to Gretzky and the rest to Cup wins by the NY Islanders and Montreal. During the 1990s, the eleven fronts were almost evenly shared between the Great One, Mario Lemieux, and Mark Messier. But in the first decade of the new century, hockey graced the cover only eight times, and was completely shut out between 2003 and 2008—unless you want to count a July 2007 tribute to the movie *Slap Shot,* featuring fictional minor-league goons the Hanson brothers. Sidney Crosby, the game's greatest current star, made it for his Stanley Cup win with the Penguins in 2009 and his Olympic gold the next year. Alex Ovechkin, who thanks to his exuberance on and off the ice seemed poised to become a cross-over sensation (the global management agency IMG made him their only hockey client in 2009), has never made the cover. And with his points total and the Washington Capitals steadily heading south ever since, that won't change soon.

Hockey just doesn't count for much outside of its usual precincts. The Celebrity 100, an annual list of the world's most influential entertainers, musicians, and sports figures compiled each year by *Forbes* magazine, featured nineteen athletes in 2011 (Lady Gaga occupied the number-one spot). Two were golfers, four played in the NBA, three kicked soccer balls for a living, and five played tennis. The NFL and baseball each had two representatives. NASCAR had one. And the NHL was shut out.

But even in its Canadian hotbed, hockey has produced surprisingly few household names in recent decades. Beyond Crosby, the only current NHL players who enjoy major national endorsement deals in Canada—for anything other than gear—are Ovechkin for the Mr. Big chocolate bar and the Blackhawks' Jonathan Toews with Canadian Tire. The Flames' Jarome Iginla used to have one with Scotiabank. Other league stars either rise and set too quickly or offer only regional appeal.

And "Sid the Kid" has sometimes seemed ambivalent about being the face of the game, even before the concussion problems that kept him off the ice for the better part of two seasons. When the Pens came to New York to play the Rangers in the wake of his gold medal–winning goal at the 2010 Winter Games, Crosby was asked to go on Letterman and read the Top Ten list, but he refused. He has North American–wide deals with Gatorade and Reebok, who first signed him when he was still playing junior and recently inked him to a $10-million, seven-year extension. But at home in Canada, he frequently turns down endorsement offers, including one from a car company that would have given him a seven-figure payday in exchange for about four hours of work standing in front of cameras for TV spots and print ads. He currently lends his name and face to a chain of sporting goods stores, a bread company, and Tim Hortons, the country's dominant coffee and doughnut emporium. Although that relationship seems deeper— his uncle Rob Forbes, who was a teammate of Mario Lemieux in the Quebec junior league, is the company's director of national promotions.

The reality in Canada is that the game is so omnipresent and evokes such strong feelings among consumers that professional pitchmen aren't really needed—any kid in a toque and skates will do. And the main difficulty for companies that want to cozy up to the NHL brand is finding space. All the major sponsorship categories—beer, financial services, automotive, telecom, consumer electronics, retail, and airlines—are sewn up, most under long-term agreements. "It's a crowded and diluted marketplace," says Brian Cooper, a former MLSE executive who now heads the S&E Sponsorship Group, a Toronto firm that brokers arrangements between sports leagues and businesses. "Although if you find the right activation, you can sell anything with hockey." The answer for many firms has been to go bigger, and deeper, with their support of the game. Cooper points to a series of deals that he has helped negotiate over the last number of years for Scotiabank, both at the team and the league level, where the bank has paid rights fees ranging from $4 million to $30 million, then spent tens of millions more in advertising and promotion. Yes, the firm has its name on the home rinks of the Ottawa Senators and the Calgary Flames, but it also sponsors 3500 minor-league teams across the country. In the crowded financial field, such initiatives have not only helped the bank differentiate itself from its competitors—they're now the hockey one—it's also given them powerful new ways to reach out to consumers who are passionate about the game.

One of the bank's newest initiatives is the ScotiaHockey NHL Visa card, sporting the league shield or personalized with the logo of a favourite team. Cardholders earn "hockey points" they can redeem with other league sponsors and get a 20-percent discount at the NHL.com website—which may distract them from the $29 fee and 19.99-percent annual interest rate. But Scotiabank's most successful play has probably been its sponsorship of the Stanley Cup's visits to smaller cities and towns across the country, where fans are offered the opportunity to get their photo taken with the NHL's Holy Grail down at the local branch. When they hit the front of the line, people are given a website address and a pin number so they can later access and share the shot. But to log on, they have to provide some basic information like their name and email address. So, too, with the friends and family they forward the photo link to—fourteen different people on average. The promotion, which has now touched down in more than forty-five communities, costs the bank about $25,000 a stop but nets thousands of new business leads every time. "Sponsorship today is hand-to-hand combat," says Cooper. "I don't think people realize the depth of research and planning that goes into the marketing of this game."

The NHL certainly understands the value of collecting data about its fans and tracking their behaviour—then offering up what it has mined to its clubs and partners. If you shop on NHL.com, join one of the league's fantasy pools, purchase a Center Ice cable package, enter a contest, download the iPad app, or buy a ticket to a game with your credit card, that information is sent on to a central database. And, over time, the league is able to develop a pretty good picture of the teams and players that you follow and to tailor its offers—everything from deals on mobile apps for the displaced fans to promos for ticket resale sites for the local team where the NHL gets a cut—to match your tastes. By 2011, the league already had detailed information on more than 500,000 fans in its Canadian database alone, and claimed to know the favourite team of 87 percent of them. Thirty-four thousand were defined as "Ubers"—male displaced team supporters who are married with children; frequently engage with the game online; spend freely on sweaters, hats, and T-shirts; and are highly profitable. At its current rate of data accumulation, the league projects it will have 2.5 million profiles of Canadian fans by 2014, which will be made available—at a price—to its partners, so they can cross-reference the information with their own databases and better target their own hockey upsells and promotions.

It's not a sinister practice, although it may be slightly out of keeping with a marketing plan that sells the game as unspoiled and authentic old-time entertainment. But all this sudden sophistication does seem surprising to those who have followed hockey's evolution as a business. Rodney Fort, an economist and professor of sports management at the University of Michigan, says the NHL has always stood out for its "weird" reluctance to even try to increase the value of its brand or improve its marketing. As the other major leagues took off, hockey seemed content to stand still, tied to an ancient gate-driven business model and without a significant US television deal. And when player salaries exploded in the 1990s, the owners became obsessed with containing costs rather than looking to the other side of the ledger and also seeking to grow revenues. The NHL commissioner deserves a lot of credit for the change in business strategy, says Fort, even if it was slow in coming. "Bettman is God. How else can you view it? They went from an industry of $400 million to $3.3 billion in 20 years. The guy is as good as gold. How can you fault what he has done to hockey? Especially given what came out of the lockout." It's not just hype; the league is picking up steam with its NBC contract and sponsorship success, he says. But in a way, those recent successes only serve to underline the emormousness of the challenge. "They're still between $1 billion to $6 billion behind the revenues of the other major sports," notes Fort. "And their spectator base is still a fraction of the other leagues." Centrally generated sponsorship, TV, and merchandise revenue now accounts for a little more than 10 percent of the NHL's bottom line, compared to more than 50 percent of the NFL's $9.3-billion annual revenue. That league's thirty-two clubs spilt more than $4 billion in TV, radio, and digital rights fees every year. And its marketing agreements dwarf the NHL's—$720 million over four years from Verizon, $1.2 billion over six years from Anheuser-Busch, and $1.1 billion for a five-year gear deal with Nike. The revenue gap isn't just limited to other pro sports either. The NCAA's TV deals for the March Madness basketball tournament brought in $666 million in 2012 alone.

Since the end of the lockout, the NHL has increased its revenues by more than $1 billion a season—a 50-percent increase in just seven years—but that sort of growth will be difficult to sustain over the long haul. First, there's the issue of the Canadian dollar. In a league where the seven franchises located north of the border account for more than a third of all revenue, the rising loonie has been a gift for Gary Bettman, with each cent gained against the US greenback adding $8 million more to the NHL's coffers. Between 2006 and 2011, the value of the Canadian dollar went up almost 15 cents—a currency swing that now inflates northern revenues by approximately $120 million a year. Canada's relatively strong economy also enabled its franchises to substantially hike their ticket prices over that same period, further multiplying the effect. (In the first three seasons after the lockout, ticket revenues in Canada went up 25 percent versus just 6 percent in the United States.) In 2008, a *Toronto Star* report based on internal NHL documents claimed that Canada's soaring loonie was responsible for as much as half of the league's then $500-million-a-year improvement to the bottom line.

Then there's the question of capacity. The box office remains the number-one cash source for the NHL—accounting for almost half of all revenues—but the seven years of record attendance that Bettman likes to trumpet would seem to leave little room for improvement. Official NHL figures suggest that sixteen of its clubs—including all the Canadian ones—sell out each and every night, and that overall its rinks are filled 95.6 percent of the time. And while twenty teams increased their ticket prices for the 2011–12 season, they were mostly modest hikes, with the price of the average NHL seat rising only 5.4 percent. Many of the best markets are tapped out. In Toronto, where the Leafs haven't made the playoffs since 2004, the average price is now $123.77. Winnipeg, with the smallest building in the NHL, charges the second most on average at $98.27 (125 percent more than the team was able to command in Atlanta). Montreal's average rose just 0.3 percent to $88.67. The Flyers, who had both the best attendance and worst prices in the United States, charged an average of $66.89. Boston, winners of the 2011 Stanley Cup, announced plans to hike their tickets by an average $5.25 apiece for the 2012–13 season to just over $64, but few teams will be able to follow suit.

The truth is that outside of the major hockey markets, it's often harder than the league makes it look to fill the seats. The best season the Ottawa Senators ever had at the gate was 2007–8, the year after they lost the Stanley Cup to the Anaheim Ducks, when they had 13,000 season ticket holders and sold out thirty-eight of their forty-one home dates. "And for 30 of those games we were selling tickets right up to the wire," says Cyril Leeder, the club president. He looks at Toronto, Montreal, Vancouver, and now Winnipeg and just shakes his head. In 2011–12, when his team made the playoffs for the first time in three years, the Sens' season ticket base started at just 10,000, leaving the organization with more than 9000 seats to flog every night. "We gotta work it," Leeder explains. "I try to go to as many sales meetings as I can—at least two a week, and more if I can fit them into my schedule. It can be a big corporate partner, or somebody buying a 20-game plan. I don't care, they're all important." Buoyed by the unexpected return to the post-season—it was supposed to be a rebuilding year—and the excitement around the 2012 All-Star Game, the club ended up with its second-best year ever, selling out twenty-six of its forty-one home games. (The league attendance table showed them at 100.9 percent of overall capacity, thanks to overflow standing-room crowds on many of those nights.) Increased demand doesn't necessarily translate to a price hike, however. Ottawa's tickets, which range from $15 to $200, already bump up against what Leeder feels is the local ceiling. "Everybody loves hockey in Canada—they get it, they understand it. But what we've learned over the years is that our business community can only support so many premium seats. It's the high-price tickets where we're restricted," he says. "That's the real challenge of a smaller Canadian market. You have to find revenue from other sources to grow."

Some NHL markets are simply bad. In Columbus, where season tickets can be purchased for as little as $599, and $25 will get you a seat at a Saturday game as well as a hot dog, a Pepsi, popcorn, and an ice-cream cone, the team attracts just 14,500 fans a game, 80 percent of Nationwide Arena's capacity. The sad-sack Islanders, decades removed from their Cup triumphs but still stuck in the ancient Nassau Coliseum, play before 3000 empty seats most nights, spectacularly failing at the challenge of filling the second-smallest building in the league. Dallas, with an average ticket price of just $29.95—the cheapest in the league and $27 less than the NHL average—plays to 75-percent capacity.

And for all Bettman's braggadocio about the current state of the game and his own hand in fixing it—"The NHL has never been healthier," he told a Boston sports conference in the spring of 2012—record revenues don't necessarily translate to record profits. *Forbes'* annual ranking of hockey's most valuable clubs— based on information the magazine pulls together and public and private sources—estimated that the NHL's collective before-tax operating income on $3-billion business for the 2010–11 season was just $126 million, down 21 percent from the previous year. An 11-percent hike in player costs was partially to blame, said the publication. But more worrying were its suggestions that eighteen of the thirty clubs actually lost money. Take away the $81 million in pretax earnings churned out by the Leafs, $47.7 million from the Habs, $41.4 million from the Rangers, and $23.5 million from the Canucks, and hockey looks like a pretty anemic business. The lowlights include a $24.4-million loss for the league-run Phoenix Coyotes (which would be almost $16 million less than an estimate that team president Mike Neely provided to *Maclean's*), $13.7 million in red ink for the Blue Jackets, and $8 million for the Islanders. Although as the NHLPA will point out, the losses attributed to several other teams—$4.4 million for the Carolina Hurricanes and $2.7 million for the St. Louis Blues—fall within the range of rounding errors, or creative accounting.

There are no magic solutions. The arena building boom, which saw twenty-five NHL clubs move into new digs in the 1990s and 2000s, vastly increasing their cash flow from luxury boxes, club seats, restaurants, and other bells and whistles, is all but over. The Pittsburgh Penguins, who opened the Consol Energy Center in

August 2010—and added $20 million to their bottom line that season—were the latest beneficiaries, leaving just the Oilers, Islanders, Flames, and Wings playing in old-style barns. (Madison Square Garden, the home of the Rangers, remains the oldest rink in the league, but is in the midst of a three-year, $850-million face-lift.) The golden goose of a second Toronto-area franchise, which could provide a one-time cash infusion of $400 million or more, remains to be plucked. But further expansion in the United States—or Europe, as John Ziegler once schemed—remains a distant dream. American TV rights, the engine of all major-league prosperity, is locked in at $200 million a year—a lot for the NHL, a pittance for anyone else—for the next decade. New broadcast agreements have been concluded for every European country (all 1230 regular season NHL games are now available on Swedish television) and all other plausible markets. And while the league is betting heavily on mobile and digital platforms as the engine of future growth, it will be a good long time before web revenue eclipses the old media money from NBC and CBC.

Sitting in a Toronto rink, watching draft prospects being put through their paces at an NHL research and development camp, Bettman is sanguine about the way forward, and more than a little proud of the way he has transformed the game over the past two decades. League revenues are now eight times what they were when he came into the job. Attendance is up from 14 million a year to more than 20 million. The two work stoppages weren't lost seasons, he says, they were hockey's most crucial ones, full of reimagining, planning, and analysis: "We needed the game to be better than it was. It was being bogged down because of the economics and the style of play. And we did that. We were able to completely turn the dial."

But he keeps coming back to the changes to the sport's geography as his true accomplishment. "People can be as critical as they want about the Sunbelt strategy—which was actually about going to big markets where we weren't—but it clearly worked," he says. In the United States, hockey is now a national property. Bettman ticks through the list of NHL partners on his fingertips: Honda, GEICO, Bridgestone, Molson Coors. "Look who our sponsors were 15 years ago, and it's night and day." (Although Nike, Budweiser, Coke, and MasterCard, who were among the companies who had deals with the league back in the mid-1990s, would surely disagree.)

It's too argumentative to be considered optimism, but Bettman is relentless when it comes to the future—the business is growing, the franchises are healthy, more and more people are connecting with the game, there isn't a cloud in the sky. Even the NHL's status as the least-major league is somehow an advantage. "Our fans tend to be more avid and connected than the fans of any other sport," he says. "And we want to feed that. We want them hooked." It's a stark contrast to the doom-laden scenarios he sketched out in the run-up to the last two lockouts. And one wonders how the pitch will be recalibrated when he soon has to justify asking the players to take a smaller share of the pie. Although as the game's chief salesman, he's never lacked confidence in his spinning abilities. The upside is what you peddle to advertisers. Tradition is what you flog to the fans. And when all else fails, you sell them both hope.

7 Between the Wars

The tough work of free agency was accomplished over a lengthy dinner—and several bottles of fine red wine—ten days before the race would be run. Brad Richards, his agent, and a financial planner sat around a table at Bern's Steak House in Tampa, Florida, for the better part of six hours that steamy June 2011 night, playing "What If?" It was already clear the thirty-one-year-old centre was going to be the most sought-after player on the open market when the NHL's bidding window officially opened at noon EST on July 1. But Pat Morris, the man who has represented Richards since he was a skinny teenager, wanted clear directions. So he and Rand Simon, a colleague at Newport Sports Management, the Toronto-area firm that's responsible for many of hockey's biggest stars and contracts, had their files and laptops set out among the glasses and cutlery. And over the course of the evening they went through every possible suitor in great detail. How would Brad fit into the lineup? Would he get along with the coach? Were there players on the squad whom he disliked? Did the team have a shot at winning the Stanley Cup? And most importantly, did the club have the salary-cap room to pay him what he was worth?

In his first season, 2000–1, Richards scored sixty-two points and was the runner-up for the Calder Trophy as rookie of the year. He finished tenth in league scoring in 2003–4 with seventy-nine points, and then added twenty-six more—including seven game-winning goals—as he helped the Tampa Bay Lightning to a Cup and himself to the Conn Smythe Trophy as playoff MVP. In the last two years, playing for the Dallas Stars, he'd finished seventh then tenth in overall scoring. And through eleven seasons in the league, he had averaged just under a point per game in both the regular season and the playoffs. Durable and big enough at 6-feet, 195 pounds, Richards is the type of playmaking centre that is coveted by general managers, and usually compensated accordingly.

The last deal he had signed in 2006—five years at US$7.8 million a season, or exactly 20 percent of the then $39-million cap ceiling, the maximum allowed—had briefly made him the highest-paid player in the league. Dallas had offered to re-sign him at $6.75 million for the next four years, $650,000 more than the Sedin twins—winners of the last two scoring titles—were getting in Vancouver. But Richards was looking for a contract that would again vault him to the top of the money list and keep him there for a good long time.

A hockey agent's job is to make his client sound like a bargain, no matter how much money a team is shelling out, building the case through hard statistics, carefully selected "comparables," and testimonials that speak to less-tangible gifts like leadership and grit. Morris, a grave-looking and gravel-voiced fifty-two year old, skilfully marshals all of those arguments for Richards and then takes it one step further: the pride of Murray Harbour, Prince Edward Island, has always been somehow undervalued. As a fourteen and fifteen year old playing for Athol Murray College of Notre Dame, a famed hockey boarding school in tiny Wilcox, Saskatchewan, it was Brad's friend and roommate, Vincent Lecavalier, who got most of the attention. Morris was the first agent to reach out to Richards, and even he didn't travel to see the kid play, signing him instead via a call to the dorm's single pay phone. And despite notching eighty-seven points for the Notre Dame Hounds in just sixty-three games in 1996–97, no one in the Ontario Hockey League, Canada's biggest junior circuit, bothered to draft him. It was the Rimouski Océanic of the Quebec Major Junior Hockey League who picked him seventh overall, reuniting him with Lecavalier, their top selection the year before. His first season in the Q, Richards scored thirty-three goals and added eighty-two assists for a total of 115 points—the exact same total as his better-known teammate. That June at the NHL draft in Buffalo, Tampa made Lecavalier the first overall pick. When their turn came up again in the third round, Brad was still available and the Lightning took him as well, sixty-fourth overall.

A pattern was emerging. That fall, Lecavalier made the NHL right out of training camp, while Richards was sent back to junior where he racked up 131 points. The next year, Tampa again dispatched him to Rimouski, telling Morris that they didn't think his client could skate at the big-league level and that they'd probably never sign him. That season, 1999–2000, Richards tallied seventy-one goals and 115 assists, then counted thirty-seven more points during a twelve-game playoff run that saw the Océanic win the Memorial Cup and him named the tournament MVP. When the dust settled, he had won ten individual awards, including Canadian junior hockey's Player of the Year. And he finally got his NHL contract.

Even with all his success during the first few years in Tampa, Richards never enjoyed the profile and perks of an undisputed

superstar. It was Martin St. Louis who won the scoring championship and the Hart Trophy—the league's most valuable player
award—the year they won the Cup. (Richards was third in team
scoring during the regular season, behind St. Louis and Cory
Stillman.) And it was his buddy Lecavalier who was team captain,
the cover boy and spokesman for EA Sports' *NHL 06* video game,
and the winner of the 2006–7 Rocket Richard Trophy for most
goals with fifty-two. By the time the franchise's fortunes started
to turn with an early exit from the playoffs that year and then a
disastrous beginning to the 2007–8 campaign (the Lightning
would go on to finish dead last), Richards was starting to feel
like the odd man out. The team was in the process of being sold,
and the incoming owners, Oren Koules, the producer of the *Saw*
horror films, and Len Barrie, a British Columbia real estate developer, didn't like the looks of the books. In their estimation, Tampa
could no longer afford quite so many big contracts, and they let
it be known that their plan was to clear cap space with an eye to
re-signing Lecavalier. So on December 15, 2007, after a 3–2 loss at
home to the Washington Capitals, Richards sent a text to Morris,
indicating he was ready to waive his no-trade clause in order to
extract himself from an unhappy situation. "Get me out of here," it
read. His preferred destination was Dallas.

The deal, struck just before the late-February trade deadline,
saw Richards packaged with goalie Johan Holmqvist in exchange
for forward Jussi Jokinen, Jeff Halpern, and backup goaltender
Mike Smith. A little over $8 million in salary shipped to "Big D,"
and just $4.75 million heading back to Tampa. In his first game
with the Stars, Richards counted five assists—a career high—in a
7–4 thumping of the Chicago Blackhawks, setting up new linemate
Niklas Hagman for his first NHL hat trick. Dallas cruised into the
2008 playoffs, beating the defending Cup champions Anaheim in

the first round, and then the San Jose Sharks in the second, before losing in six games to Detroit in the Western Conference Final. Richards had fifteen points in eighteen games. And it seemed that he had found a new long-term home.

But the kind of ownership woes that had chased Richards out of Florida soon surfaced in Texas. Tom Hicks, the leveraged buy-out billionaire who had purchased a struggling franchise from Norm Green in the aftermath of the first NHL lockout, and then bankrolled it to the 1999 Stanley Cup, was now himself in deep financial trouble. His worldwide sporting empire, which also included Major League Baseball's Texas Rangers and Liverpool FC of the English Premier League—in partnership with George Gillett, then owner of the Montreal Canadiens—was collapsing under its debt load. In the spring of 2009, Hicks Sports Group missed a US$10-million interest payment on $525 million in loans secured against the hockey club, its rink, and the baseball team. The NHL started to fund the team with "advances" from its share of future league revenues, pumping $19 million into the club in just over seven months. And by early 2010, Hicks was the owner in name only as the league quietly took over the operation and began to seek a buyer.

Committing to players was a complicated business. Joe Nieuwendyk, Dallas GM, felt out Richards about a new deal that May, but things never really progressed beyond the exploratory stage. Even to make an offer, he required the permission of the league and eleven different creditors. (Documents filed when the club entered into planned bankruptcy in September 2011 indicate the Stars had lost US$91.5 million over the previous three years and expected to go at least $31 million more into the red during the 2011–12 season.) When the $6.75-million-a-season pitch finally did come in early 2011, Richards and his camp were disappointed.

And more than a little pissed that the team had made locking up defenceman Trevor Daley for six years at an average $3.3 million their first priority. Free agency beckoned.

The relationship between Richards and Morris has more than a little Jerry Maguire vibe to it. Not only does it stretch back more than fifteen years, it sounds unusually close. During Tampa's 2004 Cup run, the pair had a ritual where the agent wished his client good luck, either by phone or in person, before all twenty-six games the team played that spring. And no win was complete until Morris texted Richards a countdown of the number of victories still to go. "It was stupid, and superstition beyond belief, but it worked," says Morris. On the night of June 7, when the Lightning triumphed over Calgary 2–1 in a nail-biting Game 7, the message simply read, "No more." And the agent was there at ice level, with crossed fingers hidden under folded arms, when Gary Bettman announced Richards's name as the playoff MVP.

It's a partnership that is also defined by a common competitive spirit. In the off-season, the two like to wage titanic tennis battles. The guy with the gaudy Cup ring—featuring a lightning bolt and Lord Stanley's trophy offset with 134 white and blue diamonds—is more than a little bugged that he can't manage to dominate on the court the way he does on the ice. (Although he's been getting closer thanks to tips from his friend John Isner, an American who now ranks as one of the world's top ten players.) But for Morris, the arena of frustration has become hockey's backrooms. On his right wrist he wears a memento of his own championship from the fall of 2000: a gold Rolex with the inscription, "Pat, thanks for all your hard work, Chris #44." It was a gift from another client, Chris Pronger, when he signed a three-year contract with the St. Louis Blues totalling US$29.5 million. Even coming off a season where the then twenty-five year old had won both the Norris Trophy as the league's best defenceman and the Hart Trophy as the NHL's most valuable player it was a monster deal. More significantly, it placed the going rate for a top rearguard at the heights of the salary list, alongside offensive stars like Jaromir Jagr, Paul Kariya, and Peter Forsberg. Few hockey players have ever earned as much per season. Even now, six years after the cap reset the salary grid, it bests the contracts of current stars like Alex Ovechkin and Evgeni Malkin. And it was a personal benchmark that Morris was determined to surpass when it came to Richards's new deal.

Newport Sports may be the biggest agency in the NHL, but its offices are decidedly down-market, located in an aging, half-vacant office tower across the street from a shopping mall near Toronto's airport. On July 1, 2011, however, they were the official centre of the hockey universe. The satellite trucks were already parked outside when Richards arrived mid-morning, coffee in hand. Morris had been at work since 8 A.M., taking reservations.

The first team to make their pitch—at the strike of noon— was the Toronto Maple Leafs. Vice-president of hockey operations Dave Nonis, Claude Loiselle, the assistant GM, and special adviser Cliff Fletcher had brought an iPad with a video message from team president Brian Burke, who was visiting Canadian troops in Kandahar, Afghanistan. And despite the camouflage and desert backdrop, the content was all hockey. The Leafs, who hadn't made the playoffs since 2004, were on the upswing, posting one of the league's best records in the second half of the 2010–11 season. Goalie James Reimer looked like an emerging star. And Phil Kessel was a premium sniper, just begging for a set-up man. In Toronto, Richards would be king—on and off the ice. And paid like one. The one hitch was something Burke had been very open about—he wasn't willing to entertain any deal longer than six years.

Even as that presentation was going on, Morris's phone was ringing. The first call was an unexpected one—Calgary GM Jay Feaster, announcing the Flames' intention to table an offer for Richards when he had a few moments to listen. The next was Glen Sather of the Rangers, who was dangling big money and a seven-year term. New York hadn't sent a delegation, but they too had a presentation to make. A courier had delivered a finely crafted mahogany box with the team crest inlaid on its top. Inside was a DVD for Brad to watch. The ten-minute film had plenty of chutzpah—come play in the best city in the world, in the best building in the world, in front of the world's greatest fans. There were shots of the Manhattan skyline and the crowd at Madison Square Garden cheering and celebrating. John Tortorella, who had coached Richards to a Stanley Cup in Tampa and was now the Rangers bench boss, made a short pitch. The video also highlighted other advantages, like the Rangers' sparkling training and practice facility in Tarrytown, New York, with its steam rooms, ping-pong tables, leather couches, and forty-two-inch HDTVs. And oddly, it included a personalized message from TV hosts Regis Philbin and Kelly Ripa. "Brad, we *need* you in New York," Ripa vamped to the camera, as a studio audience chanted his name. It was followed up by a phone call from team owner James Dolan, who delivered the same message—in a slightly less breathy tone.

Next up was Los Angeles. Their nine-person squad—including GM Dean Lombardi, coach Terry Murray, and Tim Leiweke, the high-powered president of the Anschutz Entertainment Group, owners of the Kings, Lakers, and Galaxy—had flown in that morning on a private jet. The first thing they did was place the NBA's Larry O'Brien Championship Trophy and Kobe Bryant's Finals MVP award on the boardroom table to prove that their owner's commitment to winning wasn't just theoretical. Then they broke out some well-researched gifts. Knowing that Richards was into wine, they had brought along an exclusive and expensive Napa red. As a budding musician, he received an autographed guitar that had previously belonged to Eagles front man Glenn Frey. His love of golf was taken care of with a sponsorship form for the exclusive Bel-Air Country Club, already filled in with the requisite five signatures, including that of Lakers great Jerry West. Like tennis? How about these prime seats for Wimbledon?

Then there was their video, produced by Hollywood mogul Jerry Bruckheimer, a hardcore hockey fan. Jay Leno, Cuba Gooding, Jr., and Jeremy Piven of HBO's *Entourage* all pitched Richards on LA's attractions. (Although Piven's frantic promises that they would "hang out at the Playboy mansion every night" were apparently a toned-down version of his original contribution.) The Lakers' Bryant delivered a message. So, too, did ex-King Wayne Gretzky: "It's the greatest place to play." Afterwards, Richards huddled in a side office with coach Murray for forty-five minutes, discussing just how he would be used.

Steve Yzerman's presentation was a lot less showy. Just the new Tampa GM, making the case for a prodigal player to bury the past and come back to the Lightning. Richards, who still makes his off-season home in the city, didn't need to be sold on its virtues. Although the former Detroit great still left behind an information package on its schools, beaches, weather, and other advantages. "Florida does not impose any state personal income tax," reads its first line.

By now, it was almost the dinner hour. Morris called Feaster back to get Calgary's offer. The money was good but the five-year term didn't impress. The Flames GM, who in a previous incarnation was the guy who inked Richards's first three contracts for Tampa, asked for more time. And within a few minutes, he was on the phone again. Morris won't say exactly how much the offer was—the rumour in the hockey press was nine years at $64 million—just that it started off impressively and only improved. And suddenly, Brad Richards was contemplating winters in Alberta.

Sather called, spitting nails as usual. He wanted to know what was taking so long. Morris told him that they were considering all the offers, but would soon pick a single team to negotiate with. Before Richards left for the night, his agent laid out Photoshopped hockey cards of him in each team's uniform. The best fit, it was decided, was Broadway Blue.

Talks went on through the night and into the next morning. The Rangers upped both the amount and the term. And at 3 P.M. Richards came back to the office to sign a contract that will carry him through his fortieth birthday, paying him US$60 million over nine years.

The deal was heavily front-loaded, giving the centre $12 million in salary his first two seasons, then $9 million, then $8.5 million for two years, then $7 million. Starting in 2017–18, his pay will be just $1 million year. But it was the $28 million in signing bonuses and the way the agreement is structured that really set a new standard for the NHL. By the time the collective bargaining agreement expires on September 15, 2012, Richards will have already been paid $30 million. If he sticks around to the end of year six, right around the time he turns thirty-seven, he'll have earned $57 million. The "cap hit" for the Rangers—the averaged value of the deal—is $6,666,667 each season through 2019–20.

Any way you sliced it, Brad Richards was once again the highest-paid player in the game. And his agent was in line for a new watch.

PATRICK KANE KNEW IMMEDIATELY. The harmless-looking wrist shot he tossed at the Philadelphia net when he was almost even with the goal line had somehow passed through Michael Leighton's legs and into the back of the mesh. But almost no one on the ice or in the stands had seen it happen. The Chicago winger circled the crease, pumped his right arm in the air, and let out a joyous whoop. His teammates seemed puzzled at first, but as Kane carried on past them running on the tips of his skate blades, shedding his stick and gloves in celebration, it dawned on them, too—the Blackhawks had won their first Stanley Cup in forty-nine years.

It took a video review to make the anticlimax official. Just over four minutes into overtime of Game 6 and the 2010 Final was over. Chicago's young guns had fulfilled the promise of a 112-point, third-place-overall season—knocking off Nashville, Vancouver, San Jose, and now Chris Pronger's Flyers—and restoring some much-needed lustre to one of the NHL's original six.

Only four years earlier, ESPN had christened the team "the worst franchise in professional sports." It may well have been true. The Blackhawks made the playoffs just twice between 1996 and 2009, losing in the first round on both occasions. Their last great draft pick had been Jeremy Roenick in 1988. Average attendance was a little over 12,500 a night. And "Dollar" Bill Wirtz, the team's old-school owner, had seemingly gone out of his way to antagonize the few remaining faithful, jacking ticket prices, keeping home games off of TV, and generally letting things deteriorate to the point that the *Chicago Tribune*, the biggest paper in town, no longer even bothered to send a reporter along on road trips.

The turnaround began quietly with the selection of Jonathan Toews in the 2006 draft. The next spring, then GM Dale Tallon used the first overall pick to add Kane. When Wirtz passed away in September 2007, and his son Rocky took over, the process accelerated. John McDonough, a former Cubs executive, was brought in as the new team president and set about revitalizing the business. Ex-greats like Bobby Hull, Stan Mikita, and Tony Esposito were welcomed back into the fold after years of getting the cold shoulder. By the beginning of the 2008–9 season, every single home and away game was again available on television. The coffers were pried open to lure in big free agents: an eight-year, US$57.1-million deal for defenceman Brian Campbell and $22.4 million over four years for goalie Cristobal Huet in July 2008, then twelve years and $62.8 million for winger Marian Hossa the next summer. And the fans responded. The season ticket base, which at the nadir had dwindled to just 3400, was quickly rebuilt to upwards of 14,000. Chicago vaulted from the bottom of the league's attendance table to the very top, selling out the United Center—the biggest building in the league—every night.

The tickertape victory parade, held in Chicago's downtown on Friday, June 11, 2010, drew an estimated 2 million people. But the party atmosphere didn't last for long. When Stan Bowman, the man who had taken over from Tallon as GM in the summer of 2009, met with the media the next morning, he confirmed what those who had done the math already knew: Chicago was about to hit the salary wall. Those big acquisitions, plus a decision just before the midpoint of the season to lock up Toews, Kane, and defenceman Duncan Keith with new long-term deals—$135 million worth of commitments unveiled on the same December day—had seen the team finish right up against the NHL's $56.8-million salary cap. Bonuses due to Kane and Toews, the winner of the Conn Smythe Trophy, would push them millions over— money that would be deducted, dollar for dollar, from next season's limit. With $57 million already committed to just fourteen players for the coming year, there was little room to manoeuvre and zero chance of re-signing all of the team's pending free agents. "We'd love to have everybody back, and that's just not a possibility, so we've got to move on," said Bowman. His legendary dad, Scotty, had once coached the Montreal Canadiens to four Cups in a row, and later won back-to-backs with Detroit. Chicago's renaissance, however, was to be strictly a one-shot deal.

By the beginning of the 2010–11 season, ten of the Blackhawks' core players, and a bunch of spare parts, were gone. Antti Niemi, the Finnish goaltender who had gone 16–6 in the playoffs as a rookie, won an arbitration hearing that took his salary from $827,000 to $2.75 million and was allowed to walk, signing with the San Jose Sharks. Dustin Byfuglien, Ben Eager, and Brent Sopel were packaged to the Atlanta Thrashers for veteran forward Marty Reasoner and two AHL prospects. Centre Andrew Ladd followed them a week later, dealt for another prospect. Kris Versteeg was traded to the Maple Leafs for inexpensive rookie Viktor Stalberg. Colin Fraser went to Edmonton for a sixth-round draft choice. Adam Burish signed with Dallas. John Madden, who previously won two Cups with the New Jersey Devils, skipped off to Minnesota. And Huet, who had played exactly one period in the entire Cup run, was lent to a Swiss league team—still drawing a Chicago paycheque, but no longer counted on their books. Bowman's rejigged Blackhawks went 44–24–9 in 2010–11, earning ninety-seven points and backing into a playoff spot on the final night of the regular season when Dallas lost to the Wild. In the first round, they drew Vancouver, losing in seven games. The next year, they finished sixth in the West, and then dropped their first-round series against Phoenix 4–2.

When the Great Lockout officially ended in July 2005, following a 30–0 vote by the owners in favour of the hard-won collective bargaining agreement, the predictions were bold. A new dawn was at hand for the National Hockey League and its players. "An era of economic stability for our franchises, an era of heightened competitive balance for our players, an era of unparalleled excitement and entertainment for our fans," promised Gary Bettman. "When you look back in a year, five, ten, this era in history—today in particular—will be viewed as a pivotal point in time."

On the ice, a crackdown on obstruction and holding and the elimination of the centre red line would buy space for skill and speed, killing the defensive "trap" that was choking the life out of the game. Off the ice, the lifeblood of competition would be restored as well. Free-spending teams in New York, Toronto, or Los Angeles would no longer be able to stuff their rosters with proven performers and effectively buy their way into the post-season. All NHL management would be on the same footing, forced to live within their budgets and build winners through canny draft picks, good scouting, and strong developmental systems. Little markets would compete with big, and players and owners alike would share in the profits. The cap would rule supreme, he vowed.

Seven years later, much of what was foreseen has come true. Small-market Carolina triumphed over even-smaller-market Edmonton for the first post-lockout Cup in 2006. Non-hockey hotbed Anaheim beat Ottawa the following year. And by the end of the 2011–12 season, twenty-nine of the league's thirty teams had qualified for the playoffs at least once under the new system. (Only the game's richest franchise, Toronto, remained a post-season wallflower.) NHL revenues steadily increased, even through a global recession. So did return on investment for the owners. During the 2003–4 season, the last before the lockout, *Forbes* magazine pegged the average franchise value at US$163 million. By the fall of 2011, the figure was $240 million.

But the Bettman-designed cap has also created changes that no one predicted—at least not in public. In the age of parity, hockey dynasties have become a thing of the past with only two teams, Pittsburgh and Detroit, even making it back to the final in consecutive years. A new class system has been created in which veteran players are pushed out of the game in favour of younger, cheaper bodies, while management and agents collude to exploit the system's loopholes and find ever more creative ways to reward the game's stars. The fans now seem to obsess as much about what an NHLer earns as what he does on the ice. Players who don't live up to the expectations associated with fat contracts increasingly find themselves earning big-league money to play in minor-league rinks. And despite the ever-increasing size of the pie, the owners and the union again seem set to fight over the width of the slices.

The July 2005 collective bargaining agreement runs 475 pages, including preambles and appendices. Yet the words "salary cap" never appear. The relevant section, Article 50, bears the neutral title "Team Payroll Range System." And within its thicket of legalese hide the dry-as-dust mechanics of tying compensation to overall revenue. The agreement provides for a sliding scale: if total league revenues in any year are below $2.2 billion, the players get a 54-percent cut. Between $2.2 billion and $2.4 billion and it becomes 55 percent. Between $2.4 billion and $2.7 billion, 56 percent. And if they top $2.7 billion, the players' share becomes 57 percent.

The first season the contract was in force, the maximum team payroll was set at US$39 million and the minimum at $21.5 million. But revenues bounced back a lot faster than Bettman and the owners had anticipated, and the salary pool expanded accordingly. In 2006–7, when the league brought in $2.3 billion, the cap ceiling was $44 million and the floor $28 million. Even in 2008–9, in the teeth of the worst economic recession in generations, the

NHL's $2.65-billion performance pushed the team salary range to $56.7 million at the top and just over $40 million at the bottom. For 2011–12, coming off a $2.9-billion year, the upper limit of the payroll range was $64.3 million and the lower threshold $48.3 million, which was almost $10 million above the initial cap ceiling of six years earlier.

The season before the lockout the average player salary in the NHL was $1.83 million. Aided by a 24-percent across-the-board rollback the players conceded to as part of the settlement, it dropped to $1.46 million when play resumed in the fall of 2005. By the end of the 2007–8 season, it stood at just over $1.9 million. For 2011–12, it was $2.4 million.

Of course, actual compensation in the NHL depends on who you are and which team you play for. The maximum possible salary for the 2011–12 season—still set at 20 percent of the cap ceiling—was US$12.86 million. Four players—Brad Richards, Vincent Lecavalier, Flyers goaltender Ilya Bryzgalov, and Buffalo defenceman Christian Ehrhoff were making $10 million or more. Twenty-five more were making between $7 million and $9 million a season. And in total, sixty-four guys had hit at least the $6-million plateau.

Contrast that with those players hovering down around the bottom of the salary ladder. It's only the greenest AHL call-ups that take home the league minimum salary of US$525,000. But increasingly, NHL clubs are filling out their rosters with cheap bodies. The Colorado Avalanche, with a listed team payroll of $49.4 million for 2011–12, had seven players making $1 million or less a season. The New York Islanders, who finished the year with $300,000 less committed to payroll, had eighteen players signed for similarly discounted salaries. The Philadelphia Flyers, bumping right up against the cap limit all season long, had thirteen such players, so did the Rangers. Buffalo, another top spender, boasted nine. Despite the surging revenues and payrolls, the income gap in the dressing room is as big as it's ever been.

Like most guys in the NHL, Kyle Wellwood was once a star. As an undersized and underaged Junior B player for Tecumseh, his hometown just outside of Windsor, Ontario, he racked up sixty-three points in fifty-one games in 1998–99. Taken sixteenth overall in the Ontario Hockey League draft by the Belleville Bulls, he notched fifty-one points in his rookie season, then thirty-five goals and eighty-three assists in 2001–2, winning the scoring title as a seventeen year old. The next season, he was traded to the Windsor Spitfires for another promising junior—and future number-two overall NHL pick—Jason Spezza. And in his final OHL season, Wellwood totalled one-hundred points and played for Canada's World Junior team, contributing a goal and four assists as part of a silver medal–winning effort.

Prospect reports from his NHL draft year make reference to Wellwood's "Gretzky-like vision and twine-splitting wrist shot," but there were always doubts about his size—even now generously listed at 5-foot-10, 181 pounds. The league's Central Scouting Bureau ranked him as the ninety-fourth best bet in North America. And when the Toronto Maple Leafs finally picked him, it was in the fifth round, 134th overall.

In two years with the Leafs' AHL farm club, then located in St. John's, Newfoundland, Wellwood piled up 142 points in 156 games. The season after the lockout, he made it to the NHL, playing eighty-one games for Toronto and chipping in with eleven goals and thirty-four assists, finishing tied for sixth in team scoring. In 2006–7, he started even stronger, racking up forty-two points in just forty-eight games before his season was cut short with a sports hernia. He was going to be a big part of the Leafs' future.

But when Wellwood returned for training camp that fall, he promptly reinjured himself and again required surgery. Leafs coach Paul Maurice publicly grumbled about his somewhat estranged relationship with the gym. A touchy situation that wasn't helped by Kyle's father telling a Toronto newspaper that his son really liked "to take time off and rest himself mentally" during the summers.

That next June, coming off a season where he only scored twenty-one points, the Leafs ran out of patience and placed Wellwood on waivers. The Vancouver Canucks took a chance, signing him to a one-year deal for $997,500. But another groin injury and a broken leg in the off-season saw him show up at camp in beer-league rather than big-league shape, tipping the scales at 200 pounds. The team put him on a strict diet of lean meat and vegetables. And Kyle Wellwood's name was forever linked to Jenny Craig's.

After a decent 2008–9 season playing on Vancouver's third and fourth lines, the Canucks re-signed him for another year. But they took a pass when he became an unrestricted free agent in July 2010. As it turned out, there was little interest in the services of a twenty-seven year old who had just pocketed $1.2 million in exchange for twenty-five points. Wellwood was eventually invited to the Phoenix Coyotes' training camp, but was beaten out for a spot by Kyle Turris—another former junior star who was having trouble sticking in the NHL. In early October, Wellwood signed a $1-million contract with Atlant Moscow Oblast of Russia's Kontinental Hockey League. The unhappy experiment lasted just twenty-five games, and by mid-January Wellwood was back in the NHL, initially signed by St. Louis then plucked away by San Jose as he passed through the mandatory waiver process to re-enter the league. Deemed too expensive in the summer, he was a bargain by spring, playing thirty-five regular season games and eighteen more in the playoffs on a prorated $650,000 deal, ultimately earning $277,000. But he didn't fit into the Sharks' long-term plans, and in the summer of 2011 he again found himself waiting for the phone to ring.

"If you don't get that call, or expressions of interest, it's very difficult to stay motivated about your career and what you are doing," Wellwood says as he sits in the press box, high above the ice at Winnipeg's MTS Centre. "The lifestyle seems like it should be great, but you constantly have to deal with challenges." Short, now whippet-thin, and dressed in a dark suit he looks more like an usher than a player, which is certainly part of his problem. Wellwood's talents have never fit with the NHL's vision of what he should be. In the course of six seasons and more than 400 games, he has been used as a power-play specialist, a checking centre, and a strictly five-on-five player, among other things, yet has never found a natural role. And as he has learned, under the cap, today's top prospect is tomorrow's dispensable journeyman: "If you miss your opportunity with your first club, and then fail to catch on with another one, it's very easy to gain a stigma." Although, as he rightly points out, being a Toronto draft pick has been more of a curse than a blessing over the last couple of decades.

A few different teams sent out feelers, but it was only the reborn Winnipeg Jets who were willing to put even halfway-decent NHL money on the table—a one-year deal at $700,000. So Wellwood and his girlfriend packed up their newborn son and moved to the Prairies, with the hope that he might finally earn a place and some security. Entering what should have been the prime of his career he's not bitter, just pragmatic: "I'd like to get the points and be that guy. And I'll probably have more opportunity on this team than one with a superstar." Winnipeg, with a team payroll of just over $52 million for the 2011–12 season, had only four players earning $4 million or more—Andrew Ladd, Nik Antropov, Dustin Byfuglien, and Ron Hainsey—none of them exactly household names. By season's end, Wellwood had made a pretty fair case that he deserved to stick around in the big leagues—a forty-seven-point performance over seventy-seven games, finishing fifth in Jets scoring. It was his best-ever NHL season. And in July, the Jets finally re-signed him to another one-year deal.

Under the cap there is an identifiable trend toward younger players. As of 2005, the average age of NHL skaters—which had been steadily climbing since the league first merged with the WHA in 1979, and then added still more teams through the 1990s and early part of the 2000s—started heading in the other direction. By 2012, defencemen were close to a year and forwards almost half-a-year younger than they were before the last labour war. (The average age of goalies has actually increased, although the sample size is so small that a thirty-eight year old like Tim Thomas or a forty-year-old Martin Brodeur surely skew things.)

The seeds of that change were planted during the first lockout. One of the major concessions Bettman won in 1994 was the imposition of an entry-level contract, which set a maximum base salary beginning at $850,000 for a young player's first three seasons in the league. The idea was to save the owners from themselves. In June 1992, the Philadelphia Flyers had sent six players, two draft picks, and $15 million to the Quebec Nordiques for the rights to a teenage holdout named Eric Lindros. A week later, they inked him to a six-year, $18-million deal and threw in a $2.5-million signing bonus. Without ever having played a shift in the NHL, Lindros became its fifth highest-paid player, making as much as Mark Messier, winner of five Stanley Cups and two MVP awards. (Although in retrospect, the Flyers got a lot more value for their money than the Ottawa Senators, who signed Alexandre Daigle, their top pick in the 1993 draft, to a $12.25-million contract over five years.)

In practice, however, the original entry-level system proved to be something less than airtight. While signing bonuses were limited, there were no effective constraints on rewards for performance. In 1997, for example, Boston gave first overall pick Joe Thornton an incentive-laden contract that guaranteed him just $925,000 a year in salary, but offered as much as $1.8 million more if he hit some middling targets. The next year, when Lecavalier signed with Tampa, the bonus package was even bigger, pushing the potential value of his three-year deal to $11 million. By 2002, the Atlanta Thrashers were paying more than $4 million each to first-year players Dany Heatley and Ilya Kovalchuk. And the rising rookie tide was lifting all other salary boats.

During the 2005 negotiations, Bettman and the league went to great lengths to bring the youngsters to heel. Not only was the base salary for entry-level players rolled back—in 2010–11 the maximum was US$925,000, including signing money— but the new CBA now limited performance payments to $850,000 a season. A breakout star who sweeps all available hardware at the NHL Awards could earn as much as $2 million more. But teams were given a powerful disincentive to be even theoretically generous—all such bonuses, whether earned or not, count against their cap.

At the same time, the agreement significantly raised the stakes for teams that wanted to add a veteran presence to the lineup. Since the lockout, if a player thirty-five or older is signed to a multi-year contract, his average salary (a.k.a. cap hit) stays on a team's books for the duration of the deal, even if he retires. As a consequence, greybeards are now mostly hired on a season-to-season basis, and their market value has plunged dramatically. In 2003–4, Mark Recchi, still a remarkably consistent offensive force in his mid-thirties, was earning $5 million. After the lockout, his salary dropped to $2.28 million, then $1.75 million, even as his points total stayed relatively steady. His final three seasons in the league (Recchi retired after winning the 2011 Stanley Cup with the Bruins, finishing fifth in team scoring at the age of forty-three) his paycheque was $1 million a year.

Where the players have actually done better under the cap than many anticipated has been through free agency. And not just for the superstars like Richards. Prior to the lockout, players didn't go on the open market until after the season in which they hit age thirty-one. But under the 2005 deal, that threshold dropped to age twenty-seven or at least seven years' service in the league, which meant that kids who made the NHL straight out of junior could now cash in as young as twenty-five. For some clubs, it was a painful adjustment. "I have no hesitation in saying that we were probably hurt more than any other team in the league with that change," says Cyril Leeder, now the president of the Ottawa Senators and a senior executive with the club since its 1992 inception. "We had the best group of guys in that 23 to 27 age range and the new rules meant you couldn't really keep them all." Marian Hossa was shipped to Atlanta for Dany Heatley just prior to the 2005–6 season. That next summer, the team signed centre Jason Spezza and defenceman Wade Redden to new contracts, but let another key rearguard, Zdeno Chara, walk off to Boston. Martin Havlat, a year away from free agency, was traded to Chicago. The rebuilt Senators were still good enough to make it to the Stanley Cup Final that season, but fell in five games to the Ducks. "Sometimes you've got to decide before you get there," says Leeder. "You can't have five guys making over $6 million. It's not going to work under this system."

But it was the adjustment to restricted free agency that really ended up altering the salary dynamic. Since 2005, players coming off of entry-level contracts have been able to opt for either arbitration or to test the market—able to accept offers from other teams but bound to stay put if their club matches the deal. The NHL's negotiators included what they figured would be a poison pill in the provision—any team signing a restricted free agent must compensate his former club with draft picks. And the bigger the contract, the more it hurts: a $2-million to $3-million player costs a first- and a third-round selection; $3-million to $4-million, a first-, second-, and third-round pick. Sign someone away for $5 million or more and the price is four first-rounders. Similar penalties in past collective bargaining agreements hadn't exactly frozen the free agent market. In 1995, Chicago offered Winnipeg's Keith Tkachuk $17.5 million over five years. In the summer of 1997, the Rangers tried to pry Joe Sakic away from the Avalanche with $21 million over three years. And the Carolina Hurricanes dangled $38 million over six years for Detroit's Sergei Fedorov in 1998. But those players were all established stars, and with no limit on payrolls, the only impediment to matching the offers was common sense. All three clubs chose to open the vaults and keep their marquee names.

Kevin Lowe of the Edmonton Oilers was the first to push the new envelope, offering Buffalo's Thomas Vanek, a young winger coming off a forty-three-goal season, $50 million over seven years when his entry-level deal expired in July 2007. The Sabres, who had just lost Chris Drury and Daniel Briere to free agency, didn't even wait a day to match the payout. But Lowe wasn't dissuaded. Three weeks later he went after Anaheim's Dustin Penner, offering $21.5 million over five years.

Penner was a jewel in the rough. Not only undrafted, he didn't even make junior, getting cut three different times by the local club back home in Winkler, Manitoba. But a stint playing for a college in North Dakota led to a scholarship with the University of Maine and one pretty decent NCAA season. Intrigued by his 6-foot-4, 245-pound size and scorer's touch, the Mighty Ducks signed him to a three-year entry-level contract in the spring of 2004. The year after the lockout, playing for their AHL affiliate the Portland Pirates, he had eighty-four points in just fifty-seven games. And once he was called up to the NHL his potential as a power forward quickly came into focus. In his first full season with the Ducks, 2006–7, he notched twenty-nine goals. And during the playoffs that spring he had eight points in twenty-one games, including a game-winning goal in the Stanley Cup Final.

Brian Burke, the Ducks GM, was apoplectic over Edmonton's offer sheet, calling Lowe both classless and gutless during a conference call with the media: "I think it's an act of desperation for a general manager who is fighting to keep his job." (Behind the scenes, the spat was even more intense. Incensed by an interview Lowe subsequently gave to a radio station, Burke issued a challenge via the Rangers GM Glen Sather, who had coached Lowe to Stanley Cups in Edmonton and New York: "I said, I'm gonna be at Lake Placid at the US junior camp. I gave him three dates. I told him I'd rent a barn. I picked the address and the time, and I'd fight Kevin Lowe," Burke told a Toronto TV station in December 2011. Gary Bettman got wind of the plan and called both Burke and Lowe to read them the riot act, promising to suspend them indefinitely if they didn't cool the rhetoric.) But in the end, Anaheim, which was struggling with its own cap issues, was in no position to match the deal. Penner joined the Oilers, and the Ducks received a first-, second-, and third-round pick for the 2008 draft.

Clubs still occasionally try the offer-sheet ploy when they see a competitor brushing up against the ceiling. Like San Jose's four-year, $14-million offer for Chicago defenceman Niklas Hjalmarsson, which was matched in the summer of 2010. But GMs have taken Anaheim's experience to heart and now move aggressively to lock up their core young talent with deals that carry them through their restricted years. In the course of a couple of weeks in September 2011, Los Angeles made twenty-one-year-old Drew Doughty one of the highest-paid defencemen in the league with an eight-year, $56-million deal. The New York Islanders gave John Tavares, who still had a season to go on his entry-level deal, a six-year, $33-million extension. And Brian Burke, now with Toronto, inked defenceman Luke Schenn, their fifth overall pick in the 2008 draft, to a five-year, $18-million contract.

It's a trend that, predictably enough, doesn't make the Leafs GM very happy. "I'm not sure that the right guys are getting paid in this system," says Burke, who ended up trading Schenn to Philadelphia for winger James van Riemsdyk just nine months later. "The Vanek and the Penner offer sheets changed all of us, and now we lock these guys up." He points to his own experience that summer in Anaheim, which led a couple of months later to a five-year, $26.265-million extension for Ryan Getzlaf, then just twenty-two. "I would rather at that point have paid some of the better players on the team more."

But the thing that might be in shortest supply under the salary cap is patience. When the free agency window opened in July 2008, one of the most sought-after prizes was Ottawa's Wade Redden. He was just thirty years old, and over the course of an eleven-year career had amassed 410 points in 838 games. Glen Sather called him "one of the best passers in the game." But even then, the New York Rangers' decision to lock him up for $39 million over six seasons, at a cap hit of $6.5 million a year, raised a lot of eyebrows. Redden's thirty-eight points the previous season had tied him for twenty-first among NHL defencemen. He was thirty-first in terms of plus/minus and fifty-third when it came to ice time. Solid numbers, but well short of superstar territory.

In his first year in New York, Redden contributed twenty-six points in eighty-one games, and was −5 on the season. In 2009–10, things got worse. Benched on several occasions by the Rangers' fiery Tortorella, he ended with just fourteen points in seventy-five games and ranked 158th among defencemen for ice time, averaging seventeen-and-a-half minutes per game. The press was unanimous in its assessment: Redden wasn't "living up" to his big contract. And the coach wasn't doing much to hide his disdain for the big defenceman. After the team failed to make the playoffs, Tortorella mused aloud about the need to make changes in the dressing room: "I think some people need to be weeded out."

Clubs are allowed to terminate contracts under the 2005 CBA, but the NHLPA has made sure that it will be at a steep price. Players under twenty-six get one-third of the remaining value of their deal. For older players, the walking money is two-thirds of what is left on their agreement. In Redden's case, with US$23 million owed over the remaining four years, it would have cost the Rangers $15.33 million to buy him out. And under the cap system, the team would still have to take a hit for any money they sent his way—spread out over twice the remaining life of the contract—as a punishment. Making up for Glen Sather's mistake would cost the club at least $1.9 million a season in payroll space for the next eight years.

That September, however, the Rangers found a loophole. After training camp, they dangled Redden on waivers, and when no other team bit, assigned him to their AHL affiliate, the Connecticut Whale. Playing in the minors, he'd be earning every dollar of his NHL contract but it wouldn't be counted against their cap, and that was all that mattered to a rich club like New York. Faced with a choice between riding the buses or retiring, and not getting what he was owed, Redden accepted the demotion. Two seasons later, the two-time NHL All-Star was still playing in Hartford, earning the AHL minimum salary of $37,500 in just over a period of play—collateral damage from Bettman's shock-and-awe victory in the last lockout.

Other GMs took notice of the dodge—pioneered by New Jersey in 2006, when they sent Alexander Mogilny, then thirty-seven years old and suffering from a bad hip, down to the Albany River Rats—and started to bury their problem children deep in the development system. Sheldon Souray, who had demanded a trade from Edmonton, ended up with the Hershey Bears instead, earning $5.5 million. (At the beginning of the 2011–12 season the Oilers bought out the final year of his contract and he returned to the big league, signing a $1.65-million deal with the Dallas Stars.) The Flyers' Michael Leighton, just a few months removed from the Stanley Cup Final and a new two-year, $3.1-million contract, was kicking out pucks for the Adirondack Phantoms. And Mike Commodore, a good-humoured fan favourite who played in the 2004 final with Calgary and won a Cup two years later with Carolina, found himself earning $3.8 million as a member of the Springfield Falcons after things went sour with the Columbus Blue Jackets. It was not without irony. During the lockout, when he was an up-and-comer still on a two-way contract, Commodore spent the season in the AHL playing for the Lowell, Massachusetts, Lock Monsters. And he was among the first players to break ranks, telling a Calgary radio station that he would personally accept a salary cap. "If that's what it takes, the sport has to go on," he said. "I don't want to spend however long my career lasts playing in the American Hockey

League." Happily for Commodore, the Blue Jackets bought out the remaining two years of his contract in June 2011, and he returned to the NHL, signing a one-year, $1-million deal with the Detroit Red Wings (who later flipped him to the Tampa Bay Lightning for a seventh-round draft pick).

What an NHL player makes has always been of interest to fans, especially since the Players' Association started disclosing its members' salaries in the fall of 1990. Alan Eagleson, who was both the union head and the game's biggest agent, had long resisted the trend, which started with Major League Baseball and the NBA. But when his hand was forced, the dividends were immediate. That summer, New Jersey's Brendan Shanahan, a restricted free agent, went to the St. Louis Blues for $5 million over four years, considerably more than the $700,000 a season the Devils had been offering. Adam Graves, who had been earning $145,000 in Edmonton, was suddenly making half a million in New York. For agents, there was no more guessing about what the going rate was for a twenty-goal scorer, or a top-line centre. And everyone down at the bar could join in the debate about whether a player was really worth all that money.

But the cap has taken that natural curiosity about how much our hockey heroes earn and turned it into an obsession. A guy who fails to play up to his contract isn't just overpaid, now he's eating up precious space on the payroll, and preventing your favourite team from trading for the final piece of the puzzle or signing that big free agent. What used to be a problem just for owners is now a preoccupation for almost every fan. And that might ultimately be the biggest change Gary Bettman has wrought at the NHL—the public now sees the sport as a business, much the same way he does.

Matthew Wuest studied computer science at the University of New Brunswick, but he'd always really wanted to be a hockey writer. So after undergrad he took the journalism program at King's College in Halifax, and then landed a job covering the QMJHL Mooseheads for the local tabloid newspaper. Watching junior players every day, Wuest had an epiphany that he might be able to make a name for himself by introducing NHL prospects to a wider audience. So in his off-hours he started a website dedicated to the draft picks of his favourite team, the Detroit Red Wings. It didn't get much attention, but it led him to his next venture.

In the spring of 2009, a lot of the online discussion among Red Wings fans was focused on whether the team, coming off a loss to Pittsburgh in the Stanley Cup Final, could afford to re-sign Marian Hossa. The Slovakian winger had scored forty goals and amassed seventy-one points during the regular season, adding fifteen more during the playoffs, and was seeking a long-term contract. Wuest went surfing for information and found a lot of websites that compiled team salaries, but nothing that allowed him to figure out how much payroll space the Wings had. So he built a cap calculator and made it available online.

Hossa ended up going to Chicago for $63.3 million over twelve years, but Wuest's little innovation still had legs. Soon he was receiving emails from fans of other clubs, asking him to build cap calculators for their teams. Within a couple of months his new website, CapGeek.com, had player contract details and the cap hits for all thirty NHL franchises. Soon the guys on TSN were name-checking it in their reports. "I really thought it would be more confined to a niche group of core fans," says Wuest. Today, CapGeek draws about 45,000 unique visitors during an average month and more than 100,000 around free agent time. And most of the thirty-three year old's time is spent hunting down details of the latest transactions around the league. "Unless you hack into the NHL system you're not going to get better numbers."

But the site's most popular feature has turned out to be its buyout calculator, which disgruntled fans can use to figure out just how much cap space it would cost to get rid of the stiffs. On the splash page of his website, Wuest maintains a list of the top ten bye-bye wishes. And for the better part of two years, Montreal's Scott Gomez has been number one with a bullet. It was the New York Rangers who signed the Alaskan-born forward to a $51.5-million, seven-year free agent deal in the summer of 2007, then flipped him to the Habs at the end of the 2009 season as the centrepiece of a seven-player trade. In his first season in Montreal, Gomez had fifty-nine points. In his second, he had thirty-eight points and was −15. Then there was the drought. On February 6, 2011, in a game against his former team, Gomez flipped a puck over a sprawling Martin Biron for his seventh and final goal of that season. A full calendar year later he had yet to bulge the twine again and sat stuck with seven lonely assists. True, he'd been injured, missing thirty games with a groin strain and a torn lat muscle. But Habs fans, staring at his annual cap hit of $7,357,143 through the end of the 2013–14 season, were not inclined to be forgiving. At the Bell Centre, during a 3–0 victory over Winnipeg, they celebrated the first anniversary of his scoring funk with signs, borderline-racist Bandito costumes, and rousing choruses of "Bonne Fête," the French equivalent of "Happy Birthday." The next day, Gomez told the *Montreal Gazette* that the fans had every right to boo him, but he was more focused on the team's spot near the bottom of the standings than his personal statistics: "Trust me, I want to score as much as anyone. But I'm dead serious about this—if it took me not scoring for two years for us to win in Montreal, I'd take it."

Three days later while visiting the Islanders, Gomez finally broke the goose egg on the power play, beating Evgeni Nabokov with an off-balance slap shot that clanked off the inside of the post. He gave a discreet fist pump as his teammates rushed in to congratulate him on his first goal in 369 days. The Montreal fans in the stands stood and bowed in their best I'm-not-worthy mockery. Someone threw a hat on the ice.

THE FIRST THING THAT PLAYERS and their agents see when they enter Laurence Gilman's office is a picture of the Grinch. The animation cell, signed by the great Chuck Jones, captures that moment when he first hatches the idea of stopping Christmas from coming and his bilious green face crinkles in evil delight. The image is there because Gilman, the Vancouver Canucks vice-president of hockey operations, assistant GM, and resident "capologist," is a big fan of cartoons. But it also serves as a reminder that an enhanced spirit of generosity is not one of the requirements for his position.

Back in 1994, Gilman was in law school at the University of North Dakota, with designs on becoming a player agent, when a professor prevailed upon him to use a paper he'd written about the arbitration case of Winnipeg goalie Bob Essensa—the first NHL player to break the $1-million award barrier—as a job application. The Jets, who had just fired the man who lost that case, general manager Mike Smith, hired the twenty-nine year old to assist his replacement, John Paddock, and help negotiate all future deals. (The fact that Gilman was dating the niece of Barry Shenkarow, one of the team's owners, also didn't hurt. Although it wasn't a mercenary alliance—he's now been married to Michelle for more than fifteen years.)

The instructions he received were pretty simple: Treat the team's money like it's your own. Make sure you spend it wisely. And save it in tranches of no less than $25,000. If the club and a player ended up $50,000 apart, the gap was to be regarded as unbridgeable as if it were a gulf of $500,000.

When the franchise moved to Phoenix after the 1995–96 season, Gilman went along. His expectations were that the job might change under new ownership in a big US market, but the focus on frugality remained the same. "The only thing that got bigger was the amount of money we were losing," he says. By the early 2000s, the Rangers and Detroit had payrolls that were pushing $70 million a season. The Coyotes were spending around $30 million. He remembers watching a Colorado Avalanche power play one night and realizing that the six guys on the ice—Joe Sakic, Patrick Roy, Peter Forsberg, Milan Hejduk, Ray Bourque, and Rob Blake—were making more than the entire Phoenix team. Gilman learned to be aggressive in every deal and arbitration hearing and find bargains wherever he could. "The ink was turning a deeper shade of red every year."

In the spring of 2008, he joined the Canucks as an assistant to their new GM Mike Gillis, a former Boston Bruins winger turned lawyer, who until a few weeks before had been enjoying a career as one of the most successful player agents in the sport. The team had just missed the playoffs for the second time in three seasons. The roster needed an overhaul. But more than that, the club needed a new philosophy about how to deal with life under the cap. The idea was to be clear, respectful, and tough-minded, and to transform Vancouver into the kind of franchise that players longed to join. No expense would be spared to make the club a winner. The dressing room was given a $3-million facelift. Sleep experts from the US military were hired to help players overcome the rigours of a west coast–based travel schedule. Nutritionists were on call to fine-tune meal plans and ensure that healthy snacks were always on hand. A $50,000 high-tech "shooting cage" was added in the

Rogers Arena mezzanine to help fine-tune accuracy. The budget for prospect development almost tripled. Blueprints were drawn up for a new $50-million waterfront practice facility. But there was a fixed limit to what they could spend on salary.

Gillis and Gilman sat their players down and laid out everything on the table. "We showed them our cap plan; that our owner was committed to spending right to the ceiling every season," says Gilman. "And we told them that we weren't going to argue with them in negotiations. That we would give them the most money we could. But that over a certain point, every extra dollar inhibits our ability to sign someone else and win the Cup."

Alexandre Burrows was the first to buy in. In the spring of 2009, in the midst of a season when he scored twenty-eight goals playing on the first line and received the league minimum salary in return, the twenty-seven year old re-signed for $8 million over four years—well below his market value. That summer, Daniel and Henrik Sedin were heading to free agency, in line for a huge payday. Negotiations with their agent, J.P. Barry, had gone on for months, but Vancouver's offer to the twins remained firm—$6 million apiece. A couple of days before the July 1 deadline, Gilman met Barry for a drink in the bar of Montreal's Hotel Nelligan and was told it wasn't going to be enough. The next night, he and Gillis boarded a flight for Sweden, surprising the agent in the business-class cabin. When they landed in Stockholm, they all went to dinner and made one last effort to hash things out. The following morning, June 30, Daniel and Henrik met them at the airport and agreed to sign for five more years at $6.1 million each a season. At that moment, Toronto's Brian Burke, who had drafted the twins back in 1999 when he was the Canucks GM, was in a plane somewhere over the Atlantic on his way with a much more lucrative offer. He heard the news when it touched down in Frankfurt, and caught the next flight home.

Staying up near the cap's ceiling, or just above its floor, is a complicated affair. Every player transaction—call-ups, trades, long-term injuries, waivers, signings—has a cascading effect on the current season and beyond. Sometimes you even have to be mindful of what time it is when you pull the trigger. Anyone on the roster as of 5 P.M. EST, or who has practised, played, or travelled with the team that day, counts against the limit. The NHL maintains a database that every team can tap into. In Vancouver, Gilman uses a 3-D spreadsheet to keep track of what the Canucks and their competitors are spending, down to the penny.

Not everyone is as adroit. The Calgary Flames made the biggest splash at the 2009 trade deadline, acquiring Olli Jokinen from the Phoenix Coyotes and Jordan Leopold from the Colorado Avalanche. It was the kind of gamble that characterized Darryl Sutter's tenure as the Flames GM—a total of three players and a couple of high-round draft picks for a young defenceman and veteran centre whose point production swung wildly from year to year. But the additional cap hits—$5.25 million for Jokinen and $1.5 million for Leopold—were almost $4 million more than the players Calgary had shipped out. And by early April, as the race for the playoffs came down to the wire, the Flames were feeling the squeeze. Robyn Regehr, Adrian Aucoin, and Cory Sarich were all injured, but not badly enough to go on the reserve list that would take their salaries temporarily off the books (and require them to be kept on the shelf through the beginning of the post-season). Bumping up against the ceiling, the team didn't have the option of calling up reinforcements from the minors without sending a well-paid veteran down—a move that would require the player to be placed on waivers first, where he could be snatched up by another team. So Calgary ended up playing three games, including a crucial tilt against Vancouver with first place in the Northwest Division on the line, with fewer than the NHL-mandated minimum of eighteen skaters. They fell to the Canucks and Minnesota, but somehow managed to beat Los Angeles. And the league offices chose to look the other way, as they did at the beginning of the 2010–11 season when New Jersey ran into similar injury troubles and iced just fifteen skaters for a couple of games.

At the time, rival clubs complained that the Flames and Devils were unfairly being allowed to bend the rules. But salary caps have a way of fostering creative interpretations of league regulations. That was Bettman's experience—and battle—as guardian of the NBA's system in the early years. And hockey has proven no different. "Teams—and I say this in a positive way—in their attempts to be successful, be competitive, be victorious, will push the limits to give themselves whatever edge they can get," says the commissioner. "And what we're trying to do is create a system that has as few opportunities for creativity as possible."

The most popular work-around in the NHL in recent years has been front-loaded, big-money contracts that carry players deep into retirement territory. In the summer of 2009, the Philadelphia Flyers acquired Chris Pronger in a trade with Anaheim, and promptly signed him to a seven-year, $34.4-million contract extension that would carry him through his forty-second birthday. The salary was more than $7 million a season in the first four years, but dropped to $4 million in year five, then the league minimum for the last two years, meaning the cap hit averaged out to just $4.9 million a season. Marian Hossa's twelve-year deal with Chicago, which will also carry him through to age forty-two, drops from $7.9 million annually over the first seven years to $1 million in the final four, dragging the cap charge down to $5.25 million a season. Roberto

Luongo's twelve-year, $64-million extension with Vancouver that finishes in 2022, when he, too, will be forty-two, was similarly structured.

The NHL has looked at the issue, but to date, the only contract it has rejected was New Jersey's seventeen-year, $102-million offer to Ilya Kovalchuk, which would have seen him earning $95 million over the first ten years and just $550,000 a season over the last four, reducing the cap hit to $6 million a year. When the union objected, an arbitrator looked at the deal in the summer of 2010 and backed the league up, ruling it had "the effect of defeating" the team payroll range system. Under the terms of the CBA, Bettman fined the Devils $3 million for the offence and made them forfeit a first- and a third-round draft pick. "The cap has to be respected," the commissioner told reporters. "I've been very clear all along that in the event of a circumvention, in particular in a case where you have an independent system arbitrator finding a circumvention, it has to be punished." New Jersey ended up signing Kovalchuk to a fifteen-year, $100-million contract with a salary that bounces between $11.8 million and $1 million a season—and carries a charge of $6,666,667 against the cap.

But there are other manipulations that draw far less attention. The New York Islanders, a franchise that has languished near the bottom of the standings and league attendance reports since the lockout, had the lowest reported payroll in 2011–12, with a cap hit of $49.1 million. But the amount they were actually paying players on the ice was likely well below the floor of $48.3 million. Performance bonuses—difficult to hit playing for a basement dweller—inflated John Tavares's cap hit to $3.75 million and Nino Niederreiter's to $2.795 million, far beyond their guaranteed salaries of $900,000 each. Jay Pandolfo, with a $1.4-million cap hit, was due only $600,000. And $1.8 million of Kyle Okposo's

$2.8-million hit was similarly bonus money. The Islanders were also carrying charges for the buyouts of Alexei Yashin at $2.24 million and Brendan Witt at $833,330. All told, the actual amount of money the franchise was paying out could have been as low as $40 million for the season, with just $36.8 million going to its current players. Colorado, a team that was also close to the floor, was in a similar situation with Matt Duchene and Gabriel Landeskog, carrying a combined hit of $6.75 million thanks to performance bonuses, but having actual salaries of just $900,000 each. There's no punishment because the clubs are technically in compliance with the system—so it's more like tax avoidance than tax evasion. However, such realities are at odds with the NHL's boasts that the cap has fixed the competitive balance. With payrolls only policed at the top end, the actual gap between the league's elite teams and its patsies is certainly closer to $30 million than $16 million.

And then there's the one detail that never quite seems to register with the hockey media or the fans: Since the cap came into being, contracts have rarely been worth their face value. The ceiling and floor theoretically keep the spending of each individual team within a certain band. But what the players take home is ultimately determined by the collective worth of their deals and the amount of revenue the entire league generates in a given year. They are entitled to a 57-percent share of overall revenues, and that's what they get to keep, regardless of whether the total dollar value that GMs have committed to pay them is more or less. That's why the players put a portion—it was 12.7 percent in 2011–12, but went as high as 25 percent in 2008–9—of their paycheques into escrow during the season. The NHL and the union then spend the summer poring over the books and tussling over how what the CBA calls Hockey Related Revenues (HRR) are accounted for, in order to figure out how much they actually deserve.

The first season after the lockout, business was stronger than expected, and the owners ended up owing the players 4.65 percent more than the contracts they signed. And the same thing happened in 2007–8, although the bump then was just over half a percent. But since the recession hit, the growth in league revenues hasn't kept pace with the optimistic, long-term deals now favoured by its GMs. In 2008–9, the players took home just 87.12 percent of the stated value of their contracts, refunding almost $200 million to the owners. In 2009–10, they got 90.59 percent, handing back around $150 million. In 2010–11, a year of record revenues for the league, the players got to keep 97.7 percent of what they had been paid, forking over $38.5 million.

There is one sure way for NHL players to get the full face value of their deals, however: to be optioned to the minors. One of the quirks of the cap is that the escrow provisions don't apply to the players buried in the AHL. Since he shipped down to Hartford in 2010, Wade Redden has made $150,000 more a season playing for the Connecticut Whale than if he'd still been patrolling the blue line in Manhattan for the Rangers. The extra dough has surely been little solace. Gary Bettman's new system lessened inequality between the NHL's teams, but it's hardly fair.

8 Managing Up

It's not exactly the middle of nowhere, but it's close. A thirty-minute freeway ride from downtown Phoenix (although it can take more than twice as long in rush-hour traffic), out past even the far western edges of suburban sprawl. Fifteen minutes from the main strip of the former cotton-farming town that paid $183 million of its $220 million construction cost. Beside a shopping mall and entertainment district—sunglasses stores, a Body Shop, and sensory-overload chain restaurants like Jimmy Buffett's Margaritaville—that was repossessed by the banks in 2011 and found no buyers at auction. In the shadow of a gargantuan NFL stadium named after a mostly virtual university that sits empty for 340 days a year. Jobing.com Arena is surely the loneliest building in the NHL.

And on game nights, things are scarcely better. The Phoenix Coyotes have been in the lower third of the league attendance table for a decade, and scraping its bottom for five straight seasons. On average, they draw just over 12,000 fans, playing to 72-percent capacity. But those figures are significantly goosed by the near-sellouts when Boston, Chicago, or Detroit come to town, not to mention the 1000 or so ducats the club gives away for every game. For a midweek tilt against a team like Los Angeles or Dallas, especially in the early part of the season, the crowds are in the single-digit thousands, leaving more empty chairs than full ones in the 17,800-seat rink. Promotions such as Bud Light Chill Nights ($25 for a ticket, beer, and T-shirt) or the Military Heroes Appreciation game ($20 a seat and a free bobblehead of Senator John McCain) aren't enough to fill the barn. And even on-ice success—three consecutive post-season appearances, including a 2012 run that featured an opening-round victory over Chicago, then a five-game triumph against Nashville, before finally falling to the LA Kings in the Western Conference Final—hasn't helped. The Coyotes' season ticket base remains one of the smallest in the league. In a media market of 4.4 million people, their average audience for the non-playoff games carried on local television is 6000.

There are no good old days to hearken back to, either. The franchise has never once turned a profit since moving from Winnipeg at the end of the 1995–96 campaign. And in fifteen years in the desert, the club's cumulative losses are well in excess of US$400 million. In the first three years under the salary cap, the new fiscal system that the commissioner promised would fix the game's inequities, the team spilled $73 million in red ink, or more than $24 million a season. By the end of 2010–11, Mike Neely, the club president, was publicly predicting a $40-million operating shortfall. And while the deep playoff run in the spring of 2012 put the Coyotes in their best fiscal position in years, they still bled more than $20 million. As a business proposition, pro hockey in Arizona ranks somewhere behind the lingerie concession for Afghanistan, or perhaps even Somali vacation villas.

Small wonder then that it took the league almost four years to find a new owner for the team. And that when Greg Jamison finally did agree to take on the Coyotes in June 2012, it was on the basis of a deal that will see Glendale, the Phoenix suburb where the rink is located, provide him with $324 million in direct subsidies over the next twenty years. In the interim, the NHL itself was forced to purchase the Coyotes out of bankruptcy for $140 million in the fall of 2009 to foil an attempt by Jim Balsillie, the billionaire founder of the BlackBerry manufacturer Research In Motion, to move the franchise to southern Ontario. The intervention, which capped a messy court battle, was cast as necessary to uphold the league's right to determine the fate of its teams and who gets to own them, as well as protect the rooting interests of fans in Phoenix and elsewhere. But the long-running saga of the Coyotes is also a monument to the stubbornness of Gary Bettman and the power he now wields over both the game and the men who employ him.

When Jerry Colangelo, the owner of the NBA's Phoenix Suns, and his partner Richard Burke, a Minnesota health-care executive, bought the Jets for US$68 million in December 1995 and announced plans to move them 3000 kilometres south, it almost made sense. The greater Phoenix area was one of the top fifteen media markets in the United States and growing rapidly thanks to an influx of older snowbirds from the Midwest and Canada. In addition to the basketball team, it already boasted the NFL's Cardinals—who had relocated from St. Louis in 1988—and would soon be the home to another Colangelo project, Major League Baseball's expansion Diamondbacks. There was even some puck history in the city, dating back to 1967 when a Western Hockey League franchise moved from Victoria, BC, and became the Roadrunners. In 1974, that club graduated to the WHA, and for three years there was sort of big-league hockey in town. The star was Robbie Ftorek, who won the Gordie Howe Trophy as the circuit's MVP in the 1976–77 season, scoring forty-six goals and seventy-one assists. Like so many of the WHA's experiments, however, the Roadrunners made no money and were quietly euthanized.

Initially, the Coyotes—a name picked via a fan contest with no apparent cartoon irony—showed promise, finishing third in the Central Division in their inaugural campaign and playing before sellout crowds at the America West Arena. During their first-round series against the Mighty Ducks in the 1997 playoffs, the Phoenix fans even paid homage to Winnipeg, dressing all in white to carry on the tradition of the "whiteout." But the seven-game loss also perpetuated another Manitoba custom—post-season futility. (When the Coyotes beat Chicago in the spring of 2012, it was their first series win in eight trips to the playoffs and the franchise's best showing since 1987, when the Jets beat Calgary.)

And once hockey's novelty wore off, the club quickly found itself in fiscal difficulties. Their home building was in the downtown and was state of the art, but it had been specifically designed for basketball and barely fit a regulation-length NHL ice surface. Several sections of the upper deck jutted out over one end of the rink, totally obscuring the view of the net for anyone who sat there. After their first season, the Coyotes were forced to reduce capacity from 18,000 to 16,000—although actual attendance soon plummeted far below that. Colangelo dumped his interest in 1998, and Burke, now the majority owner, started looking for the exit himself, declaring that the team either needed a new building or a new city. Microsoft billionaire Paul Allen was said to be waiting in the wings to move the franchise to Portland, Oregon.

When the Coyotes were officially put on the block in early 2000, it was Bettman who found a buyer, brokering a deal with Steve Ellman, a local real estate magnate, that hinged on a plan to turn an abandoned shopping mall in nearby Scottsdale—a moneyed community that was home to many fans and most players—into an NHL-ready rink and entertainment district. The process, however, didn't unfold as envisioned. Ellman had difficulty finding partners and raising funds toward the $87.5-million purchase price. The commissioner, determined to keep hockey in Phoenix, pulled out all the stops, first convincing Wayne Gretzky to join the ownership group and lend it some star power. (His equity was initially supposed to be just his name, but the NHL's all-time scoring leader eventually threw in more than $1 million of his own money, acquiring a 1.5-percent stake.) Then he helped Ellman in his lengthy search for financing, leading him not only to a Japanese bank, but then finding an insurance broker to secure the $60-million loan as well. And when further money issues threatened to crater the agreement just before the February 2001 closing deadline—the total cost had risen to $125 million thanks to the team's ever-swelling operating deficits—Bettman recruited one more local investor, Jerry Moyes, the owner of Swift Transportation, one of the largest trucking firms in the United States. His initial contribution of $5 million put the deal over the top.

The team they inherited was a mess. Two players—Jeremy Roenick and Keith Tkachuk—accounted for one-third of the $39-million payroll. Goalie Nikolai Khabibulin was in the second year of a holdout, after turning down a $3-million-a-season contract offer. Attendance was hovering around the 14,000 mark, and the club was mired near the bottom of the standings. Khabibulin was packaged to Tampa and Tkachuk shipped off to St. Louis. The club rallied enough to climb into a tie with Vancouver for eighth place in the Western Conference with ninety points, but missed out on the playoffs because the Canucks had a superior win–loss record.

The Scottsdale plan was also stumbling. Unable to extract the kind of tax and development breaks he was seeking from the municipality, Ellman jumped at a superior offer from an inferior place—Glendale. It was far away from the fans and the consumers, but the hope was that the rink and flashy shopping plaza would become a destination in itself and spur further retail and residential building. The Glendale Arena—later changed to Jobing.com in a ten-year, $30-million naming rights deal—opened to a standing-room-only crowd of 19,052 on December 27, 2003, and a 3–1 loss to the Nashville Predators. The Coyotes went on to finish the season well out of the playoffs, with just sixty-eight points. And whatever bump the franchise got from its impressive new digs was promptly wasted when the NHL locked out its players for the entire 2004–5 season.

Moyes had steadily upped his investment in the team, mostly by answering the cash calls when the Coyotes needed money to cover their losses, and had become full partner in Ellman's plans to build the Westgate City Center shopping mall next to the rink. But in the fall of 2006, tired of the slow pace of development, he struck a deal to take full control of the hockey club and the arena and let Ellman have the surrounding acreage. The plain-spoken former trucker—he started Swift with one rig and built it into a 19,000-vehicle company—wasn't in it for the love of the game. "I can't even spell puck," he joked at the time. Moyes just figured he had enough business acumen to clean up the mess, put the franchise on a solid footing, and then get out with some of his capital intact. He provided a new $95-million line of credit for the organization, and he also hired Jeff Shumway, a corporate attorney, to be the CEO and tasked him with restructuring the club's debt and cutting a better lease deal with the City of Glendale. The city council flatly refused his request for $12 million a year in arena-management fees, and the banks weren't willing to help either. In Moyes's first season of full ownership, the club lost $36.5 million. In his second year in charge, 2007–8, it lost $29 million.

By the summer of 2008, Moyes's own financial situation was also deteriorating. He had spent $2.4 billion to buy back the public shares in his trucking company and take it private just before the global recession hit, and now the cash-strapped banks were calling his loans. He no longer had money to spare for charity cases like the Phoenix Coyotes. Moyes reached out to the league for assistance and received a $6-million advance on broadcast and revenue-sharing funds due to the club. Then in October he met with David Zimmerman, the NHL's general counsel, in Glendale and informed him that he was officially broke and could no longer bankroll the team. Two weeks later, he flew to New York and delivered the same message to Bettman. In just seven years as an NHL owner, the transport king figured he had spent $380 million on a sport he didn't even like. And almost all of the money—$300 million at least—was gone.

The league took over the funding of the club, advancing it a further $31.4 million to ensure the rink lights would stay on and player paycheques wouldn't bounce. And Moyes signed an agreement giving control of the franchise to the commissioner— something that was kept strictly confidential to spare both him and Bettman the negative publicity. The trucker would continue to be the public face of ownership and oversee day-to-day operations, but all the big decisions were now being made in Manhattan.

Moyes instructed his lawyer, Earl Scudder, to start looking for someone to buy, or at the very least invest in, the team. And Bettman, who has always demanded that his owners keep him in the loop about all potential transactions, was also working diligently to find new backers. It just wasn't going very well. The commissioner facilitated some introductions and forwarded a few names, but the leads didn't pan out. And after one of his regular phone chats with Scudder in April, he summarized his frustrations for Bill Daly and Zimmerman. "I reiterated that we're running out of time," Bettman wrote in an email that was submitted as evidence in the bankruptcy hearing. "But this is looking more and more difficult since no one seems to be excited about a team losing 40 [million] ... I told him that at some point, if we don't have an alternative, I will have to start looking at the moving option." It was at that juncture in the conversation that Scudder informed him that outside interests were already sniffing around, and more specifically, that it was Jim Balsillie via his Toronto lawyer, Richard Rodier.

When Moyes took the Coyotes into a planned Chapter 11 bankruptcy on May 5, 2009, filing an asset purchase agreement with the court in which the BlackBerry billionaire offered $212.5 million cash (later upped to $242.5 million) for the team—provided he be permitted to move it to Ontario—the league professed shock and outrage. Bettman had flown into Phoenix that morning, they told the media, to present a purchase offer from Jerry Reinsdorf, the owner of the NBA's Chicago Bulls and baseball's White Sox, a deal that had been brewing for weeks. But as the commissioner's email would later make clear, Scudder had basically laid out the plan in advance. The team would wiggle out of the remaining twenty-five years on its lease with Glendale by declaring itself insolvent and then move on. And Bettman was hardly at a loss for a response. He threatened legal action to keep the Coyotes tied down in Glendale for at least another season, and if that failed he vowed to kill the franchise and go after Moyes for the money the NHL had spent to keep it running. The greater Toronto area wasn't going to get a second team on the cheap via relocation; the richest untapped hockey turf in North America was strictly reserved as a "league opportunity." And if the club ultimately had to leave Phoenix, Bettman was determined that "it should first be offered to Winnipeg."

It wasn't a question of means—Balsillie ranked 430th on *Forbes'* 2009 list of the world's richest people with a net worth of $1.7 billion. (Today, following RIM's market plunge and his resignation from the company, his wealth has dropped by half and threatens to tumble even further as he goes through a divorce.) And the forty-eight year old from Peterborough, Ontario, a lifelong Habs fan, has an undeniable passion for the game. Sometimes it even borders on an obsession, like the twice-a-week, hour-long 5:30 A.M. practices that he pays a former junior star to put him through each summer in preparation for his season as a beer-league right-winger.

But the hard-driving entrepreneur's two prior attempts to buy his way into the league had ended with hard feelings all around. He proved to be too intense and ruthless, even on the bell curve of NHL owners. And now they, and their chief bouncer Bettman, were determined to keep him out of the club.

The roots of the antipathy dated back to March 2006, when Balsillie sought out Bettman to share his dream of bringing a second NHL franchise to southern Ontario. The idea had been germinating since 2003, when he established a front company, HHC Acquisitions, and quietly took out an option on a lease agreement for the civic-owned Copps Coliseum in downtown Hamilton, sixty-five kilometres southeast of Toronto. The 17,000-seat building, built in the mid-1980s to lure an NHL expansion team that never arrived, was elderly, but he was willing to pay for a full-scale renovation, as well as the league fee and indemnification for the Maple Leafs and perhaps even the Sabres. (Buffalo is 115 kilometres from Steel City, but draws most of its fans from the Canadian side of the border.) Bettman was unmoved by the pitch—the league had blown off multiple Hamilton bids over the years, including efforts to relocate the Jets and the Nordiques, and remained unimpressed with both the building and the gritty industrial community. The commissioner did, however, have a team he was willing to sell to Balsillie—the Pittsburgh Penguins.

California billionaire Ron Burkle and Mario Lemieux, who had joined together to rescue the franchise from bankruptcy in 1999, were looking to get out. Negotiations with the city and state to fund the construction of a replacement for the decrepit Mellon Arena, built in 1961, were dragging, and the club was losing cash despite the presence of rookie sensation Sidney Crosby. Bettman cautioned Balsillie that the league wanted the team to stay in Pittsburgh and would only consider moving it years down the line—after all reasonable efforts to secure a new building had failed. But the tech titan wasn't dissuaded. He entered into negotiations, and within a few months, had reached a tentative agreement to buy the Penguins for US$175 million.

The process had been fitful—at one point Balsillie had told the commissioner he was abandoning the pursuit, only to return full bore a couple of weeks later—and Bettman remained suspicious about his underlying motives, even after he cancelled his Hamilton lease deal. Perhaps they were a little too much alike—a pair of overachievers from humble backgrounds with forceful personalities and a tendency to rub people the wrong way—to trust each other. The league insisted the BlackBerry maker sign an agreement with an explicit commitment to keep the team in Pennsylvania for at least seven more years. And when he met with the board of governors in New York City that December to seek final approval for the transaction, they piled on even more conditions, including a demand that Bettman be allowed to take over the arena talks. "There was a concern that he was going to sandbag the negotiations so that he could move the club," the commissioner would later testify. "There was an issue related to Mr. Balsillie's credibility. Did he mean what he said?"

Accounts of what happened next differ. In the NHL version, Balsillie verbally agreed to all the changes but then refused to sign when they were put down on paper. According to his camp, when the purchase agreement came over the fax machine at his Waterloo, Ontario, office a few nights later, there were two dozen alterations that had never been discussed. Either way, the result was the same: Balsillie pulled the plug on the deal, blaming the league's "insulting and unnecessary" extra undertakings. Lemieux issued a press release expressing his shock and distress, although the $10-million deposit that he and Burkle retained as a cancellation penalty surely eased the pain.

Whatever the rift was between the parties then, it clearly wasn't that large, because a little more than a year later Balsillie was back at the table, negotiating to purchase the Nashville Predators. The NHL owners might have felt strongly about the need to preserve the Penguins, a franchise that had been in place since 1967 and had won two Stanley Cups, but the hockey team in Music City was another story. Craig Leipold, a Wisconsin businessman who married into the SC Johnson household products empire, had paid an $80-million expansion fee for the club in 1997. And he looked like a genius that next winter when the Predators had 12,000 season ticket holders and drew more than 16,000 fans a game. However, as player salaries grew and fan interest started to dwindle, he soon found it impossible to turn a profit. By 2002–3, Nashville had the worst attendance in the league, with an average crowd of just over 13,000. And things didn't improve after the lockout season. In 2007, with his cumulative losses approaching

$70 million and revenues of just $45 million—the third lowest in the NHL—Leipold put the team on the market. Thanks to a clever provision he had inserted in his thirty-year lease for the municipally owned Gaylord Entertainment Complex, he could all but guarantee that the club could be moved. If fan attendance fell below 14,000 a game for two consecutive seasons, then the City of Nashville was either required to buy enough tickets to make up the shortfall—at a cost of millions a year—or void the rental agreement. "I was selling the Nashville Predators as a mobile franchise," Leipold would later admit in a court deposition. "So it could move to Kansas City. It could move to Las Vegas." The commissioner and the other owners sympathized with him over the challenges of the Tennessee market—the Preds were in first place and still drawing flies—and had made it clear they wouldn't stand in the way, he said.

When first approached that February, Leipold agreed to keep things quiet. But as talks progressed, he felt out Bettman about letting Hamilton into the league. "I'm not going to bother you while you're watching the playoff game, but I would like you to think about this offer from Balsillie," he wrote in an email late in the evening of May 5. It was for $50 million more than from the group that wanted to move the Predators to Kansas City, Leipold explained, and either way, he was forging ahead with his plans to try and break the lease. The commissioner wrote back to warn that there might be an issue with some of the league's executive committee, based on past history, but he didn't object: "Of course, the offer needs to be considered."

As it turned out, whatever concerns the other owners had were easily satisfied. In late May, Leipold emailed Richard Rodier from a board of governors' meeting to say that "there is unanimous support to move the team out of Nashville ... Your job will be to convince the BOG to where." He even offered to retain a

20-percent ownership stake to help smooth the path to Ontario. In another message, he provided some advice about how Balsillie should approach a scheduled meeting with Bettman. Leipold's first suggestion was that the tech billionaire should apologize "for any misunderstanding involved with the Penguins situation." Then he should indicate his willingness to follow the NHL's lead on relocation. "Should the [lease] termination occur, out of necessity, you will be investigating other markets to move the team to, such as Kansas City, Hamilton, Winnipeg, to name a few," he coached.

That meeting didn't go quite as smoothly as hoped—having lots of money means never having to say you're sorry—but it still wasn't enough to derail the deal. On May 24, 2007, Leipold held a press conference in Nashville to announce that he was selling the team to Balsillie for $220 million. He lamented the lack of support from local business and his own failure to find a Tennessee-based investor despite five years of effort. And when he was asked if the team was moving, he didn't exactly lie. "Jim Balsillie is buying this team in Nashville as the Nashville Predators. As long as the lease is in force, he's going to stay here."

But the Waterloo entrepreneur just wasn't the type to leave anything to chance. In early June, Leipold travelled to RIM's headquarters to meet with Balsillie and Rodier in an effort to finalize their agreement. (Perhaps mindful of his Penguins experience, the BlackBerry chief had delayed placing his $10-million down payment in escrow.) There, he was allegedly instructed to sue the City of Nashville for bad-faith negotiating, so that once the transaction closed at the end of the month the new owners would have an excuse to "back up the trucks" and move the team north. And when Leipold balked, suggesting the NHL wasn't going to be happy with that plan, Rodier reportedly promised to sic the government on them, issuing what may be the best threat in legal history: "Do you want to spend the winter in Ottawa with the Canadian Competition Bureau?" he asked. "Do you want to be the person responsible for your other partners at the board of governors spending their winter in Ottawa in front of the Canadian Competition Bureau?"

A couple of weeks later, Balsillie filed a formal application with the league to relocate the club. And then, just to make his intentions absolutely explicit, he concluded a new lease for Copps Coliseum and launched a season ticket drive. In a matter of days, he had collected pledges for 15,000 seats and all eighty corporate boxes, despite asking for deposits that ranged from $500 to $5000. In an email exchange the night before the announcements were made, Bettman tried to warn him off: "Your activities may have the effect of the Board calling into question your bona fides as a good business partner willing to abide by League procedures and rules and acting in the best interest of the League. In short, my best advice to you is focus solely on completing your ownership application." The commissioner was particularly irked at the timing—the campaign started on the day the NHL Awards were being held in Toronto and practically blew the trophy presentations out of the sports pages.

Less than a week later, Leipold sent a letter to the board of governors informing them that he was calling off the transaction because Balsillie had failed to conclude a legally binding agreement. The Competition Bureau did investigate, but ultimately determined that the NHL's policies on ownership transfers and franchise relocation didn't contravene Canadian law. The BlackBerry maker had again underestimated Gary Bettman's power. But even with two strikes against him, he somehow still believed the count was in his favour.

THE 2009 PLAY FOR PHOENIX was hostile from the very beginning. In the days after filing his bid with the bankruptcy court, Balsillie made the rounds of the media and sought to cast himself in a new light—as a champion for Canadian fans. "We're the source of the game, the players, the money, and I think we should have a seventh team," he told the *Toronto Star*. "I spent five years looking for a front door … We couldn't find a front door. I found a side door." Bettman was the dragon guarding hockey's treasure, and he was the knight who was going to slay him. The pitch had broad populist appeal. On Parliament Hill, Rodger Cuzner, the Liberal Party whip, got a standing ovation from all sides of the House when he made a statement praising Balsillie's chutzpah and calling on the NHL to finally recognize southern Ontario's untapped puck potential. And when the RIM boss launched a hastily constructed internet campaign— www.makeitseven.ca—it quickly became a national sensation. Over the website's first week, 55,000 people pledged support for his campaign; by the end of June, more than 200,000 had signed on. Corporations like Labatt—an official NHL sponsor—and Home Hardware rallied to the cause, becoming patrons. There was even a theme song penned by the GMOs, a band fronted by a couple of University of Guelph researchers: "C'mon, let's make it seven teams. The writing's on the wall. All you fans in Canada, stand up and heed the call. Hockey is our nation's game—apologies y'all. Gretzky's team is coming home. We'll see you here next fall."

A few years removed, Bettman now shrugs off the vilification: "He chose a tactic to make me appear anti-Canadian, and he may have got a sympathetic ear from some people who are inclined to believe that. But if you look at my record, that's ridiculous." At the time, though, there was little doubt that he and the owners were outraged. Legally obliged to at least examine the bid, along-side those filed by Jerry Reinsdorf and Ice Edge Holdings, a group

of Canadian investors who said they wanted to keep the team in
Phoenix, they invited Balsillie to meet the executive committee,
and then the full board of governors, at the end of July. Daly had
prepared a thirty-page memorandum on "historical facts and
materials relevant" to the proposals. The sections devoted to the
other two bids were about six pages each. The one on Balsillie ran
for twenty, providing chapter and verse on his past undertakings
and transgressions. At the session with Bettman and the executive
committee, Craig Leipold made a special appearance and tabled
his own "J'accuse" letter. The former Nashville owner, who finally
flogged the Predators to a group of local buyers for $193 million in
December 2008 and then promptly turned around and paid $250
million for the Minnesota Wild, was still bug-eyed angry: "I plan
on voting against Jim as a potential owner, and it has nothing to do
with Jim's desire to move an NHL franchise to Hamilton, Ontario.
Rather, I simply don't trust Jim, and don't believe he would be
a good partner." And he levelled new charges that the Canadian
billionaire had been trying to destabilize the Predators long before
he ever bid on them. In February 2005, Rodier had contacted
Nashville's director of finances to point out that the struggling
hockey team appeared to be in violation of a lease provision that
required it to maintain a net worth of at least $30 million—the
amount Nashville had given Leipold toward the expansion fee. The
city filed suit in the wake of the call and withheld money that was
due to the club, worsening the owner's losses.

Jeremy Jacobs, the chairman of the board of governors, went
on the attack, accusing Balsillie of undermining not only the franchise in Nashville but the one in Montreal, too, by falsely claiming
it was up for sale in a 2008 interview with *La Presse*. George Gillett,
the owner of the Canadiens, joined in, delivering an impromptu
lecture on the importance of trust among the NHL owners. The

only person in the room who didn't enter into the fray was Bettman. The final vote was 26–0 in favour of rejecting Balsillie, with the three franchises he had tried to purchase and the Leafs, whom he accused of trying to veto his bid, abstaining. Jacobs would later testify that it was the least active he had ever seen the commissioner in propelling a discussion; there was no need for him to intervene. All the owners already knew what Gary wanted and how far he was willing to go to get his way.

That cool detachment was again on display later in the summer at a downtown Phoenix courthouse. During the bankruptcy hearing, Bettman sat a few feet away from Balsillie, directing the NHL's team of lawyers but refusing to even acknowledge his foe. The silent treatment would have continued but for a chance encounter in the men's washroom where greetings and handshakes were finally exchanged. "Yeah, I said, 'Oh, hello,'" the commissioner later told *Maclean's*. "I mean, where else should you be more cordial than in the restroom?"

The ruling, which came down at the end of September, actually rejected both the NHL's and Balsillie's bids for the team. The first was found to be too cheap—especially since the league was proposing to pay itself in full while cutting Moyes, who was seeking $104 million, and Gretzky, owed $8 million in salary, almost totally out of the picture as "unfavored creditors." Here's your hat, there's the door. The second was spiked because Judge Redfield T. Baum determined that he didn't have the power to move the club over the objections of league headquarters and the other owners. Balsillie gave up the chase that afternoon, but not before lobbing a parting shot at his nemesis. "From the beginning, my attempt to relocate the Coyotes to Hamilton has been about Canadian hockey fans and Canadian hockey. It was a chance to realize a dream," read his statement. "All I wanted was a fair chance to bring a seventh NHL team to Canada, to serve the best unserved hockey fans in the world."

A rejigged NHL bid, cutting their counterclaim against Moyes from $30 million to $15 million and providing $11.3 million to be divided between the former owner, Gretzky, and the City of Glendale, was approved in November. It was a costly victory. In addition to the purchase price, the league had spent more than $10 million in legal fees, estranged the sport's greatest player, and laid bare the brutal economics of hockey in the Sunbelt. But Bettman had prevailed, and proven once and for all that he alone controls the game.

Three seasons later, the Coyotes were still in place, and still searching for an owner. The nearest miss came in 2011 when Matthew Hulsizer, a Chicago fund manager, agreed to purchase the club for $210 million. The reality, however, was that he would have been paying just $13 million out of his own pocket. The remainder was to come from the City of Glendale—$100 million for the rights to the parking lots around the arena (which, according to some legal experts, they may have already owned) and $97 million more to operate the building on their behalf for five-and-a-half years. The notion was that the municipality would recoup the investment over the three decades that Hulsizer was promising to keep the team in place via parking fees and sales tax. But many observers had doubts. And plans for a bond issue to raise the cash were scuttled by the threat of legal action from a conservative Arizona think tank, the Goldwater Institute.

But despite the league's lengthy search for a buyer, and Phoenix's continued financial woes, there weren't any public complaints from the folk writing the cheques—the other twenty-nine franchisees. And that, perhaps, is the truest measure of Bettman's power and the savvy way he wields it. In triumphing in what came down to a titanic clash of egos, the NHL commissioner still managed to satisfy the people who matter. For those owners in rich markets, the court's decision to uphold the NHL's entry rules means they don't have to live in fear of carpetbaggers. And for those stuck in poorer climes, it preserves an expansion payday that will surely be worth more than $10 million a team. Not only that, the drag the Coyotes put on the league's bottom line has helped to slow the growth of player salaries. And most importantly, the actual cost to the league and owners to keep hockey in Phoenix has been minimal. Faced with the prospect of losing the anchor tenant for its white elephant arena, Glendale agreed to cover up to $25 million a year of the franchise's losses until a buyer could be found. Tack on the revenue sharing that flows to the team—almost $20 million a season that is partially funded from players' escrow accounts—and the red ink starts to look almost black. Not coincidentally, math was Bettman's best subject in high school.

In fact, the biggest losers have been the taxpayers of Glendale. In addition to the original construction costs and the direct subsidies to the NHL, and now the new owners, they're also paying more than $12 million a year in interest on the rink's debt. In a coffee shop across the street from city hall, Phil Lieberman, a dissenting councillor, jots the figures down on a napkin. The municipality of 253,000 now owes more than $270 million for Jobing.com Arena, once the interest is factored in. Add the Cardinals' stadium and Camelback Ranch—a spring training facility for the LA Dodgers and Chicago White Sox that opened in 2009—and the city's total sports-related debt is closer to $500 million. The bursting US real estate bubble has sliced more than a billion dollars off local property values since 2008. And the sales tax revenue from the shopping mall and entertainment district that was supposed to be filling city coffers has never materialized.

(All of the $7 million a year realized from Westgate City Center goes toward the arena's annual debt payments.) In 2011, Glendale managed to balance its budget by dipping into a contingency fund for sewer and waterline repairs, giving its employees thirteen unpaid days off, shedding more than ninety workers through attrition, cutting opening hours at the public library, and cancelling children's sports leagues. For 2012, they were facing an even larger shortfall—$35 million plus the $17 million in arena-management fees that the city was preparing to pay Greg Jamison—and the budget-balancing options under consideration included cuts to police and fire services, laying off fifty more employees, and shutting down youth programs, in addition to hikes in property and local sales taxes.

And should the latest Coyotes deal survive ongoing courtroom and ballot-box challenges, the crunch will only worsen. The arena-management fees increase to $20 million annually for the next three years, and then drop to $18 million a season through 2019–20. (The average over the agreement's two-decade lifespan will be $15 million.) Then there's the additional $24 million the city has promised Jamison for capital improvements to the building. It's the sweetest lease arrangement in the whole of the NHL. Glendale will get some of the money back in rent and via a surcharge on tickets for both hockey and other events. But an analysis prepared for the *Arizona Republic* newspaper found that even if the Coyotes went all the way to the Stanley Cup Final for the next twenty seasons, and the rink hosted thirty sold-out concerts each year, the city would still lose $9 million annually. And the only justification for such a massive transfer of taxpayer dollars to a millionaire businessman is the fear that the city might lose even more—as much as $500 million over thirty years, according to one consultant's report—should the team leave and the arena sit vacant.

Lieberman, a Midwesterner who moved to what was then a dusty country town in 1968 to open a motorcycle shop, runs a hand over his tonic-slicked hair and sighs. "I'm not against the Coyotes. I like them here. But this just isn't the deal we voted for." Glendale went looking for a partner to help put the city on the map, but what it found instead was a league with a singular focus on its own interests. Approaching his mid-eighties, he's decided not to run for re-election.

Neither will Mayor Elaine Scruggs, the woman who built Jobing.com Arena and brought the team to town. Once the NHL's biggest booster, she has become a vocal critic of the Jamison deal and the league's attempts to foist it upon the city. "We're not in control and quite honestly, I'm kind of tired of everybody pointing the finger at us," she told a local paper. "They misled us … And maybe some places should know what they're getting involved in when they get involved with the NHL." When the deal went before Glendale council in June 2012, Scruggs joined Lieberman and another councillor in voting against it, but the motion passed 4–3.

The concrete patio outside Jobing.com's Gate 6 is where the true Coyotes fans meet up for a beer and a smoke before home games. It's not an overwhelming contingent, but they're as zealous as any partisans in the league. Scott Busby grew up in southern California and was an original season ticket holder for the expansion LA Kings, and later, when he moved to San Jose, the Sharks. He's been coming to games since the team arrived in 1996. The commute from his home on the far side of Phoenix is forty miles each direction. Heather McWhorter grew up in a small baseball-obsessed town in southern Georgia and wasn't even aware that there was an NHL team in Atlanta. She saw her first hockey game when she moved to Arizona and was instantly hooked. A drug addiction counsellor, she even changed jobs to get off the night shift so she could buy season tickets—seats in the upper bowl that cost her just $1300 for forty-one games. In some ways, she's wistful about the Coyotes' playoff success—prices will go up, the experience won't be as intimate. Although it is nice to finally be in vogue: "Winning is going to help. We've got tons of hockey fans in the valley, but they only used to come out to watch the Blackhawks or the Wings— their teams."

The one thing that won't change is their view of Gary Bettman. In the long, twisted story of hockey in the desert, he's the unlikely hero. Patient, protective of fan interests, and committed to keeping the game going in an inhospitable climate. Now they can even fantasize about what it might be like if Phoenix ever went all the way and captured Lord Stanley's mug. "This might be the only place in the NHL where he could award the Cup and not get booed," says McWhorter. Proof that Arizona is a very different hockey market indeed.

TWENTY YEARS AGO, meetings of the NHL's board of governors were free-flowing affairs. Not just in terms of what was being consumed during the cocktail hour aboard Bill Wirtz's hundred-foot yacht, *The Blackhawk*, but when the boys finally got down to business, too. It was a smoky room full of large personalities: self-made entrepreneurs who were used to getting their way and had strong opinions about almost everything. "It was generally just the owners chiming in to talk about the work that they did in their city, and why that was the right way to do it," recalls Cyril Leeder, who has been attending such sessions on behalf of the Ottawa Senators since their expansion bid in 1990. Often, the meetings descended into petty squabbling around the issue of the day—realignment, proposed rule changes, and most especially money. "The teams really ran the League, and the president was there to serve the teams," he says.

One of Gary Bettman's first innovations as the new NHL commissioner was to place microphones around the board table. The owners now had to wait for the little red light to go on to speak, and more importantly, there was a means to cut them off. The agendas became more formal, too, with reports, presentations, and brief discussion periods rather than formless crosstalk. And it all unfolded according to *Robert's Rules of Order*, just like the high school debating club back on Long Island. The format hasn't changed in two decades. When the league's power-brokers meet, it's Bettman who takes the floor and frames the issues. He's obsessive in his preparations for these encounters with his bosses, briefing himself and then quizzing his staff to make sure that they know the details as thoroughly as he does. "I've always thought from a league standpoint that it's our job to know as much as possible, more than anyone else about anything we're doing," says the commissioner. "When you lead, you don't do it by the seat of your pants. You do it by being as far out in front of the agenda as possible."

Information is power. Bill Daly tells a story about his first conference call with the executive committee, delivering an update on the sale of a franchise. Still green in the job and nervous, he stumbled and stuttered his way through the presentation. Afterwards, Bettman took him aside and gave him some advice. For the foreseeable future, he should write up a script and memorize it before he opened his mouth.

The NHL may be the fourth largest, and cheapest to buy into, big league in North America, but it still has plenty of high-powered owners. Jeremy Jacobs, the chair of the board of governors since 2007, acquired the Bruins for $10 million in 1975 and today has a net worth of almost $2 billion courtesy of his food and hospitality company Delaware North, which runs rink concessions for many of his colleagues. Mike Ilitch, the founder of the Little Caesar's pizza chain, also worth $2 billion, bought the struggling Red Wings for $8 million in 1982, and then a decade later paid $85 million for the Detroit Tigers. Stanley Kroenke, a Missouri real estate baron who is married to the daughter of Walmart's founder, has a fortune of $3.2 billion and now owns the St. Louis Rams, most of the English Premier League club Arsenal, and all of the Denver Nuggets and Colorado Avalanche (although control of the latter two franchises technically rests with his son, Josh, to conform with the NFL's cross-ownership rules). David Thomson, the money man behind the Winnipeg Jets, is worth $17.5 billion. And there's also Phil Anschutz, the deeply conservative and pathologically private—he hasn't given an interview in more than a decade—owner of the LA Kings. His Anschutz Entertainment Group (AEG), which promotes concerts and sporting events and owns stadiums around the world, including London's O2 arena, is now bidding to get the NFL back to Los Angeles. A pricey proposition, but one he can well afford, with a net worth of $7 billion.

All told, the NHL now boasts eleven billionaire owners, according to the *Forbes* magazine rankings, just as many as the rival NBA. And its second tier are hardly paupers, most possessing fortunes that count in the upper hundreds of millions. They are important men—for the club remains all male—who are used to being treated deferentially and don't suffer fools gladly. And from the very beginning, Bettman has proven to have a knack for stroking his betters. He emails. He calls. He remembers birthdays and anniversaries. And he listens. "I try not to let more than two or three weeks go without talking to each of the owners," explains the commissioner. "Just to hear their voices and make sure that they don't need anything. That there aren't any problems." Bettman has learned through experience—his own as well as what he's absorbed from David Stern—that the troublemakers deserve the most attention. "The tendency is to stay away from the guys you think are giving you a hard time. But that's exactly who you have to deal with." The key is to be candid and transparent. "The people that own teams are smart, sophisticated business people. You don't go around trying to manage them or bullshit them." For all the power that Bettman wields has ultimately been loaned, not granted. And the easiest way to hold on to it is to keep his bosses happy.

Ted Leonsis, who made his fortune in new media during a fourteen-year run at America Online, starting as a marketer and rising to upper management, has a net worth that hovers just below the $1-billion mark. But his backstory is among the most compelling in sports. Born and raised in Brooklyn, where his mother was a secretary and his father a waiter, serving breakfast and lunch at a greasy spoon, his first exposure to hockey came through charity—Rangers tickets left as tips for his dad. The only version of the sport he played growing up was on blacktop with a flattened tin can for a puck (he still has a scar on his shin from a friend's spinning slap shot). But while attending Georgetown University in the mid-1970s, he fell in love with the expansion Washington Capitals. The team was awful—they won only eight games in the 1974–75 season and set the league record for futility with just twenty-one points—but they provided cheap entertainment for a teenager trying to make ends meet on student loans. Five dollars got you a ticket, a Coke, and a hot dog.

In 1983, Leonsis was aboard an Eastern Air Lines flight that had to make a rough belly landing after its flaps and gear malfunctioned. The brush with mortality changed the then twenty-six-year-old's outlook. He created a bucket list of 101 things he wanted to accomplish in his remaining time on earth. The first entry was "fall in love and get married." "Pay off college debts" was number twelve. He wanted to own a convertible Porsche or Mercedes-Benz and travel to Egypt, Bali, and play golf at Pebble Beach. Over the years, he has crossed off seventy-four of those items. Number forty, "own a sports franchise," was accomplished in May 1999 when he bought the Capitals from Abe Pollin for $80 million.

The team performed woefully on the ice and worse on the books, bleeding $110 million during his first five years of ownership. There was even talk of contraction. But Leonsis kept faith in his franchise and in Bettman. The 2004 lockout was the turning point, he says, providing stability for the business and true competition for the game. By 2008, things were bright enough at the box office for the Caps owner to sign his budding superstar Alex Ovechkin to a thirteen-year, $124-million contract extension. "Gary's a very good businessman," says Leonsis. "He's done a remarkable job of having a foot in the camp of the traditionalist Canadian franchises, but at the same time being very, very cognizant that we have to adapt or die." He cites the Winter Classic as a prime example. Leonsis was so taken with the concept that he emailed Bettman before the first edition was even halfway through to request that Washington get to play in one. (They eventually did in 2011, taking on the Penguins and volunteering as guinea pigs for the first HBO *24/7* documentary series.)

And he has lots of praise for the commissioner's proactive management style. Bettman's regular calls aren't just to provide information; he's often seeking advice. Leonsis, who is a high-tech evangelist—he provides free WiFi at the Verizon Center, blogs incessantly about the club, and personally answers more than 500 fan emails every week—loves the league's push into the digital realm and mobile apps. But he knows that his colleagues somehow feel that their own pet projects are equally high on the agenda.

A neat trick given all the Type A personalities that Bettman must mollify. "Everyone who owns a team has had some level of success," explains Leonsis. "I look around that room at board meetings and I can tell you that I'm not the most educated, not the fittest, not the smartest, nor the richest guy. And that's why it's so tough to win a championship." (The admiration apparently flows both ways. In 2010, when the Washington owner published a book, *The Business of Happiness: 6 Secrets to Extraordinary Success in Work and Life*, the NHL commissioner was among those to offer a blurb review for the jacket. "If happiness is your goal, Ted Leonsis puts the stick in your hand, gives you the puck and tells you how and where to shoot!" enthused Bettman.)

The commissioner's powers of persuasion also seem to work equally well on hockey's old guard. Ed Snider, the irascible owner of the Philadelphia Flyers, also counts himself as a big Bettman fan. Conservative to the core—he recently bankrolled a film adaptation of Ayn Rand's *Atlas Shrugged*, a personal favourite for more than fifty years because "it is the only book that provides a moral defense of capitalism"—he appreciates what the league has done for his bottom line. The salary cap "is an absolute necessity in pro sports," says Snider. He also praises Bettman's "masterful job" during the lockout, keeping the owners united and focused on the big picture. "I've never once, in all the years that he's been commissioner, felt that he was telling me anything other than the truth." Bettman doesn't pit owners against each other, like past league presidents did, says Snider. It's all about "the good of the game." And despite Snider's Objectivist bent, it's apparent that even he can sometimes be persuaded to take one for the team. For the 2012 edition of the Winter Classic at Citizen Bank Park, the host Flyers welcomed back dozens of alumni for the celebrations and a Saturday afternoon old-timers game played before more than 45,000 people. There was a warm welcome for stars of the mid-1970s Cup teams, like goalie Bernie Parent and forwards Bill Barber and Reggie Leach. But the loudest ovation was reserved for big number 88, Eric Lindros—the not-quite-a-superstar who acrimoniously parted with the team after the 2000 season amid allegations of malingering, disloyalty, and greed. Lindros, who hadn't spoken with Bob Clarke—then the Flyers GM, now a senior VP—in more than a decade, found himself on the same oldtimers team for the afternoon, and old grudges were buried before the cameras with a handshake and some smiles. It was a feel-good topper for the league's showcase event. Ask Snider about it, however, and it becomes apparent that the ill feelings were simply papered over for the day. "It's none of your goddamn business if I talked to Eric Lindros before or after the game!" he snarls.

Still, smooth talk and flattery will get you only so far. A key to Bettman's success is his understanding that the job is as much a lion tamer's act as anything else, and one should never enter the cage without both a whip and a chair. Section 6 of the NHL constitution, drafted in large measure by Bettman during his 1992 negotiations with the league, outlines the powers and duties of the commissioner. It provides him with exclusive authority to arbitrate and resolve disputes between the owners, establish committees, change the schedule, and interpret league rules. It also gives him sweeping disciplinary powers. If the commissioner determines that a club has violated the constitution or its bylaws, he can suspend or fire the offending employee, impose a fine of up to $1 million, or transfer players and take away draft picks.

Over the years, Bettman has frequently slapped around misbehaving owners and their representatives. In 1999, he fined the St. Louis Blues $1.5 million for tampering in their 1994 pursuit of free agent defenceman Scott Stevens, even though the case was built on information that was voluntarily disclosed after a change in club management. Ted Leonsis is a serial offender. In 2000, the Capitals owner received a stiff fine for telling *The Washington Post* that he was certain there would be a labour disruption when the collective bargaining agreement next came up for negotiation. Then in January 2004, he received a $100,000 penalty and was banned from all contact with his team for a week after he got into an altercation with a fan. The twenty-year-old season ticket holder had been holding up a sign in front of the owner's box suggesting a linked pattern of failure on the ice and at AOL during a 4–1 loss to Philadelphia. When they met up in the hallway afterwards, Leonsis grabbed him by the neck and threw him to the ground—although he later apologized and the two men made up, sharing beers and watching a game against Tampa in his suite. Pat Quinn of the Leafs, Pierre Boivin of the Habs, and Tim Leiweke, the president of the LA Kings, were all docked significant amounts of money in the run-up to the last lockout for offering predictions about how things might unfold. And Steve Belkin, then lead owner of the Atlanta Thrashers, was handed a $250,000 fine in October 2004 for telling a Boston paper that the league intended to use replacement players for the 2005–6 season if they didn't get their cap.

But that all pales in comparison to the whuppin' Bettman handed the owners of the New York Rangers when they sued the league over control of digital rights. Back in 1996, the teams had voted to let head office lead the charge onto the internet, empowering the commissioner to create a website and market the game in cyberspace however he saw fit. A decade later, all the clubs had their own online presence, but the model was largely the same— NHL.com remained the league's main portal, point of sale for all team merchandise, and it was head office that sold most of the web advertising. New York didn't like the arrangement, which it perceived as yet another way to transfer revenue from big-market teams to their poor cousins. And during the 2007 playoffs, the Rangers made an attempt to break free by setting up their own internet store, broadcasting their games on the web, and inserting some virtual ads in their local TV broadcasts. Bettman reacted by fining them $100,000 for every day their NYRangers.com site didn't conform to league policy. And the team was back in the fold forty-eight hours later.

But the Dolan family, the owners of Cablevision, Madison Square Garden, and all of the pro-sports franchises that play there, were not happy about being pushed around. That September, they filed an antitrust suit against the league, alleging that the NHL was behaving as an illegal cartel and restricting competition, while aggrandizing and enriching itself at the expense of its clubs. James Dolan, the Garden's CEO, sent a scorching letter to the other twenty-nine members of the board of governors. Not only was Bettman out of line, he was failing miserably at the job, he wrote, noting that centrally generated league revenues had actually tumbled to just 7 percent of the overall gross since the lockout. "After sacrificing a season to set our player cost economics on a proper footing, we believe that the league continues to squander opportunities to improve our business and solidify and grow our fan base." It was a clear call for a coup.

The league responded with a counterclaim accusing the club of violating the NHL constitution by even seeking to sue their partners. And in November, a New York District Court judge handed Bettman an unequivocal victory, ruling that MSG was not only bound by the original web policy it had agreed to, but had failed to demonstrate that their interests, or anyone else's, were being harmed by the league's actions. The commissioner wasn't done, however. In June 2008, he invoked another of his powers—one he had never used before—and filed court papers to strip the Dolan family of control of their hockey team, or failing that, force them to sell. "The Rangers' ownership wasn't too happy, but the other twenty-nine thought we were doing the right thing," says Bettman. "And part of my job is to protect the league for the other twenty-nine." The matter was eventually settled out of court, and James Dolan was obliged to sign a declaration acknowledging that he was in the wrong and could indeed have been kicked out of the NHL. Something short of a head on a pike, but a potent warning for any future rebels. Dolan no longer has much contact with his colleagues on the board of governors. Asked what his relationship with the Rangers owners is like now, Bettman shrugs his shoulders: "It's okay."

The takedown of one of the league's most influential franchises and richest backers—the Dolan clan is worth $2.6 billion—illustrates just how potent the commissioner has grown in his twenty years on the job. Today, there are only a handful of owners—Ed Snider, Jeremy Jacobs, Mike Ilitch, and the Wirtz family—who predate his arrival on the hockey scene, and they are among his greatest admirers. The other twenty-six are all people that he had a direct hand in recruiting and grooming, not only guiding them through the sale process but initiating them into the league and inculcating a respect for its rules, customs, and mode of operation. The owners brought the monster to life, but he now controls the castle. And it's that status as the NHL's gatekeeper that has made Gary Bettman the most powerful figure the game has ever known. You can't get in—or out—without his patronage.

It's an arrangement that pays obvious dividends, but also carries great risks. When the league's more desirable franchises go on the block—teams with a glorious past like Montreal and Toronto, or in strong hockey markets like Buffalo and

Calgary—qualified investors line up for the chance to realize a hockey dream. But in the poorer markets—Florida, Dallas, Nashville, and even St. Louis—the job of the NHL's chief salesperson is hard and thankless. Bettman's contact file is stuffed with the names and numbers of anyone with money who has ever expressed even a passing interest in the sport. And he makes dozens of cold calls each month in an effort to turn up new ownership prospects. He has estimated that the league's troubled franchises take up about 75 percent of his time. And often it's like the plate-spinning guy on the old *Ed Sullivan Show*—in constant movement, but somehow always needing to return to the same spots.

Some question whether all that effort is really necessary. "Gary plays investment banker all the time," says one major broker of sports franchise sales. "He thinks he can put deals together, but often he's more of an impediment than a help." The NHL commissioner often gets caught up in his own hype, he says, holding out for unrealistic prices in soft hockey markets. "There's a real bifurcation of value. There's a ton of buyers for the top franchises. But for half of the league, all those Sunbelt spots, people just aren't interested in owning those teams at that cost."

And perhaps that's why the NHL has been so vulnerable to fraudsters over the years, rushing to embrace saviours for struggling clubs who quickly prove to be too good to be true. In 1997, it was John Spano, a thirty-three-year-old Dallas businessman who agreed to purchase the New York Islanders for $165 million—$80 million for the club and $85 million for its thirty-five-year-long cable deal. Spano, who was in the leasing trade, claimed to own ten companies with 6000 employees around the world and to have a net worth of $230 million. While negotiating the deal, he would regularly fly in on a private jet to attend games, and Islanders fans, desperate for a winner, took to chanting, "Help us, Spano!" Smitten, the board of governors approved the sale at a February meeting, handing him immediate control of the team. When the transaction closed in April, he made the down payment of $80 million—money he had borrowed from the Fleet Bank of Boston—but missed a number of subsequent instalments, citing excuses like an IRA bomb threat outside his London brokerage, then a fire at its offices. Later, he "mistakenly" wired $5000 instead of $5 million, or simply wrote cheques that bounced. As it turned out, Spano was worth nothing, with his only asset, a Dallas mansion, mortgaged to the hilt and in tax arrears. He had provided some crudely falsified investment statements to a Texas bank, which had in turn sent Islanders owner John Pickett a letter confirming he was a rich man. Fleet lent him the money on the basis of a family trust it never bothered to verify. And the NHL's investigation consisted of a $750 background check conducted by a former FBI agent, whose greatest claim to fame was a gig as the security guard for the NFL's Vince Lombardi Super Bowl Trophy.

It's an embarrassment that Bettman cites when asked if there's anything from his tenure that he wishes he could do over: "We learned from that, and we have better ways of checking now. We use private investigators to probe people's backgrounds—have they been arrested, have they done anything they shouldn't, talk to their references and neighbours, so you know what you are getting. And we use forensic accountants to dig in and make sure the money is really there."

Yet, a decade after Spano, it happened again. After Craig Leipold was diverted away from Jim Balsillie, the Nashville Predators were ultimately sold to a group of local businessmen and a California man who had dreams of moving the team to Kansas City. William "Boots" Del Biaggio III was the scion of a prominent Bay Area family and had been a business success, founding a bank and then a venture capital firm. In 2001, Greg Jamison, then the CEO of the San Jose Sharks, had sold him a 2-percent stake in the team. And in 2005, a round of golf with Mario Lemieux turned into a $120-million offer for the Penguins that cratered when Del Biaggio failed to find other investors, although he would go on to invest in a minor-league hockey team and a California beach house with the former Pittsburgh star. The high-rolling Californian—hot cars and an even hotter wife—was one of the sales leads that Bettman provided to Leipold when the Preds first went on the market, and they had entered into serious discussion before Balsillie showed up. So when the Nashville group was $25 million short, Leipold thought of Boots again and arranged a dinner meeting. The plan was for Del Biaggio to take a 24-percent interest with an option to buy more. But when it came time to close the deal in October 2007, Boots called to say he was temporarily short on cash thanks to an impending divorce. Leipold agreed to loan him $10 million to make the down payment. And a few days later, Anschutz' AEG, who owned and operated the rink in Kansas City, extended Del Biaggio another $7 million. The collateral for those loans, and $13 million more he borrowed from private bankers, were brokerage statements showing he had hundreds of millions in stocks and securities. The investments were real, but they weren't his—he had cut and pasted his name and address onto other people's accounts.

Del Biaggio's scam, as well as a Ponzi scheme he was using to finance his flashy lifestyle, started to unwind a few months later when the U.S. Securities and Exchange Commission launched an investigation. He declared bankruptcy and pleaded guilty to fraud, and in September 2009 was sentenced to eight years in federal prison. The NHL has since further tightened its franchise sale procedures and now requires its owners to divulge all business relationships with prospective recruits.

It was unwelcome bad publicity, and has added new layers of complication to the already nitpicky business of buying and selling a franchise. But responsibility for those debacles didn't stick to Bettman. Maybe that's because the endless succession of stories about southern franchises at death's door in the hockey media have conditioned fans to expect the odd failure, insulating him, in some odd way, from criticism when things do go awry on his watch. Or that buried deep, deep down, the public actually has some sympathy for his plight.

After all, he survived the Coyotes' bankruptcy, with all its revelations of messy double-dealing, unscathed and barely seemed to break a sweat during the endless search for new ownership. And not only did the commissioner steer the franchise away from one of Canada's most powerful men, he threw hockey's greatest hero under the wheels in the process. Under Balsillie's proposal, Gretzky would have received $22.5 million for his ownership stake and coaching severance. But the Great One stayed true to the league, throwing his weight behind Jerry Reinsdorf's bid. Now, more than three years after the bankruptcy trial, Gretzky remains in exile on the golf course in his gated California community, awaiting a cheque and an opportunity to come back to the game. "When Wayne reached his hand out to the league, he got it bit, and that's not right," says Marty McSorley, still a close confidant. "Nobody sat down with him and asked, 'What do you want to do?' Obviously, Wayne is very concerned about his image. I don't think the NHL would have found an easier guy to work something out with."

The league's position has always been that it's Jerry Moyes who owes Gretzky $8 million, not the team or them. In May 2010, the NHL filed suit against the former Coyotes owner, seeking to extract a further $61 million from his depleted bank accounts. The figure included a claim of $30 million for violating his agreements and placing the club in receivership, $20 million in compensatory and punitive damages, and $11.6 million to offset what the league had to pay to the club's unsecured creditors. The NHL also reserved the right to try and collect on Gretzky's behalf—if a judge rules that he's actually entitled to anything.

Mediation talks in the winter of 2012 failed spectacularly. And now it looks like the action, which has ping-ponged between courts in New York and Arizona, could drag on for years. It has already served to make certain points, however. The commissioner takes a back seat to no one. You underestimate him at your own peril. And once you're on Gary Bettman's shit list, it's awfully hard to get off.

9 Faceoff

The history lesson is in full swing, and it's clearly one that Donald Fehr has given countless times before. Go back and comb through the dusty archives, he commands, or unspool the microfilms down at the public library and trace the path of professional baseball from the first salaried squad, the Cincinnati Red Stockings, way back in 1869. Look at the contemporary coverage of the founding of the National Association of Professional Base Ball Players in the early 1870s, or its successor National (1876) and American (1901) leagues. Follow the thread through wars and economic depressions, the breaking of the colour barrier, and expansion all the way to the modern era, including most of the twenty-six years he served as executive director of the players' union. What you will find, he says, is that there was never a time when the owners thought the game was sustainable. "It was the most remarkable industry in history, because every year there wasn't enough pitching, there wasn't enough money, and people were going bankrupt. Yet somehow it never quite happened."

When his mentor, Marvin Miller, formed the Major League Baseball Players Association (MLBPA) in 1966, the average baseball salary was $19,000. By the time Fehr took over the reins in 1983, it was $289,000. And when he left the job at the end of 2009—ostensibly to slow down and enjoy life—it was $3.24 million. Extracting the money was rarely easy. There were walkouts in 1972, 1980, 1981, and 1985, a lockout by the owners in 1990, and the 232-day strike in 1994 that wiped out the World Series and fixed Fehr as public enemy number one in the minds of millions of North Americans. Tribunals and court rooms also became baseball battlefields. When clubs suddenly stopped signing free agents in the mid-1980s, Fehr accused them of collusion and made the charges stick, winning the players a $280-million settlement plus interest. War was a way of life.

But somehow, through it all, baseball not only survived, it prospered. Overall attendance rose from 38.7 million in 1977 to 57 million at the beginning of the 1990s to 73 million for the 2011 season. League revenues in 1985 were $718 million. By 1990, they were almost double that at $1.4 billion. In 2001, they were $3.55 billion, and a decade later they stood at $7.2 billion. The sponsorship deals grew by multiples, and so did the TV contracts, now worth more than $900 million a season. Eventually, things got so good that Bud Selig, owner of the small-market Milwaukee Brewers and the sport's commissioner since 1992, had to stop crying poor and demanding concessions. Fehr's baseball tenure ended on a streak of three efficient, if not exactly cordial, settlements and a dozen years of labour peace.

The new executive director of the NHLPA sits back, purses his lips, and locks his pale blue eyes on his subject. Decades of collective bargaining have made him a master of the uncomfortable pause. From outside his corner office overlooking Toronto's Air Canada Centre, there is the thrum of distant traffic. Finally, he delivers the coda. There's no reason that he can see why negotiating a contract for hockey players should be any different. Maybe it will be quick, or maybe it will be a prolonged struggle, but the NHL is a cartel, just like pro baseball, basketball, and football, and behaves the same. The owners divide up markets, fix the prices for tickets and TV rights, and do their level best to stave off any competition—internal or external—that serves to drive salaries higher. The cap system they imposed the last time around gave the players a fixed share of revenue, but it doesn't constitute a partnership. And whatever case Gary Bettman and his bosses want to make about the salary floor, the struggling southern franchises, or the troubles stalking their business, Fehr's not buying. His bottom line is that the league has set new revenue records for seven straight seasons, and that the total annual take is now over $1 billion more than it was before the last lockout—despite a persistent US recession and a global economic downturn. "It's hard to see imminent demise in such numbers," he says dryly.

Bob Goodenow got the better of Bettman in the 1994–95 dispute by waiting out the fractious owners and then offering just enough to let them save face. In the rematch a decade later, the commissioner cancelled an entire season and forced the players to blink, extracting the toughest salary cap in pro sports. But his near-total victory, and the years of turmoil it sparked within the NHLPA, have set the stage for yet another confrontation in the fall of 2012. And this time his opponent is in an entirely different weight class. At sixty-four, Fehr is the most experienced bargainer in all of the big leagues; unflappable, coolly calculating, and entirely unsentimental about whatever game he's dealing with. He kept a far richer and more powerful set of owners at bay for three decades—baseball remains the only major league without player compensation limits. And as he enters into battle with the NHL, in what will surely be the final set of negotiations in his career, he has no intention of sullying that record. The man Bettman is facing off against is not just his equal—in many ways he's his mirror image.

When Fehr was in charge of the MLBPA, he always maintained close contacts with the other big-league unions, offering support and strategic advice. He got on well enough with Goodenow, for example, that some NHL executives voiced suspicions that he might have been pulling his strings during the two sports' overlapping 1994–95 labour disputes. The struggle against salary caps was a common cause for all pro athletes, he reasoned. "There is nothing more central to players' rights in professional team sports than maintaining a free market," Fehr wrote in a memo to his members and their agents in 2005, pledging the baseball PA's support for their locked-out NHL counterparts. "Simply put, this is a battle over free agency: the hockey owners want to eliminate it, and the players want to preserve it." When Goodenow was forced out in the wake of the settlement, Fehr offered counsel to Ted Saskin on how to rebuild the divided union. And when Saskin was turfed in 2007, he came to Toronto to meet with the player reps and preach the baseball union gospel of transparency and effective communication—the members should be making the decisions for their leaders, not the other way around. So it wasn't exactly a surprise when Chris Chelios, the leader of the NHLPA's dissident rump, reached out to him in the summer of 2009 after yet another executive director, Paul Kelly, had been let go. Fehr's initial involvement was limited to a few conference-call discussions about how to make a clearly dysfunctional union functional again. Then he got drawn into the actual work, helping to redraft the organization's constitution. It was strictly pro bono. (Fehr wasn't hurting for cash, having walked away from his baseball job with an $11-million severance bonus from his grateful constituents—he had spurned their offers to raise his $1-million annual salary for years.) Then he was asked to chair the search committee for the next hockey union leader. It ended up being a little like Dick Cheney's hunt for a suitable vice-president for George W. Bush: His own name was always at the top of the short list. Fehr says he was initially reluctant to take on the job; he had plans to spend more time with his family and perhaps write a book on baseball. But he eventually relented in December 2010, won over by the players themselves. "They're genuinely nice guys, and they are genuine in a way which is nice to see and nice to interact with. I think they care about each other," he says. "They want to do the right thing." It's about as close to gushing as the reserved Midwesterner ever gets—although when asked whether he's implying something about his former charges, the shades clatter back down: "I don't do comparisons between sports and individuals." It's one of Don's many rules.

Another is that he doesn't like to talk about his background, or his family. The basics of his biography are on the public record. He was born in 1948 and grew up in the Kansas City suburb of Prairie Village, the eldest of three kids. His late father, Louis, was a restaurant equipment supplier, and his mother, Dolly, worked in their shop and then later went on to become a real estate broker. Fehr was an Eagle Scout and a high school debating champion. But the most oft-repeated nugget about his early life is the fact that he read the *World Book Encyclopedia* from cover to cover when he was twelve years old. When pressed about sports, Fehr will allow that he played baseball as a kid—mostly first or third base—but wasn't much of an athlete. Although he and his brother Steve—formerly outside counsel to the baseball union and now occupying the same job at the NHLPA—were big fans of the Kansas City Athletics. One of the American League's original teams, they had relocated from Philadelphia in 1955 but provided fans with little to cheer about, turning in thirteen consecutive losing seasons before limping off to Oakland in 1967. Fehr was off studying political science at Indiana University by then, but he still grieved over the move, albeit in a slightly wonkish way. "I saw it then, and I've seen it other times since—the psychological effect on the people in a city when a team leaves," he says. "It's quite remarkable. And that's because what professional sports franchises sell, in my judgment, is actually not sports. What they sell is group identification." (Kansas City's crisis of confidence didn't last long—the Royals, an AL expansion franchise, began play in 1969.)

Indiana is also where he was first exposed to hockey. Some of his brothers from Sigma Alpha Mu—a Jewish fraternity that also counts sportscaster Marv Albert, Philadelphia Flyers owner Ed Snider, NBA commissioner David Stern, and Donny Most, the actor who played Ralph Malph on *Happy Days*, as alumni—were from Chicago and loved the Blackhawks. Fehr became enough of a fan that he continued watching when he went on to law school at the University of Missouri, although his memories of the 1971 Stanley Cup Final between the Hawks and the Habs mostly centre on the fact that the Conn Smythe winner, Ken Dryden, was also studying to be a lawyer.

After graduating in 1973, he clerked for a federal district judge then joined a Kansas City law firm. He had a budding labour practice and gained some attention defending striking high school teachers who were jailed for ignoring a court order to return to work, but his turn toward sports law was a fluke. At the end of the 1975 season, the MLBPA had filed a grievance on behalf of pitchers Andy Messersmith of the Los Angeles Dodgers and Dave McNally of the Montreal Expos. Both had played the entire year without signing a contract, tied to their clubs by the ancient reserve clause that allowed teams to unilaterally extend expiring deals for a year. The owners believed that they could just keep renewing lapsed contracts at the same terms for as long as they liked. But an arbitrator disagreed, ruling that the players were now free agents. For whatever reason, when the league sued to overturn the decision it chose the home of the Royals as the venue. And Marvin Miller, the executive director of the players' association, enlisted the local firm that represented his former employer, the United Steelworkers, to represent the union. The case landed on Fehr's desk.

The twenty-eight year old impressed Miller with his intensity and devotion to the cause. And when the MLBPA went looking for a general counsel in 1977, Fehr was one of the first people he called. Don and his wife, Stephanie, a hometown girl, flew to Manhattan for the interview. He got the job, but the celebratory lunch was ruined when someone stole her purse from under the table. They were not in Kansas City anymore.

In his thirty-three years with the union, Fehr earned a reputation as a no-nonsense, dour sort, about as likely to crack a joke as an on-duty funeral director. And despite a lifetime in baseball, he remained in many ways an outsider to the game and its culture. (His longtime number two, Gene Orza, was the one who knew the lore and could swap stories, getting on with almost everyone. Not unlike Bill Daly.) But the players appreciated his bluntness and regular-guy style—he almost always wore jeans, running shoes, and a sports shirt, layering over a blazer when occasion demanded. And even if he used lots of big words, he never talked down to them. "For Don, the players were always priority number one: help them understand the issues, first and foremost; worry about interviews and press conferences later," Doug Glanville, the former Phillies centre fielder, wrote in *The New York Times* when Fehr stepped down in 2009. It also helped that Fehr didn't just preach solidarity, he practised it, too, refusing to draw a salary whenever his charges were locked out or on strike.

Fay Vincent, the former Coca-Cola executive who served as baseball's commissioner from 1989 to 1992, praises Fehr's integrity: "He's remarkably straight. He's scrupulously honest. He calls things the way he sees them." But that vision was always limited. Vincent describes his former foe as a committed leftist who truly believes in an adversarial, "nineteenth-century" model of labour–management relations. "I'd argue that the players had an interest in the future of baseball. And his response was always that his obligation was to represent the players. Period." It was a doctrinaire approach that had the added bonus of driving baseball's owners wild. Vincent, who was pushed out in a Bud Selig–led coup that ended the era of the independent commissioner, recalls the flak he received for even extending simple courtesies to the union leader, like letting him use the office phone to call his wife when an agreement was finally struck in the wee hours of the morning to end the 1990 lockout: "That's how perverted and warped positions get during negotiations."

It was a stark contrast to Fehr, who never, ever lost his cool or made it personal. Vincent says that, like Bettman, the new NHLPA head is first and foremost a lawyer but, if anything, is even more disciplined and rigid. Fehr doesn't bargain or advance positions unless he has fully explored all the potential ramifications with his members and received their instructions. Maddening behaviour when you are locked in a room trying to save a season. Which is really the point. "I think it's difficult for people to avoid underestimating him," says the former commissioner. (Bettman, who has known Fehr for thirty years—the offices of the baseball union and the NBA face each other across St. Patrick's Cathedral on Fifth Avenue in Manhattan—but has never before tangled with him, may have already fallen into that trap. "He's quite smart and capable. I'm sure he'll do a very workmanlike job in representing his constituents," the commissioner said in the fall of 2011, damning with faint praise.)

Fehr is a conspicuously clever man—a baseball beat writer once stopped by his hotel room for a chat and found that he was reading a book on chaos theory and a biography of the Roman emperor Augustus—and has never been shy about sharing his knowledge. Like Bettman, when he interacts with the media he spends as much time deconstructing the questions as answering them. And underneath the prickly exterior there are occasional hints that he, too, has a healthy ego. For instance, since taking over the NHLPA, Fehr has often made a point of putting his baseball legacy in context for hockey writers, expressing annoyance that he's been portrayed as a villain rather than a hero. "The notion that either of the two long strikes were precipitated by the players is simply wrong," he says. Factually, that's true. In the summer of 1981, it was Major League Baseball that forced the union's hand, bringing an eighteen-month dispute over whether teams should be compensated for the loss of free agents to a head by getting a judge to rule against a walkout-delaying injunction. "I went to court to try and get permission not to go on strike, and I lost," says Fehr. "And Marvin said to me, 'Good job, Don.'" A settlement was reached fifty days later—shortly after the owners' insurance ran out.

The season-cancelling strike that he was entirely in charge of in 1994 also started with a management power play. Baseball's collective agreement had expired the previous December, and negotiations had been fitful. And when the owners finally unveiled their proposal almost halfway through the season in mid-June—featuring a hard cap limiting the players to 50 percent of league revenues and an end to salary arbitration—they knew how it would be received. The two sides hardly talked in the run-up to the August 11 deadline the union had set, or through the walkout's first month. And when Selig brought an official end to the season on September 14, cancelling the World Series for the first time in the game's history, few believed his expressions of deep sorrow. But the unflinching Fehr hardly engendered more sympathy. "It was their decision to make. They decided their circumstances were more important," was all he told the fans. Judging by the number of death threats he received—including some relayed to his young daughters, then still at home in Rye Brook, New York—he was even more hated than the commissioner.

The positions only hardened as the dispute dragged on, with the owners voting to unilaterally impose the cap, and the union seeking to have all major-league players declared free agents. President Bill Clinton got involved, ordering the players' association and baseball honchos to resume bargaining, but there was no movement toward a deal. The strike dragged on into 1995, and spring training began with minor leaguers and has-been veterans as the owners prepared to field squads of replacement players. When a resolution finally did come, it wasn't through negotiations but rather the courts. In late March, Judge Sonia Sotomayor, now a US Supreme Court Justice, ruled that the owners were engaging in unfair labour practices and reinstated the terms of the old contract. The players then voted to return to work. The strike that the owners provoked ended up costing them more than $700 million in lost revenue and won them no concessions, but it instantly vaulted Fehr to the top of those "most powerful people in sports" lists. (A new two-year deal without a salary cap, but featuring revenue sharing and a "luxury tax" on team payrolls over $51 million, was finally signed in the fall of 1996.)

The fans never did care who was in the right in a battle that pitted millionaires against multimillionaires. And when play resumed in late April, they showed their displeasure, hurling abuse, foreign objects, and in the case of some Mets' partisans, dollar bills, from the stands. Average attendance plunged by more than 20 percent, from 31,612 per game in 1994 to 25,260 per game in 1995. It wasn't until the 1998 season, during Sammy Sosa's and Mark McGwire's much-hyped chase of baseball's home run record, that the sport fully recovered. Fehr has always been the kind of guy who takes the long view, however, and has no regrets. As unpopular as the strike was, and as unpopular as it made him, it was clearly in the players' interest, he says: "We got an enormously better deal than would have been available otherwise."

That willingness to defend the indefensible was again on display through baseball's steroid crisis. The sport's problem with performance-enhancing drugs was obvious for years. McGwire's biceps measured twenty-one inches around, compared to the average man's thirteen inches, while Sosa gained sixty pounds of muscle over his first few seasons in the bigs. But even when the owners finally got around to proposing testing in 2002, the union resisted. Fehr cast it as a civil liberties issue. "How would you like to be sitting down to Thanksgiving dinner when somebody knocks on your door and tells you you're being tested? That's an invasion of privacy," was how he explained it to a prominent baseball writer. It wasn't until the trickle of admitted and unmasked steroid users became a flood that he finally consented to anonymous, conse-quence-free screening during spring training as a pilot project. (Even with lots of pre-warning, 103 major leaguers still managed to fail.) And the drug policy the union ultimately signed on to was so watered down that amateur athletes and coaches launched a drive to have Fehr removed from the board of the US Olympic Committee. His reluctant embrace of fair play remains a blight on his record. "Giving Fehr his proper due without considering The Steroid Era is like saying the 1919 White Sox were a good team and Pete Rose was a good manager and leaving it at that," Tom Verducci wrote in *Sports Illustrated* in 2009. Sometimes you can do your job a little too well.

But the performance-enhancing drug controversy also serves to underline why Bettman and hockey fans should be worried about the immediate future. Don Fehr is the kind of guy who sticks to his principles, even when he probably shouldn't. And he really doesn't give a damn about winning over the press or public. In part, that comes from an intellectual assessment that seeking support for a union, especially one representing very wealthy athletes, is simply a waste of time. According to Fehr's history lesson, unions in North America have been in decline for more than three decades, ever since Ronald Reagan broke the air traffic controllers in the summer of 1981. Yes, the walkout was illegal and they had defied back-to-work legislation, but the Republican president's decision to turn on a labour organization that had backed him in the election only ten months earlier and summarily fire 11,345 people changed the tone. Public sympathy started shifting to the bosses, and it has never come back. "There has been what is now a generation-and-a-half-long tendency to blame all the ills of the world on working people," he lectures. "They get paid too much, they want too much, they this, they that, and the other thing." And more to the point, Fehr long ago learned that caring about anything other than the best interest of your clients makes you vulnerable at the bargaining table, and ultimately in your job. He will play the heavy when required. And with more conviction than even the NHL commissioner can muster.

As with previous CBA negotiations, informal discussions between the league and the NHLPA started almost a year before the deal expired. But Fehr, who spent the better part of eighteen months touring around North America and Europe to meet with players and hammer out positions, seemed to take pleasure in making Bettman wait to start the official talks. In the summer of 2011, the commissioner was confidently saying that negotiations would commence just after the puck dropped on the regular season. Then it was after the Winter Classic, and then the All-Star break. And when he was making these bold predictions to the media, Fehr was often watching from the back of the room, waiting to scrum and deflate all optimism by proclaiming himself still not quite ready. (Bargaining finally got underway two weeks after Los Angeles' Stanley Cup victory in mid-June.) The union also set an early tone by withholding its approval of a league proposal to realign the conferences and change the playoff format beginning in the 2012–13 season. The plan, conceived by Bettman, would have seen the number of divisions shrink from six to four and provided relief to teams like Winnipeg, still stuck with the Thrashers' deep south schedule, and the Minnesota Wild, who spend much of their time in the Canadian west. It took only an hour for the board of governors to adopt it with a 26–4 vote at their December 2011 meeting. The slick stickhandling was "typical Gary Bettman," Brian Burke had enthused. "Like a Chicago election in the '30s, you know? He's got a pretty good idea where the votes are gonna come." But the commissioner clearly hadn't anticipated Fehr's veto, which was purportedly based on concerns that the new groupings might result in more travel for a select few clubs.

The biggest slap for Bettman, however, has been the team that Fehr has assembled to aid him in the bargaining process. Former player Mathieu Schneider, who once wore his hard feelings about the commissioner on the front of his helmet, is an adviser. He's hired another Kansas boy, Don Zavelo, a former attorney with the US National Labor Relations Board who worked on the 1994–95 baseball strike and the recent NFL lockout, as the new general counsel. And one of his first acts when he took over the NHLPA was to bring Jim Balsillie's hatchet man, Richard Rodier, aboard as an economic consultant. The pugnacious Toronto lawyer's last dealings with the commissioner were as his inquisitor during a couple of highly charged depositions over the Phoenix bankruptcy case.

The central issues in the fall of 2012 are the same as they were in 1994 and 2004—money and envy. Coming off a $3.3-billion year, NHL owners are facing a salary-cap ceiling that would grow to more than $70 million if the current formula stays in place, and a floor that will climb to $54 million. Numbers that make the 57–43 percent player–owner revenue split they imposed the last time around suddenly seem too generous. After a four-month lockout in the spring of 2011, the vastly richer National Football League managed to browbeat its players into reducing their share of 59.6 percent to 49 percent. Ditto with the NBA, which reduced player compensation from 57 to 50 percent of revenues after a 161-day lockout that lasted from June through December and resulted in a shortening of the 2011–12 season from eighty-two games to sixty-six. Every percentage point that hockey owners can claw back is $19 million more in their collective pockets. But the question is how far they will be willing to push a union that shows every sign of digging in and fighting. "There may be a lot of players who say, 'Wait a minute, we already gave at the office,'" Fehr's brother Steve warned just before negotiations got underway. "We made massive concessions last time that were designed to fix your so-called problems. And if it has not fixed your so-called problems, we need to have a long, hard discussion about what those problems are and what we should do about it."

The focus of that talk, and perhaps the most contentious facet of the negotiations, will be the NHL's system of revenue sharing.

Under the expiring agreement, the league is required to redistribute a minimum of 4.5 percent of overall revenues each season to help its weaker clubs. In 2009–10, that threshold worked out to US$123 million, although as has been the practice, slightly more— about $145 million—went from the rich to the not-quite-so-rich. The Players' Association points out that hockey's equalization payments lag far behind the other major leagues, and they are keen to see them improved. The NFL, which throws all of its enormous broadcast revenues into a collective pool, as well as merchandise sales and 40 percent of each team's ticket sales (excluding luxury boxes), equally divides close to $7 billion a season. (In his book, *The New, New Rules*, political comedian Bill Maher contends that's what makes football so great: socialism. "TV is the NFL's biggest source of revenue, and they put all of it in a big commie pot and split it 32 ways because they don't want anyone to fall too far behind.") Baseball redistributed $433 million, or about 6.5 percent of its $6.6 billion in total revenues in 2009. Part of that comes from the competitive balance tax, colloquially known as the luxury tax, which penalizes big-payroll teams—the Yankees alone paid $26 million that year. But the league also pools its national TV and radio deals and merch sales, and then adds another surcharge for its rich teams based on net local revenues like ticket, regional broadcast, and concession sales. (Although leaked financial documents suggest that longtime recipients like the Florida Marlins and Pittsburgh Pirates have a history of simply pocketing the cash, which often works out to more than $30 million a season, rather than using it to improve their on-field product.) And the NBA, which has moved away from the luxury tax model under its new collective agreement, is in the process of phasing in a redistributive system that will see poorer teams share around $200 million a season by 2013–14, leaving the NHL as the pikers.

Hockey's revenue-sharing rules are also a lot more Byzantine than the competition's. To begin with, the NHL ranks its clubs by the amount of locally generated hockey-related revenues (HRR) from one to thirty. The top fifteen earners, a group that now includes virtually all the Canadian teams, are immediately excluded, and so are any clubs that play in markets of more than 2.5 million households. The remaining franchises, normally about a dozen a season, are then evaluated to determine how much they actually need—the goal of the exercise is to provide the lowest-earning clubs with enough cash to lift their payrolls to around the midpoint between the salary-cap floor and ceiling—and whether they deserve all of it. To qualify for a full share, clubs must have an average attendance of 14,000 a game and be growing their local revenues at a rate that equals or exceeds the league average. If not, there's a clawback—25 percent for the first season they fail to hit those marks, which grows to 40 percent in the second consecutive year, then 50 percent after that. A perennial sad-sack franchise like the Atlanta Thrashers, for example, was only getting half of its possible payment. Although the Phoenix Coyotes, who by all rights should be in the same boat, were granted an exemption from the penalty while under league ownership. The end result is fairly wide variance in assistance payments. Some teams are getting just $1 million or $2 million a season, while the very worst franchises are netting as much as $15 million to $20 million, with the average handout sitting at around $12 million.

But what the players would really like to change is how the revenue-sharing system is funded, since to date much of it has been coming out of their own pockets. The way it works now, if the league makes more than $300 million a year in centrally gener-ated income, like national TV and sponsorships deals, it can use the excess to fund up to 25 percent of the required revenue-sharing amount. (Although 2010–11, with the advent of the NBC contract, was the first time the NHL actually surpassed that threshold.) After that, the next tranche—up to one-third of the remaining total— is covered by player escrow due back to the top ten HRR teams in years where the total value of their contracts has exceeded their 57-percent share of revenue. Then comes a tax levied on all teams that make the playoffs, which ranges from 30 to 50 percent of the value of a regular season sellout (low-revenue teams pay the least, the richest the most) multiplied by the number of home post-season games. And finally, if the revenue-sharing pool is still short, the league's ten richest clubs make up the remainder on a prorated basis.

The union feels the split is unjust because the league can effectively manipulate escrow by keeping a money-losing team like the Coyotes in Phoenix, rather than moving them to a place like Quebec City where they would turn a profit and add $30 million or $40 million more a season to overall revenues. (By some estimates, Phoenix alone is responsible for 70 percent of the clawback in recent years.) So it's not just that the players aren't getting the face value of their contracts, the money they are refunding to the owners is being used to prop up the same sick and lame franchises that are costing them the cash in the first place.

However, the NHLPA won't be alone in demanding changes to revenue sharing. Large-market teams, especially those who consistently make the playoffs, are tired of getting dinged three different ways. And the smaller-market clubs are frustrated at the requirement that they continually grow their revenues as quickly as their colleagues in greener pastures to receive a full portion. "Revenue sharing right now doesn't work," Larry Quinn, the former part-owner of the Buffalo Sabres, recently complained to the *Toronto Star*. "You can do that for a few years, but it just becomes impossible for a team like Tampa to keep up those increases." Everyone has come to the conclusion that the system is broken, but for entirely different reasons.

And there will be lots of other hills to die on. Many owners will be demanding a lower salary floor—possibly over the objections of Bettman, who considers the current parity on the ice to be one of his greatest accomplishments. There will also be a push, from the commissioner's office at least, toward further limits on cap-circumventing dodges like lengthy contracts and front-loaded deals. The way that hockey-related revenues are defined is a perennial concern, with the two sides already squabbling over the classification of things like arena-operating payments from the local government in Nashville and the subsidies that continue to flow from the City of Glendale. The players have served notice that they would like to add independent oversight to the discipline process, preferably cutting Bettman and Brendan Shanahan entirely out of the process or, at the very least, establishing some sort of neutral court of appeal. (The War Crimes Tribunal at The Hague has a relatively light caseload, and a certain amount of expertise.)

With the recent spate of head injuries and tragic deaths of former tough guys, there will be discussions about how to improve the safety of today's players and the beefing up of assistance programs for those who have left the game. The issue of drug testing—the current agreement allows the NHL to collect samples only during the regular season, essentially offering a free pass to anyone who wishes to blood dope during the playoffs or bulk up on vitamin S over the summer—may come back to haunt Fehr.

And NHL participation in the 2014 Sochi Olympics and beyond—something the players desperately desire—is certain to be used as a bargaining chip by Bettman. The owners hate having to shut down the league for the better part of three weeks and resent being treated like regular folks when they visit the Games. Ted Leonsis is among the many who came away from Vancouver 2010 unimpressed. "I'm a populist. I like to think I'm a normal person. But I lent them $200 million worth of players the last time around and all I got were tickets for me and my wife. No parking, no meal. We had to stand in line with everyone else." However, he says he's already decided to let Alex Ovechkin go and play on home soil no matter what.

Money could soothe their concerns. Bettman has long been lobbying the International Olympic Committee (IOC) for some of the cash that currently gets kicked back to the International Ice Hockey Federation (IIHF) or, preferably, a direct cut of the TV contract. (One of the holdups in concluding a deal for the Canadian broadcast rights to Sochi has been the question of NHL participation, with the networks wanting a discount of at least $30 million if the pros don't show.) But René Fasel, the mustachioed Swiss dentist who has been heading up the Geneva-based world amateur hockey body since 1994, is firmly against anybody reaching into his pocket. "The NHL is a big business; we're a non-profit organization," he says. The Olympics are special, he argues. "For sure, big money is involved, but it should be about the values." Although it's a fair bet that Fasel, a member of the IOC's executive committee since 2008, spends little of his time at the Games mingling with the masses. In Turin, the IIHF rented out an exclusive private club with white linen, silverware, and three types of wine glasses on the dining room tables as their Olympic headquarters. In Vancouver, they had their own dedicated VIP lounge and a presidential suite at the Molson Canadian Hockey House, where the general public paid between $99 and $450 a day for access to the less swanky areas of the beer tent. Still, the consensus is that the NHL will ultimately end up playing in Sochi, if for no other reason than the fact that

NBC is paying US$775 million to broadcast the Games in the United States.

But just how long it will take Fehr and Bettman—or their subordinates—to work through all these various issues is the question that no one has the answer to. The NHL commissioner's attempts to build a relationship with the new union leader have been politely received, but largely rebuffed. For his part, Fehr says the idea that you have some sort of rapport with the other side is overrated: "It's better to have one than not, but if you put me in Gary Bettman's job tomorrow and you put him over here, the positions wouldn't change very much." He says that's because it's the players and owners who are calling the shots and defining the issues, not the commissioner or executive director of the union. Bettman offers a different take. If you don't connect outside the room, he says, it increases the risk that you'll misunderstand each other at the table. And while failing to clinch a deal because your interests don't overlap is part of business, missing an opportunity because you can't get along is inexcusable.

It is hard to believe that the mix of personalities could fail to shape the negotiations. The dynamic between the commissioner and Bob Goodenow, which went from hostile to poisonous, certainly helped write the script for the two previous lockouts. And this time it will again come down to a competition between the two smartest boys in the room. The fact that Bettman and Fehr are more alike than they are different is the wild card. It could give rise to common ground, or just as easily descend into *folie à deux*.

For the worried fans, the idea of a baseball guy squaring off against a former basketball executive to decide the future of hockey isn't a comforting one. The best they can hope for is that it will be a short chapter in an already troubled history.

THERE WASN'T MUCH TO LOVE about the 2012 Stanley Cup Playoffs. In the opening round, the Vancouver Canucks, the top team in the league for a second year in a row and Canada's great hope for returning Lord Stanley's mug to home soil, washed out in just five games, falling to the eighth-seeded Los Angeles Kings. Boston, the defending champions, also face-planted at the first hurdle, losing to Washington in seven. The Pittsburgh Penguins, buoyed by the March return of Sidney Crosby from more than a year of concussion problems, were favoured to go on a deep run but couldn't overcome a run-and-gun remake of the Philadelphia Flyers. Detroit lost to Nashville. The Chicago Blackhawks bowed out to Phoenix. And the New York Rangers—the top squad in the East—barely squeaked past the Ottawa Senators, a team that had exceeded all expectations by simply making the post-season.

Worse still for the NHL, most of the media attention hockey was receiving was negative. In the first round alone, eleven players were fined or suspended for dangerous play. It was as if the season-long crackdown on headshots and illegal hits had never happened. Shea Weber, Nashville's captain, kicked things off by grabbing Detroit's Henrik Zetterberg by the head in the dying seconds of their opening match and smashing him into the glass, like a pro wrestler softening up an opponent on the turnbuckle. (Weber received a $2500 fine, and two weeks later a second straight nomination for the Norris Trophy as best defenceman.) Rangers rookie Carl Hagelin got three games for skating across the ice to deliver a gratuitous elbow to the face of Ottawa captain Daniel Alfredsson, leaving him severely concussed. Pittsburgh's Arron Asham was banned for four games after cross-checking Philly's Brayden Schenn in the face, then following up with a punch to the back of his head as he lay stunned on the ice. But it was Raffi Torres who really got out in front to lead the parade of miscreants.

In Game 4 against Chicago, the Coyotes winger found Marian Hossa admiring a pass at centre ice and delivered a leaping blind-side shoulder check to his head. The Blackhawks star was knocked out cold and had to be removed from the building on a stretcher. It wasn't the first time that Torres had crossed the line. At the very end of the 2010–11 regular season, when he was playing for Vancouver, he had received a four-game suspension for another high hit on Edmonton's Jordan Eberle. Forced to sit out the first two games of the Canucks' opening-round series against the very same Blackhawks, he returned to ice for Game 3 and promptly laid out Brent Seabrook with a similarly nasty check. But the NHL, citing the vague proximity of the puck, declined to mete out further punishment. When it all repeated in the 2012 playoffs, however, the league's new discipline czar, Brendan Shanahan, wasn't so inclined to be forgiving, handing Torres twenty-five games—tying the mark for the second-longest suspension in league history. For once, the punishment fit the crime. Although it's still not clear if Hossa, who woke up in the hospital with no recollection of the collision, will ever be the same. And Torres managed to get his suspension reduced to twenty-one games on appeal.

The level of mayhem dropped off as the playoffs progressed, but the hockey didn't get any more interesting. In the next round, the St. Louis Blues, seeded second in the west, got swept by Los Angeles, and New Jersey slogged past Philadelphia in five turgid games. The Capitals and Alex Ovechkin were dispatched in seven by the Rangers, knocking the last marquee name out of the post-season. And Phoenix, a team previously known only to family and close friends—at least judging by the size of the regular-season crowds at Jobing.com Arena—continued its unlikely march, knocking off Nashville in five. By the time the conference finals started in mid-May—Coyotes versus Kings and Devils versus Rangers—many fans had already tuned out and started their summer. And a Stanley Cup Final, which pitted Los Angeles against New Jersey, sure wasn't going to drag them back into their living rooms. Without a Canadian team or a homeboy hero to flog, CBC's ratings for the series averaged about half of the 6 million-plus viewers who had tuned in to watch each of the Boston–Vancouver tilts in 2011. (Nik Wallenda's tightrope walk across Niagara Falls drew 2 million more Canadian viewers at its peak than the final minutes of the Cup-clinching Game 6.) And in the States, it seemed like no one who was living outside of the teams' respective turfs cared at all. Game 1 of the final, carried coast to coast on NBC—the type of exposure that Bettman had worked for the better part of a decade to achieve—drew just 2.9 million viewers. For Game 2, the audience dropped to 2.54 million. One pop culture website compiled a helpful list of all the prime-time programs that had attracted more eyeballs that same week—there were sixty-six of them. The NHL's championship showcase was trounced by reality TV, dramatic series, cartoons, reruns of *America's Funniest Home Videos*, and even the NBA draft lottery. If there was a channel devoted to drying paint, it might well have bested hockey, too.

The truth about sports is that not every playoff storyline is equally compelling. Sometimes the defence-first Baltimore Ravens win the Super Bowl, or the Florida Marlins—essentially an extension of the witness protection program—fluke their way into a World Series title. And part of the job of a major-league commissioner is to try and sell the dogs just as vigorously as the timeless classics. So when Bettman delivered his annual pre–Stanley Cup state-of-the-union address, he sought to cobble together something positive out of all the post-season negatives. A championship pitting the sixth-best team in the Eastern Conference against the eighth-best club in the West was a "testament to the competitive balance that we see in our game," he said, noting that the NHL entered the final day of the regular season with twenty-seven different potential playoff matchups. The league-wide crackdown on headshots was working, resulting in a "modest decline" in concussions, even if the commissioner didn't back up the claim with any numbers, oddly stating he wasn't "at liberty" to share them. The US TV ratings during the long march to the Cup were the highest they'd been in fifteen or sixteen years—although, with all the games available nationally for the first time in league history, some improvement was all but guaranteed. He also trumpeted the league's ever-improving bottom line. Despite the challenging economy, the NHL had set another revenue record in 2011–12, pulling in $3.3 billion. There were twenty-three national sponsors in the United States and Canada—another new benchmark. And more than 21.5 million fans had gone through the turnstiles, one of the best attendance years in league history. Fiscally, at least, the game has never been better.

The buzz, such as it was, finally kicked in after the Kings took the first two games of the final in overtime and the series moved on to Los Angeles. Games 3 and 4 were events—the bars and restaurants around the rink were packed, limos jammed the downtown streets, and inside the crowd was studded with a mix of current and outdated celebrities: James Gandolfini, Channing Tatum, and Ellen Page rubbing shoulders with cryogenically preserved Kings fans from the last golden era, like game-show host Pat Sajak, former *Entertainment Tonight* poppet Mary Hart, and once-famous Canadian Matthew Perry. Wayne Gretzky, who resembles his father more and more with each passing year, showed up to drop the puck and sing the praises of his former team, skating around questions about his continued estrangement from the league as gracefully as he once deked defencemen. Mark Messier and Sidney Crosby watched from luxury boxes. While another ghost from the past, Bruce McNall, grinned his way through the concourse, exchanging high-fives with those blessed with long memories.

The former Kings owner remains tight with Luc Robitaille, once part of his stable of hockey stars, now the team's president of business operations. And the club has continued to treat him kindly, fronting tickets when he calls and including him in its major celebrations. But the man who gave Gary Bettman his NHL job remains somewhat miffed that he was so quickly written out of the commissioner's story. "When my shit hit the fan, he wanted to distance himself because everyone knew I had been the one who hired him," says the ex-wunderkind, now sixty-two. "I think he could have been a little more supportive." Other owners who went bankrupt often get invited to the All-Star Game or the Winter Classic, he sniffs. (Although, to be fair, perhaps not those who have been to jail.)

But the déjà vu experience of hockey mattering in Los Angeles left those who were there at its zenith a little sad. It had been almost a quarter century since Gretzky came to town, nineteen years since the franchise's only other trip to the final, and sixteen seasons since the Great One left. An era of great promise, not just in California but all across the United States, that simply ebbed away. "I thought that what we had going was like a locomotive heading downhill," says McNall. "There was an excitement around the league. There were all these brand new franchises. And there was an opportunity." At times, he has faulted Bettman for failing to take hockey to the next level, telling interviewers that he picked the wrong man for the job. But upon further reflection, he has come to believe that the blame should be more widely shared: "It does come down to Gary, but he's not the league." He does what his partners tell him to do. McNall characterizes it as a paucity of imagination among almost everyone associated with the game: the owners, the players, the broadcasters, and even the fans. All of them are too reluctant or slow to embrace the kind of changes needed to speed up the action and make it easier for the uninitiated to follow and understand. And unless that dynamic is altered, the sport will always be a sideshow south of the border. "Hockey in Canada is what it has always been: huge," he says. "But when Sidney Crosby walks around any US city other than Pittsburgh, people have no idea who he is. Even when he walks into the rink."

To those still actively involved in the NHL, however, the reasons behind the sport's sometimes sputtering advance seem a lot more complex. The game is undeniably faster and better played than it was even a decade ago, and the athletes are far superior to previous generations. "When I started in '67, we may have had one line, the top one, that could do what our fourth line does now. The skill of the guys—the skating, the passing, the shooting—it's all gotten better and better," says Ed Snider, the longtime Flyers owner. Yet the mass US audience is just as elusive. For hockey's reach isn't just limited by geography, it's also restricted by demographics. "One of the things we have to change, in my view, is that we have to do more with inner cities and minorities," says Snider. "If you take a city like Philadelphia, which has 50 percent of the ratings in black neighbourhoods where you get a 0, while in a white neighbourhood you get an 8 share, well it comes out to be a 4. But in basketball, it's an 8 because it's not watered down by the 0." The seventy-eight-year-old cable executive has been trying to lead by example through the eponymous foundation he created in 2005. The charity offers hockey clinics for at-risk youth, providing free ice time and equipment. And it has renovated and now runs five community arenas formerly owned by the city and is in the process of upgrading four more outdoor rinks.

It's an issue that the league would be foolish to ignore. According to a recent University of North Carolina analysis of census data, visible minorities accounted for 85 percent of US population growth over the first decade of the twenty-first century. And much of that expansion is happening in the southern states, where the NHL is either non-existent or a sporting curiosity. It's not a stretch to say that hockey may already be the fifth most popular team sport in America. Game 2 of the Stanley Cup Final, aired by NBC on a Saturday night, drew almost a million fewer viewers than a Mexico–Brazil "friendly" soccer match carried the next afternoon by Univision, the Spanish-language cable channel.

Ted Leonsis of the Capitals says it's time for individual owners to take more responsibility for growing hockey on their home territory, rather than waiting for the league to lift the sport for them: "It's up to me to build a market. It's up to me to build the franchise." He believes the best results flow from having owners who are really tied to the community, either living there or hailing from the area. (Although that's at odds with some recent NHL franchise transactions, like Vancouver businessman Tom Gaglardi's purchase of the troubled Dallas Stars.) Blaming Bettman for hockey's failures misses the point, he says. For twenty years, the commissioner has done exactly what was required by his bosses—waging the battle for a salary cap, dousing franchise fires, preparing for the next crisis. And the demands of the present have left little time for plotting the future. "But the game and the business have still both improved. And that's where you have to judge him," says Leonsis.

And it's not like the merry-go-round is slowing down. Since the tail end of the 2010–11 season, Bettman has negotiated a US TV deal, overseen the relocation of the Thrashers to Winnipeg, navigated the bankruptcy and rebirth of the Dallas Stars, found new ownership for the Buffalo Sabres and the St. Louis Blues, and addressed the many ramifications of the sale of the Toronto Maple Leafs to two rival sports channels. And in his free moments, he's been busy stickhandling the deal between the City of Glendale and the new Phoenix Coyotes ownership group, as well as trying to keep the deeply indebted New Jersey Devils afloat long enough to secure angel investors, all the while preparing for collective bargaining.

Bill Daly helps carry a lot of Bettman's load, riding herd on the franchise transactions, acting as chief labour negotiator, addressing health and safety concerns like the rise in headshots, liaising with all the other hockey bodies, and functioning as the principal media spokesperson for the league. But despite all that responsibility, he maintains that every decision the NHL makes still flows down from the top. As the number-one deputy, he has earned the right to question and push back, but the terms of his job are clear—it's Bettman's prerogative to listen or not. And more often than not, it's the boss's instincts that carry the day. "I think we've been able to juggle the balls as well as any sports league during Gary's tenure, and he's entirely responsible for that," says Daly. "That's his sense of balance that makes everything work out okay." He's a dozen years younger than the commissioner, and has long been touted as Bettman's eventual successor, but Daly claims to have settled in for a good, long haul as the NHL's co-pilot. The commissioner, he says, shows no sign, or even thought, of disengaging. "I think he's excited every day by the difficulties that are presented by operating this league," he says. "And he's never backed off from a challenge. I mean, that's what he lives for."

How much longer could Bettman carry on? The answer—barring some major fallout with the owners—seems to be: indefinitely. His current contract runs through the fall of 2015. From there, it's a short hop to the league's hundredth anniversary in 2017, and the year after that would mark a quarter century on the job. But he swears that such milestones hold little meaning for him. And if there is a record that he's aiming to beat, it probably has nothing to do with hockey.

In the offices of his former employer, the National Basketball Association, six city blocks away from NHL headquarters, three oil portraits hang on the polished wood walls of the fifteenth floor boardroom depicting the men who have run the league for the last fifty years: Walter Kennedy, a former publicity director for the Harlem Globetrotters and mayor of Stamford, Connecticut, took over the nine-team circuit as president in 1963, becoming its first commissioner four years later and eventually doubling its size; Larry O'Brien, the Democratic Party heavyweight and presidential adviser who succeeded him in 1975 and piloted a merger with the American Basketball Association (when he stepped down in 1984, the NBA named its championship trophy after him as a retirement gift); and David Stern, the former Proskauer lawyer who has occupied the top job for almost three decades now and shows no sign of ever letting go.

The man sitting at the head of the table, near the leather-covered door that leads to his office, isn't quite as well put together as is shown on the wall. There's no tie or suit jacket, and the creased white shirt looks like he might have slept in it. Now seventy and snowy haired, with square glasses and a healthy paunch, Stern has what you might describe as a grandfatherly air—if your grampy had slit the throats of twenty men in some long-ago war. He's avuncular enough, but there's an undercurrent of menace. And when a subject captures his attention, and the slow, deliberate answers become faster and more caustic, it's not hard to believe all those stories about his legendary temper.

He's not just Bettman's mentor, he's his competitor and friend.

They meet in person or talk on the phone at least once a week. Swapping stories about troublesome franchises, crappy travel schedules, and the indignities that get heaped upon a big-league commissioner. Although the exchanges are more exercises in needling than support sessions. "Whenever I see some particularly bad assault I usually call up and weigh in with my vote, agreeing with their assessment," says Stern. "Or I'll say, 'I see you're moving the team to Saskatoon, again.'"

For despite the disparity in exposure and income between their respective leagues—the NBA pulls in about $1 billion more a season in revenue—their jobs are identical. They serve the owners and simultaneously strive to keep their bosses' baser instincts in check. They promote the players as stars, all the while trying to keep their salaries within the stratosphere. And they function as handy pinatas for the media and fans whenever something is wrong with the game. A tough act, but Stern figures it all boils down to one fundamental skill that all good lawyers possess: the ability to identify issues and defuse them.

Even after twenty-nine years in the hot seat, he still gets plenty of practice. The NBA's 2011–12 season was even more restive than hockey's: the fourth lockout of Stern's tenure, threats of relocation in Sacramento, and the protracted efforts to sell the Atlanta Hawks as well as the league-owned New Orleans Hornets. Then, to cap it off, basketball had its own outburst of highly publicized violence— a flagrant elbow that the LA Lakers' Ron Artest (a chronic discipline case despite changing his name to Metta World Peace) delivered to the head of Oklahoma City's James Harden. The resulting seven-game suspension wasn't much by Artest's standards—he was banned for eighty-six games in 2004–5 for going into the stands to punch out a fan—but it did manage to divert the spotlight away from the first round of the playoffs.

Stern likens his position to being the captain of a large ocean liner that plies heavy seas. The course always needs to be corrected. The battered vessel is in constant need of repairs. And every once in a while you have to lower the lifeboats. There's no downtime, because the problems a commissioner addresses are like bad weather, passing but never truly disappearing. There's always another storm tracking toward you.

"After you've been in the job for a while, it gets to the point where you only notice the stress when it's gone," he says. The lousy hours, the constant travel, the grind of collective bargaining, screaming owners, and the beatings you take in the press are what makes it interesting. He and Bettman are part of a brotherhood of misery and take pride in being able to thrive under conditions that would send most other men running for the exits. "Masochism. That's our bond," says Stern. In short, they're not the kind of guys who retire and spend their days playing golf or puttering in the garden. Their power has been hard won and won't be relinquished easily.

If you catch Bettman in a reflective mood, he'll admit that it might have something to do with his parents having both died young. The experience left him with shorter horizons than other people, and a need to run hard and fast. It's the day-to-day stuff that drives him, not some master plan. There are still things he wants to accomplish in the job—growing the game at home, expanding it abroad, improving the product on the ice. There's also the dream of thirty—or more—hale and profitable franchises, no matter where they play. "You understand that's utopia, but you keep working for it," he says. And if in the end the fans and the media come to respect the efforts he and his head office team have made to keep hockey moving forward, that would be nice, too, but not necessary. "I largely don't function the way people think I do," says the commissioner. "Sometimes perception isn't reality."

The truth is that the NHL will probably never be as big as the owners wish and many of its fans fear. And hockey will remain Canada's game by default, if not design, for that is simply where it matters most. In twenty years under Bettman's stewardship, the sport's fortunes have risen, fallen, and appear to be on the way back up once again. It is packaged differently, played differently, and he has succeeded in transforming it as a business. Still, those fundamental facts don't change. Even the most powerful figure the game has ever known can't make the American masses care. But that doesn't mean he's going to stop trying.

AFTER SCORING JUST TWO GOALS over the first three games of the Stanley Cup Final, the New Jersey Devils finally showed up for Game 4. Facing elimination in front of a hyped-up LA crowd, they checked the Kings into the ice for two periods before Patrik Elias caught the rebound off a point shot midway through the third and backhanded it past Jonathan Quick. But their first lead of the series didn't last long. Handed a power play less than a minute later, LA tied the score on a Drew Doughty one-timer. It ended up being Adam Henrique, a Devils rookie, who was the difference-maker as he kicked a pass off his skate up onto his stick and then wristed it high over Quick's blocker with just four-and-a-half minutes remaining. Ilya Kovalchuk, New Jersey's $100-million man, added an empty-netter in the dying seconds for a 4–1 victory, and his first point of the series.

Game 5 back at the Prudential Center in downtown Newark, New Jersey, was another close affair. The Kings outshot the Devils 26–19, but Martin Brodeur, a three-time Cup winner bidding for one more taste of glory at age forty, turned away all but one, preserving a 2–1 victory. A year after Boston had fought back from a 2–0 series deficit to eventually win the NHL's crown over Vancouver in seven games, it seemed like another rally might be brewing, and the interest of fans and the media suddenly picked up. But Game 6 at the Staples Center was over almost as soon as it began.

Just before the halfway point of the first period, Devils winger Steve Bernier, a former first-round pick for San Jose, who had fallen down the depth chart to become a fourth-line checker, pasted LA's Rob Scuderi into the glass from behind. It was an uncharacteristic move—the twenty-seven year old had only twenty-one minutes in penalties the entire season—but was severely punished nonetheless. As Scuderi lay face down on the ice, bleeding from a gash on the bridge of his nose, Bernier was given a five-minute major for boarding and was tossed from the game. The Kings scored three times on the ensuing power play. First, it was a deflection by captain Dustin Brown that squeaked between Brodeur's pads. Then came a tip-in from Jeff Carter. And with just eight seconds left in the man-advantage, Trevor Lewis scooped a rebound in the crease and stuffed it in on his backhand.

By the time Carter added his second goal of the night, almost two minutes into the middle period, the party was already in full swing. And as the final seconds ticked down on what turned into a 6–1 laugher, the standing-room-only crowd of nearly 19,000, including soccer star David Beckham and his three sons, were able to savour the franchise's first-ever Cup victory. The publicity-averse Phil Anschutz, who has owned the club since 1995 and last gave a press conference in 1988, even showed up for the happy occasion, posing briefly with his team for a photo. Officially, the drought dated back to their 1967 debut as an expansion franchise. But as one wag noted on Twitter, few in attendance or watching at home—it was the highest-rated hockey game ever in Los Angeles with a quarter of all households tuning in—felt the burden of history: "Congrats LA Kings! So many of your fans have been waiting weeks for this first championship."

And maybe that at least partially explains what happened when Bettman took to the ice to present the Conn Smythe to Jonathan Quick, who finished the playoffs with a .946 save percentage, a 1.41 goals-against average, and a record of 16–4, including ten victories on the road. For the first time in years, no one booed. Even the commissioner seemed surprised. Standing on the red carpet, shoulders tensed with a tight smile fixed to his face, he began the presentation, shouting into his wireless mic like someone anticipating some stiff competition. And when he could actually hear his words pinging back off the rafters, he stumbled over his lines and then dropped his voice. By the time the Cup was carried out to centre ice a few minutes later, however, he actually appeared to be enjoying himself, throwing out compliments to the "great fans" and the Kings ownership group, and flashing a grin when the crowd screamed "Luuuuc" in response to Robitaille's name—a tradition dating all the way back to his Calder Trophy–winning rookie season in 1986. He was loose. He was happy. And for once, the presentation of the chalice wasn't overshadowed by the fans' hatred of the man giving it away.

It was the kind of polite, respectful response that is certainly his due after two decades in one of the most difficult and thankless jobs in sports. Although it was surely an aberration, fuelled by a newbie hockey crowd and the generosity born of unexpected victory. In his heart, he knows this. The instigator's role is to be feared, not loved. And Gary Bettman is way too good at the job to stop now.

Bibliography

Brunt, Stephen. *Gretzky's Tears: Hockey, Canada, and the Day Everything Changed.* Toronto: Vintage Canada, 2010.

DeGeorge, Gail. *The Making of a Blockbuster: How Wayne Huizenga Built a Sports and Entertainment Empire from Trash, Grit and Videotape.* Toronto: John Wiley & Sons, 1996.

Dowbiggin, Bruce. *Money Players: How Hockey's Greatest Stars Beat the NHL at Its Own Game.* Toronto: McClelland & Stewart, 2003.

Dowbiggin, Bruce. *Money Players: The Amazing Rise and Fall of Bob Goodenow and the NHL Players Association.* Toronto: Key Porter, 2006. (Revised and updated.)

Fischler, Stan. *Cracked Ice: An Insider's Look at the NHL in Turmoil.* Toronto: McGraw-Hill Ryerson, 1995.

Horrow, Rick, and Karla Swatek. *Beyond the Box Score: An Insider's Guide to the $750 Billion Business of Sports.* Garden City, NY: Morgan James, 2010.

MacGregor, Roy. *Road Games: A Year in the Life of the NHL.* Toronto: Macfarlane, Walter & Ross, 1993.

MacLean, Ron, with Kirstie McLellan Day. *Cornered: Hijinks, Highlights, Late Nights and Insights.* Toronto: HarperCollins, 2011.

Mellanby, Ralph, with Mike Brophy. *Walking with Legends: The Real Stories of* Hockey Night in Canada. Bolton, ON: Fenn Publishing Company, 2007.

Miller, James Andrew, and Tom Shales. *Those Guys Have All the Fun: Inside the World of ESPN.* New York: Little, Brown, 2011.

Probert, Bob, with Kirstie McLellan Day. *Tough Guy: My Life on the Edge.* Toronto: HarperCollins, 2010.

Staudohar, Paul D. *Playing for Dollars: Labor Relations and the Sports Business.* Ithaca, NY: IRL Press, 1986.

Stein, Gil. *Power Plays: An Inside Look at the Big Business of the National Hockey League.* Secaucus, NJ: Birch Lane Press, 1997.

Stursberg, Richard. *The Tower of Babble: Sins, Secrets and Successes Inside the CBC.* Toronto: D&M Publishers, 2012.

Turner, Randy. *Back in the Bigs: How Winnipeg Won, Lost and Regained Its Place in the NHL.* Winnipeg Free Press, 2011.

Willes, Ed. *Rebel League: The Short and Unruly Life of the World Hockey Association.* Toronto: McClelland & Stewart, 2004.

Acknowledgments

The credit—and at least part of the blame—for this book belongs to my friend and editor Nick Garrison, for it was his idea and he somehow selected me to write it. I also owe a large debt of gratitude to Gary Bettman, who not only gave me his valuable time but facilitated access to many of his current and former colleagues. Thanks are also due to Frank Brown and his PR and media staff at the NHL for attending to my many requests, as well as to Jonathan Weatherdon and his co-workers on the other side of the fence at the NHLPA for their similar good deeds.

I am very grateful to the dozens and dozens of people—players, management, owners, experts, marketers, and fans—who sat down for interviews and provided me with documentation. It was all highly appreciated and useful, even in cases where their names and insights failed to make it into the final product.

This book would not have been possible without the support of my bosses at *Maclean's* magazine, Mark Stevenson, Anne-Marie Owens, Peter Kopvillem, and Dianna Symonds, who offered encouragement and indulged my newly narrowed focus for the better part of a year. My thanks also go to Ken Whyte and Keith

Pelley further up the Rogers food chain. I am indebted to all my colleagues at the magazine for picking up my slack, and in particular, Charlie Gillis, Colin Campbell, Michael Friscolanti, and Phil Gohier for all the hockey-dominated conversation. Thanks to Steve Maich, Katie Fillion, and Saramishta Subramanian for sharing their publishing insights and tips.

I learned a lot sitting in the press box and in the bar with hockey writers from competing publications, and almost as much from their books. A big tip of the hat to Roy MacGregor for his advice and assistance. Thanks also to Sean Gordon in Montreal and to Gary Lawless for organizing a hell of a dinner in Winnipeg.

Penguin proved to be a great home for a first-time author. And in addition to Nick, I greatly appreciate the efforts of Sandra Tooze, Stephen Myers, Justin Stoller, Leanne Rancourt, and the rest of the team.

Back at Dunnrenton Inc. world headquarters, thanks to George Serhijczuk for his hyper-organized research, Fraser Symington for his fleet transcription services, and Derek Shapton for trying to make me look pretty.

On the home front, thanks to Esselin Stewart and June West for the support and child care that allowed me not just to write about hockey, but to get out and play it too. And lastly, my love to my wife, Andrea Laing, for the encouragement and free legal services, and to our children, Maeve and Rory, for the lunchtime hugs.

Index

INDEX